P9-CDB-581

No Smoking

PATRICK & BEATRICE HAGGERTY LIBRARY
MOUNT MARY COLLEGE
MILWAUKEE, WISCONSIN 53222

ROBERT E. GOODIN

No Smoking

THE ETHICAL ISSUES

The University of Chicago Press

Chicago and London

This work is based partially on the article entitled *The Ethics of Smoking*, by Robert E. Goodin, that appeared in the April 1989 issue of ETHICS: AN INTERNATIONAL JOURNAL OF SOCIAL, POLITICAL, AND LEGAL PHILOSOPHY (volume 99, no. 3), © 1989 by The University of Chicago; all rights reserved. The present work contains many changes and additions.

The University of Chicago Press, Chicago 60637
The University of Chicago Press, Ltd., London
© 1989 by Robert E. Goodin
All rights reserved. Published 1989
Printed in the United States of America
99 98 97 96 95 94 93 92 91 90   5 4 3 2 1

Library of Congress Cataloging-in-Publication Data
Goodin, Robert E.
    No smoking: the ethical issues / Robert E. Goodin.
        p.   cm.
    Includes bibliographical references.
    ISBN 0-226-30300-4 (alk. paper).—ISBN 0-226-30301-2 (pbk.: alk. paper)
    1. Smoking—Government policy.   2. Smoking—Moral and ethical aspects.   3. Antismoking movement.   I. Title.
    HV5735.G66   1989
    363.4—dc20
                                                89-38279
                                                     CIP

The paper used in this publication meets the minimum requirements of American National Standard for Information Sciences—Permanence of Paper for Printed Library Materials, ANSI Z39.48-1984.2⊗™

Cover illustration: Vincent van Gogh, *Skull with Cigarette*, 1886, canvas. © by the Vincent van Gogh Museum/National Museum Vincent van Gogh, Amsterdam. Reproduced with permission.

363.4
G652n
1989

Contents

Preface

For far too long, philosophical discussions of public policy have focused far too tightly upon far too narrow a set of issues. Abortion, euthanasia, capital punishment, just war, and the like are undoubtedly important. Philosophers undoubtedly have much to contribute to their resolution. But it is an error to think—as readers of standard anthologies on these topics might be forgiven for thinking—that philosophical contributions must inevitably be confined to any so narrow subset of policy concerns.

This book is aimed explicitly at getting another issue (and, in certain respects, another kind of issue) onto the philosophical agenda. Moral philosophers have a long standing interest in problems of paternalism, of course; and some philosophers have recently offered important insights on matters of medical and regulatory policy. Still, even in those areas, the impression remains that philosophy engages only with the dramatic, and hence the unusual—organ transplants or nuclear reactors—rather than with more mundane and pervasive aspects of our everyday lives.

There is also something of a sense that moral philosophy can engage with policy problems only when they are somehow "matters of conscience," beyond the ken of ordinary politics. That is not to say that the "standard topics" in applied ethics are not politically charged. Far from it. Abortion, euthanasia, capital punishment, just war, and the like all carry a very high political charge indeed. That is precisely the point, though. They are matters well above and beyond "politics as usual." They carry an exceptional moral, and hence political, charge. For some, smoking policy is like that. From the tenor of this book, it should be clear that I do not see the matter like that at all. For me, smoking is very much an ordinary political issue, albeit one on which there is clearly a correct moral stand. Advocates on either side of the issue might approach it in a "holier than thou" way. But there is no need to do so. Moral philosophy may be nonetheless relevant, even outside the context of a moral crusade.

With this book, I hope to make a contribution to ongoing debates in both the philosophical and the policy communities. First and foremost, though, I hope to have written a book that will be accessible to and interesting for students in courses concerned with applications of moral philosophy to policy problems.

*   *   *

My interest in the smoking issue was originally piqued by protracted discussions over several years with Margo Goodin, whose files I raided and whose brain I picked mercilessly in the preparation of this book. She disagrees with many of the arguments and emphases in the resulting product. Even where she disagrees, though, the arguments have been powerfully shaped by interactions with her. Under other circumstances, she might have been the book's coauthor.

In compiling the materials used in writing this book, I have also had the assistance of librarians at various institutions: Action on Smoking and Health (London); the Institute of Health Economics, University of York; Middlesex Hospital, London; the Institute for Advanced Legal Studies, London; the London School of Economics; and the University of Essex, especially its interlibrary loan librarian, Terry Tostevin. Individuals who have supplied useful materials or comments include Brian Barry, Geoffrey Brennan, Norman Care, Richard Daynard, John Dryzek, Gerald Dworkin, Debbie Fitzmaurice, Mark Flannagan, Robert Fullinwider, Alvin Goldman, Steven Hetcher, Martin Hollis, Shelly Kagan, Sheldon Leader, Judith Lichtenberg, Claudia Mills, Dorothy Rice, Mark Sagoff, Thomas Schelling, Robert Sugden, Robert Tollison, Robert Wachbroit, Kenneth Warner, and Albert Weale. I am grateful to them for their help and exonerate them from blame for the use I have made of it.

Despite having more than doubled in size, this book has its unmistakable origins in the essay "The Ethics of Smoking," published in the April 1989 issue of *Ethics*. I am indebted to that journal's editor, Russell Hardin, and senior managing editor, Steven Hetcher, for originally commissioning the piece and for patiently persevering as it grew ever larger. The Journals Division of the University of Chicago Press has been most helpful, both with the original article's publication and in sponsoring publication of a much expanded version in book form.

Wivenhoe, Essex
November 1988

1   Introduction

The early history of tobacco is a fascinating one. Native to the Americas, the plant was commonly smoked by pre-Columbian tribes in shamanistic rituals. Like syphilis, it was brought to Europe aboard Christopher Columbus's returning ships. Its early career there was checkered. Initially, it was hailed as a herbal panacea—embraced with prescient irony by the Scottish physician William Barclay as being every bit as good for whatever ails you as a dose of mercury. Soon, though, the recreational smoking of tobacco began to take hold, particularly among the lower orders of society. Eventually smoking became virtually emblematic of a dissolute life-style, with brothel keepers displaying the tobacco pipe outside their houses as an insignia of their trade. At that point, the crowned heads of Europe stepped in to curb the menace. Some outlawed tobacco consumption, and backed up those laws by draconian penalties: Turkish Sultan Murad IV was executing eighteen smokers a day, at one point; the first Romanov tsar slit their noses instead. In England, James I raised the tax on tobacco by 4,000 percent and penned the 1604 pamphlet, *A Counterblaste to Tobacco*, warning his subjects in no uncertain terms that smoking is "hateful to the nose, harmful to the brain and dangerous to the lungs." All those official attempts at curbing the use of tobacco met ultimately with little success. By the nineteenth century, tobacco consumption—principally through smoking—had become a well-established practice, at least among certain social classes and in certain social settings.[1]

Philosophically, that is where our story begins. The received wisdom on the ethics of smoking today is essentially that forged in the

---

1. This summary is based loosely on Demarest (1976), Harrison (1986), and Wilbert (1988); Infante (1985) provides a jolly, idiosyncratic commentary on the history of smoking and its place in Western culture. Full details on references given in this form can be found in the list of references at the end of the book.

1

Victorian era. Victorian moralists were prudish, but they were also pragmatic. They disapproved of smoking—along with most of life's other small pleasures. But they had few illusions about the power of their preaching to change people's behavior. So they took care to express their disapproval in such a way that their moral authority would remain unimpaired when their injunctions were widely disregarded.

The formula they struck upon—which has become the received wisdom handed down from their day to ours—is this. Smoking is undoubtedly a vice. Still, it is a paradigmatically private-regarding vice, best treated as such.

That smoking is a vice was, to nineteenth-century moralists, beyond question. It was seen as a dirty, disgusting habit, best confined to smoke rooms and male company. The words of that last great Victorian, Miss Manners, are evocative of the era:

> *Dear Miss Manners:*   Are there any legitimate rules about . . . when and where I can smoke?
> *Gentle Reader:*   Yes, and they never should have been abandoned, as they were when women began to smoke, which should never have happened, either. Smoking should be confined to certain parlors to which smokers may retire from the sensible people and make their disgusting mess. One should not smoke at the same table where others are still eating. If you wish to smoke in the presence of clean people, you must ask their permission and be prepared to accept their refusal to grant it. [Martin 1983, p. 637]

Anyone who supposes that that is altogether a spoof need only consult nineteenth-century manuals of etiquette to confirm that the Victorians were completely in earnest on those points.[2]

---

2.   One 1836 text admonishes: "If you are so unfortunate as to have contracted the low habit of smoking, be careful to practice it under certain restrictions; at least, so long as you are desirous of being considered fit for civilized society. . . . Smoke where it is least likely to prove personally offensive by making your clothes smell; then wash your mouth, and brush your teeth. What man of delicacy could presume to address a lady with his breath smelling of onions? Yet tobacco is equally odious. The tobacco smoker, in *public*, is the most selfish animal imaginable; he perseveres in contaminating the pure and fragrant air, careless whom he annoys" (Day 1836/1947, pp. 27–28). Schlesinger (1946, pp. 38–39) reports that "the ancient prejudice against men's smoking in the presence of the other sex or 'on a public promenade, where one is likely to meet ladies,' still lingered" right the way to the turn of the century; "President McKinley, anxious even about male users of the weed, refused to allow his picture to be taken with a cigar in his mouth, remarking to the photographer, 'We must not let the young men of this country see their President smoking!' Nevertheless," by the turn of

Having made their opposition to smoking crystal clear, however, Victorian moralists would promptly go on to say that its abatement is a matter for morals rather than legislation. Smoking is a vice, to be sure. But it is a private vice, harming only smokers themselves.[3] It is, therefore, best left to their personal discretion and moderation. Smoking was thus established—and has thus been handed down to us—as something best controlled through codes of etiquette and social pressure, and completely unsuited to any very much more serious social sanctions.[4]

On the broad outlines of that analysis, the great Victorian moral philosophers—John Stuart Mill (1859/1975, chaps. 4, 5), Herbert Spencer (1893, pt. 3, secs. 214–15), and Henry Sidgwick (1907, bk. 3, chap. 9, sec. 2)—all seem agreed. It is the place of society to stop us from doing things that will harm others; it is not the place of society to stop us from doing things that will harm no one but ourselves. In Mill's (1859/1975, p. 15) classic formulation:

> the sole end for which mankind are warranted, individually or collectively, in interfering with the liberty of action of any of their number, is self-protection. . . . The only purpose for which power can be rightfully exercised over any member of a civilized community, against his will, is to prevent harm to others. His own good, either physical or moral, is not a sufficient warrant. He cannot rightfully be compelled to do or forbear because it will be better for him to do so, because it will make him happier, because, in the opinions of others, to do so would be wise, or even right. These are good reasons for remonstrating with him,

the century, "increasing evidence in and out of manners books suggested that 'modern notions on the tobacco question,' even among women, were 'growing lax.' "

3. Together, perhaps, with their immediate families. That would have come, literally, to one and the same thing for those Victorians who still held to the traditional legal doctrine of "privity" within marriage, according to which a wife's legal identity is merged with that of her husband. There would have been others, even then, however, who would have allowed that, "if . . . a man, . . . having undertaken the moral responsibility of a family, . . . through intemperance or extravagance becomes . . . incapable of supporting or educating them, he is deservedly reprobated, and might be justly punished"; but, as Mill (1859/1975, p. 100) goes on to say, in that case "it is for the breach of duty to his family . . . , not for the extravagance" itself, that he is to be reprobated or punished.

4. Of course, it is also perfectly true that Victorians took their manners more seriously than we tend to do nowadays. For them, "manners were sanctified and moralized, so to speak, while morals were secularized and domesticated. . . . Manners were placed in a continuum with morals, as morals were with laws, and laws, as a last resort, with force" (Himmelfarb 1988, pp. 223, 233). Anyone reading J. S. Mill's essay *On Liberty* (1859/1975, p. 95) will appreciate that "mere" social pressure was not, for him, a form of social sanction to be taken lightly.

or reasoning with him, or persuading him, or entreating him, but not for compelling him, or visiting him with any evil in case he do otherwise. . . . The only part of the conduct of any one, for which he is amenable to society, is that which concerns others. In the part which merely concerns himself, his independence is, of right, absolute. Over himself, over his own body and mind, the individual is sovereign.

As Mill (1859/1975, pp. 96–97) goes on to say:

What are called duties to ourselves are not socially obligatory, unless circumstances render them at the same time duties to others. . . . The distinction between the loss of consideration which a person may rightly incur by defect of prudence or of personal dignity, and the reprobation which is due to him for an offence against the rights of others, is not a merely nominal distinction. It makes a vast difference both in our feelings and in our conduct towards him, whether he displeases us in things in which we think we have a right to control, him, or in things in which we know that we have not.

For Mill and his philosophical fellow travelers, smoking—along with various other forms of "intemperance" and "hurtful indulgences"— clearly falls into the latter category.

This characteristically Victorian view of smoking as a purely private-regarding indulgence, for which people are to be scolded but not sanctioned, is very much the received wisdom in our own day, as well. The lay moralists of the medical profession editorialize in the *Journal of the American Medical Association* for "tobacco for consenting adults in private only" (Lundberg and Knoll 1986). Mill could not have put it better himself.

Among professional philosophers, too, smoking has long been an area where Mill's traditional precepts have been thought largely to rule. In a classic essay on "Legal Paternalism," for example, Joel Feinberg (1971/1983, p. 11) writes:

Many perfectly normal, rational persons voluntarily choose to run . . . a grave risk of lung cancer or heart disease . . . for whatever pleasures they find in smoking. The way the state can assure itself that such practices are truly voluntary is to confront smokers continually with the ugly medical facts so that there is no escaping the knowledge of exactly what the medical risks to health are. . . . But to prohibit [smoking] outright for everyone would be to tell voluntary risk-takers that even their informed judgments of what is worthwhile are less reasonable than those of the state and that, therefore, they may not act on them. This is paternalism of the strong kind. . . . As a principle of public policy, it has an acrid moral flavor, and creates serious risks of governmental tyranny.[5]

Or, again, in his distinguished recent contribution on philosophy and health policy, Norman Daniels (1985, pp. 156–58) maintains:

> Though most of us would agree that promoting health[y] life-styles is an important social goal, we are also justifiably hesitant about permitting too much social intrusion into individual decision-making about life-styles. . . . . We resist the suggestion that there is only one acceptable conception of the good, or that self-regarding features of those conceptions must all agree on basic points, for example, in the importance placed on avoiding risks to health. . . . Only if these decisions [to endanger health] are the result of independently defined and detected failures of competency is paternalistic intervention justified. Specifically, health-threatening behaviors—smoking or not wearing seat belts—are not themselves evidence of diminished capacity for rational decision-making. Many of these behaviors, after all, are associated with natural effects—the relaxation of smoking—that are also desirable and whose payoffs individuals may weigh differently.

These and various other writings in similar veins (Dworkin 1972/1983, pp. 32–33; Wikler 1978/1983, 1987) serve to confirm the hold that Mill still has on professional and lay moralists alike. For all of us, the received view is apparently very much that smoking is a private-regarding vice, best treated as such.

In current controversies surrounding smoking, that conventional wisdom is being questioned in both its parts. The proposition that smoking is a merely private-regarding vice, harming only smokers themselves, is challenged by evidence of the harmful effects of "passive smoking" (i.e., nonsmokers' inhaling smoke given off by others smoking around them). The proposition that smoking is best treated as we would an ordinary private-regarding vice—by informal social pressure, rather than by formal legal sanctions—is also being

5. In volume 1 of his four-volume treatise on *The Moral Limits of the Criminal Law,* Feinberg (1984, p. 23) reiterates, "I object to criminalization of smoking because it is supported only by a paternalistic liberty-limiting principle that I find invalid." By the time volume three—the volume consolidating his earlier work on legal paternalism—was published, however, Feinberg (1986) conspicuously excised almost all references to the smoking example that had previously served him as a paradigm of impermissible legal paternalism.

challenged by evidence of the addictive nature of nicotine, making it difficult for smokers to start and stop at will.

These new developments make smoking a paradigm of another kind: an issue concerning the quality of social life, requiring codes that are formal rather than informal and enforceable rather than merely hortatory. Here, morally worthy goals cannot be achieved if backed by morals alone. Legislation is not only permissible but, in some ways, morally mandated.

In arguing toward those conclusions, I shall organize my discussion along Mill's classic lines. First I shall discuss "harm to self" that occurs as a result of smoking, and to what extent that justifies social intervention. Next I shall discuss "harm to others," and the extent to which that justifies social intervention. Finally I take up various arguments and counterarguments that arise in connection with those various proposals for social intervention. Although of special relevance for the ethics of smoking and its control, many of those issues recur in a wide range of other applications as well. Indeed, my own past experience suggests that the best way to discover general principles of very broad applicability is through an in-depth examination of some particular policy puzzle.[6]

6. The importance of the general principle of "protecting the vulnerable" first struck me in connection with the ethics of nuclear power generation (Goodin 1980, pp. 438–39); those two pages subsequently grew into a book (Goodin 1985).

2   Harm to Self

The first and most obvious reason we may have for wanting to restrict smoking is to prevent harms that would be done to smokers themselves by their smoking. This chapter opens with a survey of those harms and of the scientific problems in assessing them (section 2.1).

Of course, Mill and his followers would query whether "his own good, either physical or moral" is ever "sufficient warrant" for coercively interfering with a person's own behavior. But they would be the first to concede that it might be, if the behavior is not fully voluntary. If it is autonomy that we are trying to protect in opposing paternalistic legislation in general, then the same values that lead us to oppose such legislation in general will lead us to welcome it in those particular cases where what we are being protected from is something that would deprive us of the capacity for autonomous choice. Evidence of the addictiveness of nicotine, surveyed in section 2.2, suggests that even advocates of personal autonomy ought to favor smoking restrictions on those grounds.

Another class of broadly utilitarian moral theories would have us look instead to people's welfare, both individually and especially collectively. Although it turns out to be a slightly longer story than one might first imagine, that too would lead us to favor restrictions on smoking, as shown in section 2.3.

In pursuing these goals, we face a choice among several broad styles of policy. They range from "self-regulation" on the part of the tobacco industry, or "self-help" on the part of injured smokers initiating tort damage suits, through government bans on the advertising, sale, or use of tobacco products. By and large, the arguments canvased above offer slender grounds for any principled choice among those options, advising merely that we should choose whichever policy works best to achieve the stipulated goal. In section 2.4, I survey such evidence as we have on the track records of various alternative policies for restricting tobacco consumption, and I tentatively propose my own preferred policy mix on the basis of that survey.

2.1   WHAT ARE THE RISKS?

Folk wisdom has long held tobacco smoking to be unhealthy. During the first outbreak of the smoking epidemic in the seventeenth century, the authorities tried to outlaw it on grounds of public health (Harrison 1986, p. 555). From the earliest days of our own century, cigarettes have been popularly known as "coffin nails," everyone's grandmother warned that they would stunt your growth, and so on.

Proper medical evidence scientifically supporting such suspicions began mushrooming in the 1950s and culminated in the justly famous reports of the Royal College of Physicians of 1962 and of the U.S. surgeon general two years later. The subsequent scientific literature on smoking and health—now numbering over 50,000 studies (U.S. Department of Health and Human Services [DHHS] 1986, p. vii)— has merely served to reinforce those earlier fears.

The easiest way into this vast technical literature is through the surgeon general's reports: *Smoking and Health* (U.S. Department of Health, Education and Welfare [DHEW] 1964); the series on *The Health Consequences of Smoking,* published almost annually since 1967 and focusing on a different hazard each year; and consolidation volumes in that series (U.S. DHEW 1976; U.S. DHHS 1989). These reports contain both nontechnical summaries for the general reader and fuller summaries of technical literature for anyone wanting to follow up in some detail; to follow them up further, see the U.S. DHHS annotated bibliography, *Smoking and Health Bulletin,* published six times a year and collected annually as the *Bibliography on Smoking and Health.* The Royal College of Physicians reports (1962, 1971, 1983) are more sporadic but aimed more at a mass audience.[1]

In a way, though, further reading is not really necessary. The basic findings are familiar enough already. Smoking leads to cancer (especially of the lung and respiratory tract, but also of the pancreas and bladder) and to cardiovascular diseases (particularly coronary heart disease, but also peripheral vascular disease) and is the major cause of chronic obstructive lung disease.

If the basic findings are familiar, the magnitude of the effects can still shock. To say that smoking is responsible for more than 350,000 deaths per year in the United States is to say that about 15 percent of all deaths in the United States are smoking-related (U.S. DHHS 1986, pp. vii, 5–6). Put in more personal terms, "about a quarter of the young men who smoke a pack a day or so of cigarettes are killed

---

1.   The best single brief article is Fielding (1985).

before their time by smoking"; and "on average . . . [they] have lost ten to fifteen years of life" (Peto 1980, p. 45).

Another way of putting the point is in terms of age-adjusted mortality rates. Of course, the older you are the more likely you are to die over the course of the next year. But factoring out age considerations, the point remains that at any given age smokers are 68 percent more likely to die over the course of the next year than are nonsmokers; and age-adjusted mortality rates for heavy smokers are about double that. In terms of such age-adjusted mortality rates, a moderate smoker's chances of dying from lung cancer are 10.8 times greater than a nonsmoker's; of bronchitis or emphysema, 6.1 times greater; of cancer of the larynx, 5.4 times greater; or oral cancer, 4.1 times greater; of cancer of the esophagus, 3.4 times greater; of coronary artery disease or other heart diseases, 1.7 times greater; and so on down the list (U.S. DHEW 1964, p. 29).[2]

Such findings have been confirmed time and again in subsequent replications of those early studies. The surgeon general's annual reports on this unfolding literature make drearily monotonous reading.[3] The surgeon general has, accordingly, concluded repeatedly that "cigarette smoking is the largest single preventable cause of death and disability for the U.S. population" (U.S. DHHS 1986, pp. 5–6). And even President Reagan's Council of Economic Advisers [U.S. CEA] 1987, p. 184) was forced to agree: "smoking presents the largest single source of health risk in America."

In principle, the advent of low tar and nicotine cigarettes might have been expected to mitigate, if not eliminate, many of the health effects of smoking. In practice, such cigarettes are less of a health boon than they might seem. The evidence is that people smoke more of them, and smoke them more intensively, so as to sustain their nicotine intake (U.S. DHHS 1981, sec. 7; Russell 1974, p. 255). Other forms of technological breakthrough toward a "safer cigarette" may prove similarly unsuccessful, for one reason or another.[4]

In the rest of this book, I shall often refer—as a kind of shorthand—to "cigarette smoking" and "cancer" when discussing

2. These mortality ratios have remained broadly stable across time (Doll and Peto 1981, p. 1221; U.S. DHHS 1989, chap. 3). There is only a very short list of ways in which smoking contributes to longer life, as indicated by mortality ratios less than 1.0. Among them are cancer of the rectum, colorectal cancer (in women, but not in men), primary central nervous system neoplasms, and Parkinson's disease. Of these, only the latter mortality ratio can credibly be claimed to be very substantially below 1.0. See Eysenck (1986, pp. 20–21).

3. The consolidation volumes—U.S. DHEW 1976; U.S. DHHS 1989—usefully summarize findings to date. On policy responses, see esp. U.S. DHHS 1989 chaps. 7, 8.

4. In the course of recent litigation, it emerged that Liggett and Meyers had in the 1970s developed and patented a cigarette which mixed a palladium catalyst and a nitrogen salt with the tobacco, resulting in an "almost total elimination" of tumors in

these issues. But be warned, that is no more than shorthand. All modes of consuming tobacco cause significant—if not quite so dramatic—increases in the risks of contracting cancer somewhere or other in the body (U.S. DHEW 1976, chap. 10). And cancer, clearly, is not the only thing that smokers have to fear.

The evidence underlying these medical conclusions is largely epidemiological in character. They rest on analysis of statistical aggregates rather than on analysis of the aetiology of particular cases. What these studies show is simply that, in the population as a whole, smokers contract those various diseases many times more often than nonsmokers; and heavy smokers contract them much more often than light smokers. These differential rates of illness are much too large to be put down to mere chance. They seem to vary, in lagged fashion, with changes in the aggregate consumption of tobacco over time. And so on.

Strictly speaking, all that that proves is that smoking correlates with those diseases. As any first course in statistics teaches, correlation is not causation. The 1964 surgeon general's report addresses this question of causation at length, arguing, inter alia, that just as cause precedes consequence, smoking precedes cancer; just as causes are spatially contiguous to consequences, smoke touches the lung where cancer later develops; there is properly controlled experimental evidence that tars from cigarette smoke cause cancer when painted on the skin of mice and other animals; and the increases over the past century in smoking seem to correspond, in lagged fashion, so closely to increases over the same period in lung cancers that it is simply not credible that that increase in cancer could have been caused by any other factor so far suggested (U.S. DHEW 1964, pp. 19–21, 175–96; Bradford Hill 1965).

None of that yet proves causation, in an ironclad fashion. And the last point, in particular, is still sometimes challenged (Brownlee 1965; Burch 1978; Eysenck 1986, pp. 32–43). Still, the essence of scientific explanation lies in telling "plausible stories." All of that goes a substantial way toward underwriting the plausibility of the tale.

Statistical purists and tobacco apologists will nonetheless insist that the case is still "not proven" because the findings are "merely statistical" (R. J. Reynolds 1986; Burch 1978; Eysenck 1980, 1986). It

replications of the mice-painting experiments that had helped establish cigarette tars and nicotine as carcinogenic in the first place. See the *Tobacco Products Litigation Reporter* 3, no. 1 (January 1987); 8.1–8.13. The researcher responsible for this development, Dr. James Mold, disappointed that the product was never marketed, suspects the intervention of company lawyers. The company says the cigarette was never marketed because of problems with taste (Matthews 1988) similar to those forcing the withdrawal of other "nicotine-free" and "smokeless" cigarettes from the market (Freedman 1989; Morris and Waldman 1989). Experience with low tar and nicotine cigarettes suggests that, even if people were prepared to smoke the new cigarettes, they might do so in a way that mitigated the hoped-for health effects, though.

pays to consider carefully what other causal paths are being contemplated when they say that. In an early letter to the *British Medical Journal*, the distinguished statistician and geneticist, Sir Ronald Fisher (1957), identified two alternative possibilities. One is that we have the causal arrow backward and that incipient cancer is what causes people to smoke rather than vice versa. So far as I can tell, nobody has taken this possibility sufficiently seriously to investigate it properly.

The other, more worrying possibility is multicolinearity. That is simply to say that there might be some common cause that leads both to smoking and to cancer, thus rendering any apparent connection between the two wholly spurious. The textbook example of multicolinearity is that the price of rum in Havana correlates tightly with the wages of Boston preachers—not because the holy men drink up all their extra wages, thus driving up the price of rum, but, rather, because changes in the state of the world economy drive up both prices and wages (Tufte 1974, p. 19). Something similar may be going on in the link between smoking and cancer, Fisher fears.

There are, of course, a great many confounding factors involved in the relationship between smoking and lung cancer. Most of them (such as social class and workplace exposure to carcinogens) can be controlled statistically; and when they are, the relationship between smoking and cancer still remains significant. The most worrying possibilities are ones that are hard to control statistically. Primary among them is the possibility that an individual's genetic constitution causes both his smoking and his cancer, either directly (Fisher 1957; 1958; 1959; 1974, 5: 377–80, 385–432) or indirectly, through its influence on personality (Eysenck 1980).

The best test of this "genetic constitutional hypothesis" would come through a comparison of smoking and lung cancer rates among monozygotic and dizygotic twins. The former share the same genetic constitution; the latter do not, but they do presumably share much the same environment as their fraternal twins. Early studies suggested that the former were indeed significantly more alike—both in their smoking behavior and in their cancer history—than the latter. That finding lent credence to the hypothesis that there is no direct link between people's smoking and their lung cancer but, rather, that there is some third factor (their genes) that causes both. Those early studies were beset by a number of methodological problems, however (U.S. DHEW 1964, p. 190; Slade et al. 1986–87). The findings of the latest and most thorough analysis of the most comprehensive collection of twin data—the Swedish Twin Register—"speak strongly against this [genetic] constitutional hypothesis" (Cederlog, Friburg, and Lundman 1977, p. 115).[5]

---

5. Eysenck (1980, p. 157) dismisses those findings as "too slight to be convincing either way" but is forced to concede that the conclusions from his own twin studies are still merely "speculative," too (1986, p. 49).

Furthermore, that hypothesis is simply implausible, given what we know about the mechanisms governing the genetic transmission of personality characteristics and of susceptibility to cancer. Where two characteristics are coded on the same gene—as are, for example, skin color and susceptibility to sickle-cell anemia—there is a plausible genetic story to be told about how they can have a common genetic cause. But the relationship between smoking and lung cancer is not like that. Both human personality traits (like the propensity to smoke) and the propensity to develop most forms of human cancer seem to be the product not of a single gene—much less the same gene—but rather of interactions among multiple genes. As the surgeon general says, "the linkage (in a genetic sense) between multiple genes related to a habit (smoking) and a disease (lung cancer) in a heterogeneous population" is utterly implausible. It "would require numerous coincidences with small probabilities" all to occur simultaneously (U.S. DHEW 1964, p. 191).

Some researchers remain unpersuaded by those arguments (Eysenck 1986, pp. 52–53). And even if successful, all those arguments will have succeeded in doing is knocking out yet another alternative interpretation of the apparent link between smoking and cancer. But while the causal case is not quite proven, the hypothesis that smoking causes cancer will have been rendered substantially more credible than the most threatening alternative explanation of the apparent link.

Certainly carcinogens merely "trigger" tumors in those who are genetically predisposed, so not everyone is necessarily at equal risk from smoking. There may even be both "genetic constitutional" and genuinely "causal" factors linking smoking and cancer (Burch 1978). Advocates of curbs on smoking can concede all that without cost. Their case goes through perfectly well, just so long as: a sufficiently large proportion of the population is genetically vulnerable; among them, smoking makes a sufficiently large contribution in causing their cancers; and there is no way, technically or politically, to target truly effective antismoking policies only at those who are genetically at risk. Given the likelihood of each (indeed, of all) of these conditions being satisfied, antismoking policies can nonetheless be defended as important contributions to public health.[6]

Were we to regard the case against a suspected carcinogen as "not proven" for purposes of public policy-making until we identified the precise mechanism by which it caused cancer, we would have to wait until we found the cause of cancer itself before we could regulate carcinogens at all, however strong the statistical evidence linking the

---

6.   Strides are being made in identification of those at especially high risk of lung cancer and cardiac disease in consequence of smoking (Russell 1974, p. 257); but that, in itself, is not enough to undercut this case for a general antismoking campaign.

substances in question to cancer might be. By that standard, wildly carcinogenic substances like plutonium could be sold over the counter. By similar standards, thalidomide could still be marketed: we know it causes birth defects, but not exactly how or why. Or, again, by similar standards we might be obliged to ban apparently safe and effective drugs from the market until we knew precisely how they worked to effect their cures. In all those cases, such a standard of proof would be unreasonably high to require (Bradford Hill 1965; Armitage 1978, p. 460; Galbraith 1959).

In addition to questions about the standard of proof to be required, there are also questions to be raised about the allocation of the burden of proof itself. If we see ourselves as interfering with the liberty of manufacturers, we might more naturally suppose the burden of proof should lie with them to prove their product safe. If we see ourselves as interfering with the liberty of consumers, it would be a case of paternalism, and we would be more inclined to suppose that the burden lies with the government to prove products unsafe before prohibiting people from using them (Dworkin 1972/1983, pp. 33–34). Any manufactured good, cigarettes included, could equally legitimately be viewed under either description, of course; so, useful though that general principle might be in explicating the phenomenology of the situation, it is useless in providing any real policy guidance.

Those who argue against policies to curb smoking on the grounds that the case against it is still "not proven" are implicitly asking us to presume a product safe until proven otherwise. In practice, U.S. regulatory policy characteristically employs almost exactly the opposite presumption. Under the Food, Drug and Cosmetic Act, as amended in 1958, it is the manufacturer of a new drug or food additive that must bear the burden of demonstrating that the product is safe and effective, which in practice means "producing at least four and possibly more than ten valid studies involving rodent and nonrodent toxicity, cancer, and other tests. Moreover, no additive can be approved as safe 'if it is found . . . to induce cancer in man or animal' " in any measure at all (Breyer 1982, p. 134).

Now, as it happens, cigarettes stand outside the statutory boundaries governing this regulatory regime. Being classified for these purposes as neither a food nor a drug, cigarettes are beyond the Food and Drug Administration (FDA)'s jurisdiction.[7] Furthermore, under

7. Why that should be so is in and of itself an interesting story. "The item 'Tobacco' appeared in the 1890 edition of the *U.S. Pharmacopoeia*, an official listing of drugs published by the government. It did not appear in the 1905 or later editions . . . because the removal of tobacco from the *Pharmacopoeia* was the price that had to be paid to get the support of tobacco state legislators for the Food and Drug Act of 1906. The elimination of the word tobacco automatically removed the leaf from FDA supervision" (Fritschler 1969, p. 37).

that legislation, the FDA's prior approval is not required for marketing various categories of items: "natural constituents of food"; substances "generally recognized among experts as safe"; and products on the market before the 1958 enactment.[8] So even if cigarettes were brought under the ambit of FDA regulations, the carcinogens they contain might still be able to claim exemption from the regulations under the first and third of those other clauses.

All that speaks solely to the question of what the law, as it stands, happens to be. What the law ought morally to require is, perhaps, something else. In those terms, there seems to be a strong case for treating all carcinogenic consumer products the same. The most we might reasonably want to do is to presume products safe until the first sign that they might cause cancer emerges. But at the first sign that they might cause cancer, the presumption should shift; at that point, the burden of proof should fall upon those who would market potentially cancer-causing agents to prove that their products are safe. That is the way the FDA behaves in assessing most drugs and food additives. That is the way that the public at large reacts to evidence that cigarette smoking causes cancer, as tobacco companies themselves are the first to appreciate.[9]

For those things which we are 95 percent certain cause cancer or 95 percent certain do not, it makes no difference to our final decision which way we set the presumption. For those cases in which neither is true, however, the presumption will alone dictate the decision. There, it is absolutely crucial which way that presumption is set.

Alternatively, we might not want to operate with any presumption or burden of proof at all in these areas. The alternative would be to judge substances carcinogenic if, on the balance of available evidence, they seem more likely than not to cause cancer. Such a rule would avoid excesses in both directions. It would avoid banning substances at the first sign that they might cause cancer, as now

---

8.   Note, however, that "the FDA can proceed against" the latter products "by showing in court that they are 'injurious to health' " (Breyer 1982, p. 134). Thus, such products are not necessarily exempted from regulation altogether—the burden of proof has merely shifted to the government.

9.   In a confidential briefing to the Philip Morris board of directors in October 1964, its operations department stated that, thanks to the surgeon general's report, "in the public eye the burden of proof had been shifted from the accusers of cigarettes as a health hazard to the cigarette producers. It was now up to the cigarette companies to prove that cigarettes are safe or that safe ones could be made. In this connection it is our opinion that the industry must somehow find a way to make an effective *technical rebuttal* to the arguments of the anti-cigarette forces. Only in this way will the present burden be lifted from us." This document was released in connection with litigation of Cipollone v. Liggett Group (U.S. District Court for the District of New Jersey, Civil Action no. 83–2864) as Plaintiff's Exhibit no. 613; the quotation is from p. 3 of that document.

happens under the Delaney Amendment governing the FDA; but it would not go so far as to allow substances to continue being marketed as presumptively safe on equally slight evidence (Page 1978; see, further, Morrison and Henkel 1970; Atkins and Jarrett 1979).

Either way, however, tobacco surely has to be treated as if it caused cancer. It stands indicted, whether by presumption or by the balance of evidence. Indeed, on the above evidence, it would stand indicted at the .05 confidence level even if the presumption were set in favor of its safety: question as they might whether correlation proves causation, even friends of tobacco concede that, statistically (for what that is worth), there is much less than a 5 percent chance that the observed relationship between smoking and cancer would have occurred randomly.

2.2   DO SMOKERS VOLUNTARILY ACCEPT THE RISKS?

Given what we know of the health risks from smoking, we may well be tempted to "ban cigarette manufacturers from continuing to manufacture their product on the grounds that we are preventing them from causing illness to others in the same way that we prevent other manufacturers from releasing pollutants into the atmosphere, thereby causing danger to members of the community." That would be to move too quickly, though. For as Dworkin (1972/1983, p. 22) goes on to say, "The difference is . . . that in the former but not the latter case the harm is of such a nature that it could be avoided by those individuals affected, if they so chose. The incurring of the harm requires the active cooperation of the victim. It would be a mistake in theory and hypocritical in practice to assert that our interference in such cases is just like our interference in standard cases of protecting others from harm."

The courts have been as sensitive to this distinction as have moral philosophers. They appeal to the venerable legal maxim, *volenti non fit injuria*, to hold that through their voluntary assumption of the risk smokers have waived any claims against cigarette manufacturers. In perhaps one of the most dramatic cases in this area (given the well-established synergism between smoking and asbestos inhalation in causing lung disease), the Fifth Circuit refused to enjoin cigarette manufacturers as codefendants in a suit against Johns-Manville, saying that "the danger is to the smoker who willingly courts it."[10]

Certainly there is, morally speaking, a world of difference between the harms that others inflict upon you and the harms that

---

10. Johns-Manville Sales Corp. v. International Association of Machinists, Machinists Local 1609, 621 F.2d 756, 759 (5th Cir. 1980). See, further, Daniels 1985, p. 155, n. 8; cf. Anonymous 1986.

you inflict upon yourself. The question is simply whether, in the case of smoking, the active cooperation of the smoker really is such as to constitute voluntary acceptance of the consequent risks of illness and death. The question is decomposable into two further ones. The first, discussed in section 2.2.1, concerns the question of whether smokers know the risks. The second, discussed in section 2.2.2, concerns the question of whether, even if smoking in full knowledge of the risks, they could be said to "accept" the risks in a sense that is fully voluntary.

2.2.1   *Do Smokers Know the Risks?*

Here we are involved, essentially, with a question of "informed consent." People can be held to have consented only if they knew to what they were supposedly consenting. In the personalized context of medical encounters, this means that each and every person being treated is told, in terms he understands, by the attending physician what the risks of the treatment might be (Gorovitz 1982, chap. 3). For largely anonymous transactions in the market, such personalized standards are inappropriate. Instead, we are forced to infer consent from what people know or should have known (in the standard legal construct, what a "reasonable man" should have been expected to know) about the product. And in the anonymous world of the market, printed warnings necessarily take the place of face-to-face admonitions.

Cigarette manufacturers, in defending against product liability suits, have claimed on both these grounds that smokers should be construed as having consented to whatever risks that they have run (Edell and Gisser 1985; American Medical Association [AMA] 1986; Anonymous 1986). They claim, first, that any "reasonable" person should have known—and that the "ordinary consumer" did indeed know—that smoking was an "inherently dangerous" activity.[11] Their interrogatories (pretrial questions put to the plaintiff before a case comes to trial) constantly seek to establish that plaintiffs had in their youth consorted with people calling cigarettes "coffin nails," and so on.[12]

---

11.   Recent tort law revisions in California and New Jersey bar product-liability actions altogether against manufacturers of "products that are inherently dangerous and are known to be unsafe by the ordinary consumer" (Cohen 1987, p. 8; see, further, Daynard 1988, p. 12). In order to avail themselves of this protection, however, manufacturers will have to prove that their products are inherently dangerous. That would compromise their defenses against liability claims in other jurisdictions and would undermine their public standing more generally, so on balance they may well prefer to shun this option.

12.   See, e.g., those reprinted in the *Tobacco Products Litigation Reporter* 2, no. 7 (July/August 1987): 3.365–400, 3.441–60.

Of course, claiming that any reasonable person should have known smoking was unhealthy sits uneasily with the same corporations' claims—often in the very same litigation—that there is no evidence that smoking causes cancer, either in general or in the plaintiffs' particular cases (Anonymous 1986, p. 817). Caught in this inconsistency, one tobacco company recently withdrew any claims as to the plaintiff's negligence, lest it be required to answer interrogatories stating exactly what any "reasonable person" should have known about the dangers of its products (Mintz 1987).

Cigarette manufacturers have a fallback position here, though. They claim, second, that the printing of government-mandated health warnings on cigarette packets from 1966 onward has constituted further, explicit warning to users of the dangers of the products. The question, recall, is whether consumers were warned of the risks, not who warned them or why. So the fact that the health warnings were required by the Congress rather than printed voluntarily by manufacturers does nothing to undercut their value for this purpose. Indeed, according to the current run of court opinions, that might actually enhance the value of such warnings in deflecting tort liability suits.[13]

Not only are those government health warnings printed on cigarette packets useful in defending companies against claims for harms that were inflicted at some time after 1966, when they first appeared, but tobacco company lawyers defending against product liability suits have even tried to use post-1966 behavior to infer "hypothetical consent" to risks before the warnings were given. As one company attorney argued in *Cipollone v. Liggett Group,* "because Rose Cipollone continued to smoke for at least 15 years while warnings were on every pack she bought, she would have smoked before January 1, 1966, even if the defendants had voluntarily warned her about possible health consequences" (quoted in Mintz 1988a). Now, there may be certain circumstances in which hypothetical consent can be a convincing argument—some such logic must be what justifies the physician in cutting open the comatose patient in the emergency room, for example. This case does not seem to be among them, though. What we have here is more like an amateur boxer mugging you, on the grounds that since you belong to the same boxing club you obviously would have agreed to fight him if he had only asked. It takes actual, not merely hypothetical, consent to defend against a charge of assault and battery. Likewise, I would argue, in the case of the tobacco companies. That the companies

13. Reference here is to the "preemption" defense, discussed more fully on pages 49–50 below.

should try to run the argument at all is indicative, however, of the hopes that they are pinning on printed warnings to relieve them of legal liability.

In the best of circumstances, warnings—whether from government or grandmother—will only get us so far. There are some risks of which smokers have historically never been warned by either government or grandmother. Among them are things like Buerger's disease, a circulatory condition induced in often quite young people by smoking, that can result in amputation of limbs.[14]

Furthermore, the warnings of both folk wisdom and cigarette packets, in the 1960s and 1970s at least, were desperately nonspecific. A more general question therefore arises: are all-purpose warnings that "X is hazardous to your health," without specifying just how likely X is to cause just what sorts of harms, adequate warning to secure people's informed consent, at all? Certainly the psychological evidence suggests that an explicit, concrete message is a better spur to action than a vague, abstract one (Borgida and Nisbett 1977).

Problems of nonspecific warnings are not peculiar to cigarettes, of course. In principle, they might be as much of a problem with lawn mowers and insecticides. In practice, though, warnings there tend to be stated more strongly: they tend to say that certain bad things *will* happen to you if the product is misused (e.g., you will be poisoned), not just that they *may* (i.e., not just that the product "is dangerous to your health"); they mention death explicitly (often employing the conventional skull-and-crossbones symbol on the label); they suggest specific antidotes; and so on. All those factors make those warnings more successful at what warnings are supposed to do—convey a real sense of the seriousness of the hazard—than do the sorts of milquetoast warnings traditionally carried on cigarette packets.

There is a fair bit of evidence that smokers—especially young smokers—simply do not read what appears inside the surgeon general's boxed warning on cigarette packets and advertisements. One study, for example, monitored eye tracking of adolescents viewing tobacco advertisements and found that almost half of them did not cast eyes on the warning at all; when subsequently asked to identify, from the surgeon general's rotating list of warnings, which it was that appeared in the advertisement they had seen, subjects did only slightly better than random (Fischer et al. 1989). Warnings that are not—and perhaps are designed not to be—read cannot possibly be

---

14. Neither do cigarette packets warn, as some drug containers do, that the product is addictive (Garner 1980; Schwartz 1989). But if tobacco is truly addictive, then it is that addictiveness rather than the failure to warn of addictiveness that blocks consent-based defenses, as argued in sec. 2.2.2 below (cf. Wikler 1978/1983, p. 39).

effective. The evidence suggests that tobacco health warnings fall largely into that category.

As important, cigarette manufacturers take back through their advertising what is given, inside the surgeon general's boxed notice, by way of warnings (White 1988, chap. 6). There are various examples. Admonitions that "smoking is dangerous to your health," when conjoined with pictures of people enjoying dangerous sports (white water rafting, and the like), perversely serve to make smoking more attractive. Warnings that "smoking by pregnant women may result in fetal injury, premature birth, and low birth weight," when conjoined with sexually provocative photos in magazines devoted to casual sex without procreation, again perversely undercut the health message. Perhaps most important of all, advertising that appeals to the rebelliousness of youth in general and young women and young blacks in particular (the "You've come a long way, baby" campaign, e.g.) constitutes a thinly veiled invitation for them to ignore the advice of authorities. Particularly striking, in this connection, was a 1983 billboard campaign in Britain employing the caption, "We're not allowed to tell you anything about Winston cigarettes, so here's a man blowing a raspberry" (Chapman 1986, p. 16).[15]

The problem is not so much one of literally deceptive advertising, though there is evidence of some of that (U.S. Federal Trade Commission [FTC] 1981, 1984, 1985), particularly in earlier periods (Rothenberg 1988).

> Since the early 1930s, the [Federal Trade] Commission . . . brought approximately 20 actions against cigarette companies for false or misleading advertising. Many of those actions involved what the Commission considered misleading health claims. The manufacturers of Chesterfields were prohibited, for example, from claiming their product had "no adverse effect upon the nose, throat or accessory organs." Another producer was proscribed from claiming that Kools will keep one's head clear in winter . . ., give extra protection, or provide an excellent safeguard during cold months. [Fritschler 1969, pp. 29–30]

Despairing of a case-by-case strategy for controlling such deceptive advertising, the Federal Trade Commission felt compelled, in September 1955, to lay down certain mandatory "guides" for cigarette

15. Some would argue that smokers were better informed in the past, when unregulated advertisers employed "knocking copy" to point out health risks of other brands of cigarettes (Calfee 1986). Those arguments are highly suspect, though. The central claim of such advertisements, after all, was that the advertiser's own brand was free from the defects found in others.

advertising including, inter alia: "a ban on assertions that smoking had favorable effects on the respiratory, digestive, or nervous system; a ban on claims of medical approval of smoking, or of a particular brand; and a ban on any unproven claim of nicotine content" (White 1988, p. 39; see also Fritschler 1969, p. 30). Ultimately the Federal Trade Commission itself agreed even that was inadequate to curb deceptive trade practices in the tobacco industry (Fritschler 1969, pp. 70–72).

The greater contemporary problem, though, lies not in any literally false claims cigarette advertisements make for their products. It lies instead in the widespread use, in them, of deceptively healthy imagery (U.S. FTC 1981, pp. 428a, 491a). The printed warnings may say "smoking kills." But the advertising images are the very picture of robust good health. Cowboys, sports, and the great outdoors figure centrally in the ads. The U.S. Federal Trade Commission has continually warned Congress that "current practices and methods of cigarette advertising" have the effect of "reducing anxieties about the health risks posed by cigarette smoking" (U.S. FTC 1984, p. 5), "negat[ing] the effect of health warnings because they imply that smoking is a habit which is compatible with performing various outdoor activities and having a strong healthy body" (U.S. FTC 1985, p. 5).[16]

The point being made here is not that advertising bypasses consumers' capacity to reason, and somehow renders them unfree to choose intelligently whether or not to partake of the product. No one is saying that consumers of tobacco are brainwashed to quite that extent. The central point here is merely that the tobacco companies in effect are giving out—and, more important, consumers are receiving—conflicting information. The implicit health claims of the advertising imagery conflict with the explicit health warnings, and thus undercut any *volenti* or informed consent defense companies might try to mount on the basis of those warnings (Edell and Gisser 1985).

2.2.2   *Is Acceptance of the Risks Fully Voluntary?*

Obviously, people cannot voluntarily accept the health risks of smoking if they do not know what they are. Despite tobacco companies' best

---

16.   Literally, of course, it is—at least broadly speaking and in the short run. But in the medium to long term, participation even in purely recreational sport (not to mention serious sport, where peak performance is required) is impaired by the consequences of smoking. Insofar as young smokers are encouraged in the belief that they can always quit, should smoking become a problem later, that is a false belief (as shown by the addiction evidence, discussed below); and advertisements carrying any such implications once again would count as clearly deceptive advertising.

efforts, though, the great majority of people—smokers included—knows, in broad outline, what health risks smoking entails. In a 1978 Gallup poll, only 24 percent of even heavy smokers claimed that they were unaware of, or did not believe, the evidence that smoking is hazardous to health (Anonymous 1986, p. 814, n. 26; U.S. FTC 1981, p. 433a). That figure might somewhat overstate the extent of their acceptance of the statistics. There are various other false beliefs smokers sometimes employ to qualify their acceptance of those statistics and hence to rationalize their continued smoking (e.g., that the lethal dose is far in excess of what they smoke, however many that may be) (Marsh 1985, p. 8). Still, we can reasonably suppose that, in some sense or another, well over half of smokers know that what they are doing is unhealthy.

It is worth pausing, at this point, to consider just how we should handle that recalcitrant residual of smokers who deny the evidence. Having smoked thousands of packets containing increasingly stern warnings, and having been exposed to hundreds of column inches of newspaper reporting and several hours of broadcasting about smoking's hazards, they are presumably incorrigible in their false beliefs in this regard. Providing them with still more information is likely to prove pointless (cf. Feinberg 1971/1983, p. 11). People will say "if they are so bad for you as all that the government would ban cigarettes altogether." Or they will say "the government says that nearly everything is bad for you." Or they will find still some other way of rationalizing the practice.

Ordinarily it is not the business of public policy to prevent people from relying on false inferences from full information which would harm only themselves. Sometimes, however, it is. One such case comes when the false beliefs would lead to decisions that are "far-reaching, potentially dangerous, and irreversible"—as, for example, with people who believe that when they jump out of a tenth-story window they will float upward (Dworkin 1972/1983, p. 31; see also Feinberg 1971/1983, p. 7).

We are particularly inclined toward intervention when false beliefs with such disastrous results are traceable to familiar, well-understood forms of cognitive defect (Sunstein 1986, pp. 1161–64). There is something deeply offensive—morally, and perhaps legally as well—about the "intentional exploitation of a man's known weaknesses" in these ways (White 1972).

One such familiar form of cognitive defect is "wishful thinking": smokers believing the practice is safe because they smoke, rather than smoking because they believe it to be safe (Pears 1984). There is substantial evidence that smokers believe, groundlessly, that they are less vulnerable to smoking-related diseases (Leventhal, Glynn, and

Fleming 1987, p. 3374). More surprising, and more directly to the "wishful thinking" point, is the evidence that smokers came to acquire those beliefs in their own invulnerability, and to "forget" what they previously knew about the dangers of smoking, *after* they took up the habit.[17]

Another cognitive defect is the so-called anchoring fallacy (Kahneman, Slovic, and Tversky 1982). People smoke many times without any (immediately perceptible) bad effects. Naturally, people extrapolate from their own experience. They therefore conclude—quite reasonably, but quite wrongly—that smoking is safe, at least for them.

Yet another phenomenon, sometimes regarded as a cognitive defect, is "time discounting." Sometimes the ill effects of smoking would be felt almost immediately. Tonight's cigarette will make me short of breath when jogging tomorrow morning, for example. To ignore such effects, just on the grounds that they are in the future, is obviously absurd when the "future" in question is so close; it would imply a discount rate of 100 percent per hour, "compounding to an annual rate too large for my calculator," as Schelling (1980, p. 99) sneers. But most of the really serious consequences of smoking are some decades away for most of us. And since young smokers will not suffer the full effects of smoking-related diseases for some years to come, they may puff away happily now with little regard for the consequences, just so long as they attach relatively little importance to future pains relative to present pleasures in their utility functions (Fuchs 1982). Economists, of course, are inclined to regard a "pure time preference" as a preference like any other, neither rational nor irrational. But reasons can be given for thinking that a lack of due regard for one's own future truly is a form of cognitive defect.[18]

17. In the crucial study Alexander, Calcott, and Dobson (1983) administered a twenty-eight-item questionnaire about the health risks of smoking to 6,000 school children aged ten to twelve. Then they exposed them to a health education program informing them, among other things, about the health consequences of smoking. When administering the same twenty-eight-item questionnaire to the same children a year later, the researchers came upon this startling discovery: those children who had taken up smoking over the course of the year showed a decrease in knowledge on that test compared to their previous year's score, whereas other children who had not begun to smoke showed significant increases.

18. Daniels (1985, p. 99) tries to show its irrationality by inviting us to construct a notion of a "hypothetical agent, . . . abstract[ing] from certain features of individuals" as we know them. He then argues that it would be prudent for (i.e., rationally incumbent upon) such agents to take a strong interest in their futures. That amounts to a quasi-Rawlsian appeal against the *injustice* of time-discounting, though. It does not, strictly speaking, demonstrate its imprudence or irrationality. My preferred argument is this: suppose, plausibly enough, that your later self will prefer that your earlier self

All of these cognitive defects point to relatively weak forms of irrationality, to be sure.[19] In and of themselves, they might not be enough to justify interference with people's liberty, perhaps. When they lead people to take decisions that are far-reaching, potentially life-threatening, and irreversible, though, perhaps intervention would indeed be justifiable.

Interfering with people's choices in such cases is paternalistic, admittedly. But there are many different layers of paternalism (Sartorius 1983; Feinberg 1986). What is involved here is a relatively weak form of paternalism, one that works within the individual's own theory of the good and merely imposes upon him a better means of achieving what after all are only his own ends.[20] It is one thing to stop people who want to commit suicide from doing so, but quite another to stop people who want to live from acting in a way that they falsely believe to be safe (Feinberg 1971/1983, p. 10; Dworkin 1972/1983, pp. 23, 33). Smokers who deny the health risks fall into that latter, easier category.

The larger and harder question is how to deal with the great majority of smokers who, knowing the risks, continue smoking anyway. Of course, it might be said that they do not *really* know the risks. Although most acknowledge that smoking is "unhealthy," in some vague sense, few know exactly what chances they run of exactly what diseases. In one poll, 49 percent of smokers did not know that smoking causes most cases of lung cancer, 63 percent that it causes most cases of bronchitis, and 85 percent that it causes most cases of emphysema (U.S. FTC 1981, pp. 345a–364a; see similarly Marsh 1985).

Overestimating badly the risks of dying in other more dramatic ways (such as car crashes, etc.), people badly underestimate the

---

had taken its later interests more seriously. Then want-regarding moralities (utilitarianism, certainly) would put this later claim fully on a par with that of the earlier self (Goodin 1982, chap. 3). So long as earlier and later selves are instantiations of one and the same person, we can say that the earlier one is therefore "irrational" not to take properly into account his later interests. (If they are not the "same person," it is indeed appropriate to appeal to norms of justice: it is unjust for one person to take advantage of another in this way, whether or not they share the same body at different moments.)

19. The addiction evidence surveyed in sec. 2.2.2 below *is* evidence of genuine, full-blown irrationality; and it might explain why people are so prone to these more modest cognitive errors, when it comes to smoking, as well.

20. One of a person's ends—continued life—at least. Perhaps the person has other ends ("relaxation," or whatever) that are well served by smoking; and insofar as "people taking risks actually value the direct consequences associated with them . . . it is more difficult to intrude paternalistically" (Daniels 1985, pp. 158, 163). But assuming that smoking is not the only means to the other ends—not the only way to relax, etc.—the intrusion is only minimally difficult to justify.

relative risks of dying in the more mundane ways associated with smoking. This allows them to rationalize further their smoking behavior as being "not all that dangerous," compared to other things that they are also doing.

Of course, logically it would be perfectly possible for people both to underestimate the extent of a risk and simultaneously to overreact to it. People might suppose the chances of snakebite are slight but live in mortal fear of it nonetheless. Psychologically, however, the reverse seems to happen. People's subjective probability estimates of an event's likelihood increase the more they dread it, and the more "psychologically available" the event therefore is to them (Kahneman, Slovic, and Tversky 1982). Smoking-related diseases, in contrast, tend to be "quiet killers" of which people have little direct or indirect experience, which tend to be underreported in newspapers (typically not even being mentioned in obituary notices) and which act on people one at a time rather than catastrophically killing many people at once (Lichtenstein et al. 1978, p. 567). Smoking-related diseases being psychologically less available to people in these ways, they underestimate their frequency dramatically—by a factor of 8, in the case of lung cancer, according to one study (Slovic, Fischhoff, and Lichtenstein 1982, p. 469).[21]

Besides all that, there is the distinction between "knowing intellectually" some statistic and "feeling in your guts" its full implications. Consent counts—morally, as well as merely legally—only if it is truly informed consent, that is to say, only if people really know what it is to which they are consenting. That, in turn, requires not only that we can state the probabilities but also that we "appreciate them in an emotionally genuine manner" (Dworkin 1972/1983, p. 30). There is reason to believe that smokers do not (U.S. FTC 1981, p. 428a).

It may still be argued that, as long as people had the facts, they can and should be held responsible if they chose not to act upon them when they could have done so. It may be folly for utilitarian policymakers to rely upon people's such imperfect responses to facts for purposes of constructing social welfare functions and framing public policies around them. But there is the separate matter of who ought to be blamed when some self-inflicted harm befalls people. There, arguably, responsibility ought to be on people's own shoulders (Knowles 1977; Wikler 1987). Arguably, we ought to stick to that judgment, even if people were "pressured" into smoking by the

---

21. Thus, health education campaigns have begun focusing on the risks of contracting Buerger's disease from smoking, the amputation of limbs being, like snakebites, psychologically more accessible to people (especially teenagers, before they start to smoke) than rotting lungs.

bullying of aggressive advertising or peer group pressure (cf. Gewirth 1980, pp. 124–25; Daniels 1985, p. 159).

What crucially transforms the "voluntary acceptance" argument is evidence of the addictive nature of cigarette smoking. Of course, saying that smoking is addictive is not to say that all smokers are hooked and none can ever give it up. Clearly, many have done so. By the same token, though, "most narcotics users . . . never progress beyond occasional use, and of those who do, approximately 30 percent spontaneously remit" (U.S. DHHS 1988, p. v). Surprisingly enough, studies show that more than 70 percent of American servicemen addicted to heroin in Vietnam gave it up when returning to the United States (Robins 1973; Pollin 1984; Fingarette 1975, pp. 429–31). We nonetheless continue to regard heroin as an addictive drug. The test of addictiveness is not impossibility but rather difficulty of withdrawal.

There is a tendency, in discussing *volenti* or informed consent arguments, to draw too sharp a distinction between "voluntary" and "involuntary acts" and to put the dividing line at the wrong place, at that (Feinberg 1986, chap. 20). The tendency is often to assume that any act that is in the least voluntary—that is in any respect at all, to any extent at all, within the control of the agents themselves—is to be considered fully voluntary for the purposes. If we want to claim that some sort of act was involuntary, we are standardly advised to look for evidence of "somnambulism" or "automatism" or such like (Prevezer 1958; Fox 1963). Thus, U.S. Supreme Court justices wanting to argue for more humane treatment of addicts felt obliged to assert that "once [the defendant] had become an addict he was utterly powerless" to refrain from continuing to service his addiction (Fortas 1968, p. 567). That is an implausibly strong claim, given the above evidence.

There is no need to make such a strong claim, though, to vitiate arguments that the conduct was "voluntary" and the harm thus self-incurred. For purposes of excusing criminal conduct, we are prepared to count forms of "duress" that stop well short of rendering all alternative actions literally impossible. It is perfectly possible for bank tellers to let a robber break their arms instead of handing over the money; but no one expects them to do so. A credible threat of serious pain, or perhaps even very gross discomfort, is ordinarily regarded as more than sufficient to constitute duress of the sort that excuses responsibility for otherwise impermissible behavior.

So, too, I would argue should be the case with addiction-induced behavior. The issue is not whether it is literally impossible, but merely whether it is unreasonably costly, for addicts to resist their compulsive desires. If that desire is so strong that even someone with " 'normal and reasonable' self-control" (Watson 1977, p. 331) would succumb to it, we have little compunction in saying that the addict's free will was sufficiently impaired that his apparent consent counts for naught.[22]

This is arguably the case with nicotine addiction. To establish a substance as addictive, we require two sorts of evidence. The first is some sort of evidence of "physical need" for the substance among its users. That evidence is widely thought necessary to prove smoking is an addiction, rather than just a "habit" (U.S. DHEW 1964, chaps. 13–14), a psychological dependence, or a matter of mere sociological pressure (Daniels 1985, p. 159)—none of which would undercut, in a way that addictiveness does, claims that the risks of smoking are voluntarily incurred. That physical link has now been established, though. Particular receptors for the active ingredients of tobacco smoke have been discovered in the brain; the physiological sites and mechanisms by which nicotine acts on the brain have now been well mapped, and its tendency to generate compulsive, repetitive behavior in consequence has been well established. Such evidence—summarized in the surgeon general's 1988 report (U.S. DHHS 1988, chaps. 3–4; see also Leventhal and Cleary 1980; and Winsten 1986)—has been one important factor in leading the World Health Organization ([WHO] 1978) and the American Psychiatric Association ([APA] 1987, sec. 305.1) to classify nicotine as a dependence-inducing drug. (Strictly speaking, the term "addiction" is out of favor in these circles, with "dependence" taking its place; in what follows, I shall continue using the more colloquial term in preference to the more technical one, though.)

None of that evidence proves that it would be literally impossible for smokers to resist the impulse to smoke. Through extraordinary acts of will, they might. Nor does any of that evidence prove that it is literally impossible for them to break their dependence altogether. Many have. Recall, however, that the issue is not one of impossibility but rather of how hard people should have to try before their will is said to be sufficiently impaired that their agreement does not count as genuine consent.

The evidence suggests that nicotine addicts have to try very hard indeed. This is the second crucial fact to establish in proving a

22. Some would question whether drug withdrawal symptoms in general are really so severe as to justify claims of involuntariness by reason of "pharmacological coercion." Fingarette (1975, p. 437; see also Fingarette 1970) may well be right that the effects of withdrawal are largely in the addict's own mind and that they loom much larger in prospect among addicts contemplating withdrawal than they turn out to have been in retrospect after withdrawal has been successfully accomplished. Still, it is the agent's beliefs that are always the keys to coercion: if the bank tellers believed the robber's gun was loaded, they handed over the money under duress and are excused for that reason, even if it turns out that the gun's chambers were empty.

substance addictive.[23] Central among the WHO/APA criteria for diagnosing nicotine dependence is the requirement of evidence of "continuous use of tobacco for at least one month with . . . unsuccessful attempts to stop or significantly reduce the amount of tobacco use on a permanent basis" (APA 1987, sec. 305.1).

A vast majority of smokers do indeed find themselves in this position. The surgeon general reports the results of various studies showing that 90 percent of regular smokers have tried to quit (U.S. DHHS 1979, quoted in Pollin 1984). Another 1975 survey found that 84 percent of smokers had attempted to stop, but that only 36 percent of them had succeeded in maintaining their changed behavior for a whole year (Benfari, Ockene, and McIntyre 1982; see, further, Leventhal and Cleary 1980). Interestingly, graphs mapping the "relapse rate"—the percentage of ex-addicts that are back on the drug after a given period of time—are almost identical for nicotine and for heroin (Winsten 1986; U.S. DHHS 1988, p. 314 and chap. 5 more generally).[24]

On the basis of all this evidence, the surgeon general has been led to three "major conclusions" contained in his 1988 report:

1. Cigarettes and other forms of tobacco are addicting.
2. Nicotine is the drug in tobacco that causes addiction.
3. The pharmacologic and behavioral processes that determine tobacco addiction are similar to those that determine addiction to drugs such as heroin and cocaine. [U.S. DHHS 1988, p. 9]

Evidence of smokers trying to stop and failing to do so is rightly regarded as central to the issue of addiction, philosophically as well as diagnostically. Some describe free will in terms of "second-order volitions"—desires about desires—controlling "first-order" ones (Frankfurt 1971). Others talk of free will in terms of a person's "evaluational structure" controlling his "motivational structure"—a

23. There are other physical needs that we would have trouble renouncing—such as our need for food—that we would be loath actually to call "addictions." Be that terminological issue as it may, we would also be loath, for precisely those reasons of physical need and the difficulty of renouncing it, to say that we eat "of our own free will." (We would have no hesitation that someone who makes a credible threat of preventing us from eating has thereby "coerced" us.) Since involuntariness and impairment of free will are what is really at issue here, those thus do seem to be the aspects of addictiveness that ground the conclusion that we do not voluntarily consent to the risks associated with addictive substances.

24. It might be wrong to make too much of that fact, however. Perhaps heroin addicts find both (*a*) that it is harder to give up and (*b*) that they have more reason to do so. Then relapse rates would appear the same, even though heroin is more addictive, in the sense of being harder to give up.

person striving to obtain something if and only if he thinks it to be of value (Watson 1975; 1977). Addiction—the absence of free will—is thus a matter of first-order volitions winning out over second-order ones, and surface desires prevailing over the agent's own deeper values. In the case of smoking, trying to stop can be seen as a manifestation of one's second-order volitions, or one's deeper values, and failing to stop as evidence of the triumph of first-order surface desires over them. The same criteria the WHO and APA use to diagnose nicotine dependence also establish the impairment of the smoker's free will, philosophically.

For certain purposes, at least, even the courts now treat nicotine as addictive. Social security benefits are not payable to those claimants whose disabilities were voluntarily self-inflicted. But the courts have held that "smoking can be an involuntary act for some persons," and that those benefits may not therefore be routinely withheld from victims of smoking-related diseases on the grounds that they are suffering from voluntarily self-inflicted injuries.[25]

Various other policy implications also follow from evidence of addictiveness, though. One might be that over-the-counter sales of cigarettes should be banned. If the product is truly addictive, then we have no more reason to respect a person's voluntary choice (however well-informed) to abandon his future volition to an addiction than we have for respecting a person's voluntary choice (however well-informed) to sell himself into slavery (Mill 1859/1975, pp. 126–27). I am unsure how far to press this argument, since after all we do permit people to bind their future selves (through contracts, e.g.). But if it is the size of the stakes or the difficulty of breaking out of the bonds that makes the crucial difference, then acquiring a lethal and hard-to-break addiction is much more like a slavery contract than it is like an ordinary commercial commitment (cf. Feinberg 1986, pp. 71–81).

In any case, addictiveness thus defined makes it far easier to justify interventions that on the surface appear paternalistic. In some sense, they would then not be paternalistic at all. Where people "wish to stop smoking, but do not have the requisite willpower . . . we are not imposing a good on someone who rejects it. We are simply using coercion to enable people to carry out their own goals" (Dworkin 1972/1983, p. 32).[26]

25. Gordon v. Schweiker, 725 F.2d 231, 236 (4th Cir. 1984).
26. That is one way of explaining an apparent paradox surrounding "sin" taxes in general: "items such as alcohol [and cigarettes] are so commonly consumed, and so little complaint is made about large excise taxes" on them, that microeconomists are led to conclude that it simply must be in the individual's own perceived interest, somehow, to be so taxed (Crain et al. 1977).

There is, of course, a genuine difficulty in deciding which is the "authentic" self. With whom should we side, when the person who asks us to help him to "enforce rules on himself" repudiates the rules at the moment they come to need to be enforced (Schelling 1980; 1983; 1984a; 1984b; 1985).[27] But at least we have more of a warrant for interference, in such cases, than if we were never asked for assistance by the agent at all.

Much of the assistance that we have to render in such situations will necessarily be of a very personal nature, and it will be outside the scope of public policy for that reason. There is nonetheless a substantial role for public policy in these realms. Banning or restricting smoking in public places (especially the workplace) can contribute crucially to an individual's own efforts at smoking cessation, for example (Etzioni 1978, pp. 67–68; Leventhal and Cleary 1980; U.S. DHHS 1986, chap. 6).

The real force of the addiction findings, in the context of *volenti* or informed-consent arguments, though, is to undercut the claim that there is any *continuing* consent to the risks involved in smoking. There might have been consent in the very first instance—in smoking your first cigarette. But once you were hooked, you lost the capacity to consent in any meaningful sense on a continuing basis (White 1972). As Hume (1760) says, to consent implies the possibility of doing otherwise; and addiction substantially deprives you of the capacity to do other than continue smoking. So once you have become addicted to nicotine, your subsequent smoking cannot be taken as indicating your consent to the risks.

The most that we can now say with confidence, therefore, is that "cigarette smoking, at least initially, is a voluntary activity," in the words of a leading court case in this area (Brown 1987, p. 627). If there is to be consent at all in this area, it can only be consent in the very first instance, that is, when you first began to smoke. That, in turn, seriously undercuts the extent to which cigarette manufacturers can rely upon *volenti* or informed-consent defenses in product liability litigation and its moral analogues.

It does so in two ways. The first arises from the fact that many of those now dying from tobacco-induced diseases started smoking well before warnings began appearing on packets in 1966 and were

---

27. It begs this question to say that the one reflects an "evaluational" and the other merely a "motivational" judgment (Watson 1975; 1977) or that the one reflects a "second-order preference" and the other merely a "first-order" one (Frankfurt 1971). In the intrapersonal bargaining game that Schelling envisages, each side typically claims the superior status for its own preference ranking. From the wanton self's point of view, wanton preferences enjoy evaluational rather than merely motivational status.

hooked by the time those warnings reached them. Their consent to the risks of smoking could only have been based on "common knowledge" and "folk wisdom." That is a short-term problem, though, since that cohort of smokers will eventually die off.

The second and more serious problem is a continuing problem in a way the first is not. A vast majority of smokers began smoking in their early to middle teens. Evidence suggests that "of those teenagers who smoke more than a single cigarette only 15 percent avoid becoming regular dependent smokers" (Russell 1974, p. 255). Studies show that, "of current smokers, about 60 percent began by the very young age of thirteen or fourteen" (Blasi and Monaghan 1986, p. 503), and the great majority—perhaps up to 95 percent—of regular adult smokers are thought to have been addicted before coming of age (Califano 1981, p. 183; Lewit, Coate, and Grossman 1981, p. 547, n. 8; Pollin 1984; Leventhal, Glynn, and Fleming 1987, p. 3373; Davis 1987, p. 730; U.S. DHHS 1988, p. 397).

The crux of the matter, then, is just this: being below the age of consent when they first began smoking, smokers were incapable of meaningfully consenting to the risks in the first instance.[28] Being addicted by the time they reached the age of consent, they were incapable of consenting later, either.

2.3   DO THE BENEFITS OUTWEIGH THE COSTS?

In addition to Kantian-style questions about informed consent, there are also utilitarian-style questions of overall social welfare to be considered in this connection. Calculations of the social costs of smoking—both to smokers themselves and to the larger society—establish a prima facie case against smoking on such grounds, as will be shown in section 2.3.1. Before that presumptive case can be conclusive, though, we must consider two rejoinders, to be discussed in sections 2.3.2 and 2.3.3. In the end, neither is convincing, so there is a case against smoking in terms of utility as well as autonomy. But it is important to see that that case does not fall out quite so easily as we might preanalytically suppose it would.

2.3.1   *The Disutility of Smoking*

Presumably it is in straightforwardly utilitarian terms that public health measures of all sorts are standardly justified. We do not leave

---

28.   Strictly speaking, ability to consent is not predicated—legally or morally—upon attaining some arbitrary age but, rather, upon having attained the capacity to make reasoned choices in the matter at hand (Anonymous 1986, pp. 812–13). The level of understanding manifested by teenagers about smoking clearly suggests that their decision to start smoking cannot be deemed an informed choice, however (Leventhal, Glynn, and Fleming 1987).

it to the discretion of consumers, however well-informed, whether or not to drink grossly polluted water, ingest grossly contaminated foods, or inject grossly dangerous drugs. We simply prohibit such things, on grounds of public health. That appeal is justified, in turn, most standardly by recourse to utilitarian calculations of one sort or another.

Of course, we might try to dress those utilitarian arguments up as something else. To some extent, the same considerations that lead us to believe that such public health measures are justified on grounds of social utility might also give us grounds for presuming people's (at least hypothetical) consent to them, also. To some extent, we can appeal to the unfairness as well as the social disutility of external costs imposed on others in order to justify public health measures: contagious diseases and costly cures affect the community as a whole, burdening others with bills they have done nothing to incur but which the perpetrators have no (narrowly self-interested) incentive to avoid, either. While bearing those other, nonutilitarian interpretations as well, those at root seem to be most naturally seen as utilitarian considerations in favor of public health measures.

To a very large extent, though, the justification of public health measures in general must be baldly paternalistic. Their fundamental point is to promote the well-being of people who might otherwise be inclined calvalierly to court certain sorts of diseases. The ultimate ethical justification for such paternalism, in turn, must be essentially utilitarian, turning on the way that overall social utility is maximized when the utilities of all members of the society are maximized.

All of those broadly utilitarian considerations are in play in the case of smoking. Paternalistic elements have been canvassed above. There are contagion effects, too (Preston 1971; Schelling 1986b, pp. 161–62): being among smokers exerts strong social pressure upon people to start smoking and makes it difficult for people to stop; and these contagion effects are particularly pronounced among young people, whose smoking behavior is strongly affected by that of parents and peers (Leventhal and Cleary 1980). As regards externalities, smoking is believed to cause at least half of residential fires, harming family and neighbors as well as the smokers themselves (Schelling 1986a, p. 550; U.S. CEA 1987, p. 185; Botkin 1988); treating smoking-induced illnesses is costly, and even in the United States some 40 percent of those costs are borne by the public (Breslow 1982, pp. 146–48; U.S. Congress, Office of Technology Assessment [OTA] 1985); premature deaths cost the economy productive members and entail pain and suffering for family and friends; and so on (Atkinson and Meade 1974; Schelling 1986a; cf. Littlechild 1986).

Dealing just in those nonquantified terms of human costs, smoking must surely stand indicted. The U.S. surgeon general says it is "the chief, single, avoidable cause of death in our society and the most important public health problem of our time" (U.S. DHHS 1982, preface). Cigarettes kill 25 percent of their users, even when used as their manufacturers intended they be used. Suppose a toaster or lawnmower had a similar record. It would be whipped off the market forthwith. On utilitarian grounds, there would seem to be no reason why cigarettes should be treated any differently.

For those preferring hard, solid numbers, economists (focusing principally upon medical costs and lost productivity) calculate that smoking costs the American economy on net \$52–\$62 billion per year (Luce and Schweitzer 1978; U.S. OTA 1985; Rice et al. 1986). By that reckoning, too, there is clearly a case to answer against smoking, on grounds of social utility.

To say "there is a case to answer" is not, of course, to say that there necessarily is no adequate answer. Defenders of smoking do, in fact, offer rejoinders on two levels. One is a microlevel argument couched in terms of benefits to smokers themselves from the practice. The other is a macrolevel argument, querying the real costs to society from the practice. These rejoinders will be considered, in turn, in sections 2.3.2 and 2.3.3, respectively.

2.3.2   The "Willingness to Pay" Rejoinder

The first style of rejoinder to the standard utilitarian case against smoking operates in standard microeconomic terms, familiar from consumer theory and welfare economics. Essentially, it amounts to a repudiation of "human capital" calculations of costs and benefits in favor of a "willingness to pay" approach (Schelling 1968; 1986a, pp. 500–502; Robinson 1986).

Utilitarians tend to regard all capital in a society—including the capital embodied in your physique—as society's capital. Anything done to diminish that capital stock is therefore adjudged bad, on utilitarian grounds. At this point, though, a rights-based theorist would ask, Whose human capital is it, anyway? Unless we believe in forced labor, we must accept that even a highly productive member of the work force is perfectly entitled to quit his job and go live on a desert island, squandering his talents from which everyone else would have benefited so greatly. The rights theorist would say that we must accept, with the same equanimity, the productivity loss entailed in a person's (voluntary, fully informed) decision to smoke himself to death.[29]

---

29. Notice, e.g., the way Tollison and Wagner (1988, pp. x, 114) set up the problem: "Depending on whether those costs are predominantly borne by smokers or by nonsmokers, very different implications for public policy surely arise. If smokers bear the costs of their smoking, we submit that little if any issue of public policy should

There is no need to move outside the utilitarian language of costs and benefits and over into the deontological language of rights to make this point, however. There is another, perfectly respectable utilitarian way of phrasing the same basic proposition. That is simply to say that cost-benefit calculations should take into account whatever subjective pleasures smokers derive from the practice.[30] In the boldest statement of this very standard microeconomic proposition, Buchanan (1970) argues that, if fully informed people would be willing to buy the product in preference to all others on the market, then by banning that product from the market we would necessarily be making them worse off. Or at least we would necessarily be making them worse off in terms of their preference ordering, which—for Buchanan, like most economists—equates, by definition, to welfare. It may betray a defect of character that they have such preferences; but the fact remains that they do have them, and by this account we must simply respect them (Schwartz 1989).

One quick way around this argument is to reject "willingness to pay"—and preference-based standards, more generally—as a true measure of welfare or utility. It might be argued that, in reckoning costs and benefits, we should deal in terms of interests, not wants. Sometimes, as with cigarettes, people subjectively want what will objectively harm them. To pander to their wants in such cases would compromise their welfare and undermine their utility.

Certainly there would be little difficulty in establishing health (or life, anyway) as a Rawlsian "primary good," a necessary means that is a prerequisite for accomplishing any more particular ends that people might have. In that sense, health is indeed an "interest" that people have, whether they know it or not; and their welfare (or, anyway, their stock of resources for obtaining welfare) is indeed increased by any measures protecting their health.

---

arise, particularly within the normative framework of the American polity as constituting a free people. But if nonsmokers bear significant portions of those costs, tobacco taxation and regulation may be important instruments for making smokers more fully responsible for the costs of their smoking." At the end of their book, having demonstrated, to their own satisfaction at least, that the former is the case, they conclude with a plea for "the liberty of tobacco consumers to act on their free choice and mind their own business. . . . If government is going to be allowed to enact coercive measures that arbitrarily restrict the liberties and trample the rights of smokers, where will employment of this restrictive power end?"

30. See, e.g., Atkinson 1974; Wikler 1978/1983, p. 42; Woodfield 1984, p. 118. Even in tort law, a form of "risk-utility" analysis is now standardly employed in such cases: the benefits have to exceed the anticipatable losses for an activity to be deemed nonnegligent. See Edell and Gisser 1985, for a discussion of the application of this more general doctrine to the case of smoking.

Having established that health is among a person's interests, though, that argument still crucially fails to do precisely what we need it to do for us. We need to know not only what the person's interests are but also, more important, how to trade off each of those interests for one another, if we are to be able to act effectively on his behalf. The argument just sketched, insofar as it provides guidance on this point at all, argues against according a person's health interests any kind of absolute priority over the person's other interests.

Indeed, on the argument just sketched, a person's other interests should actually override his health interests, at least occasionally. The argument, recall, was that health is necessarily in a person's interests because it is a necessary means to his other ends. But if that is the only reason a person has for valuing his health—and it is the only reason our argument says he *must* have for valuing it—then by the selfsame argument we can justify unhealthy activities, insofar as they are strictly necessary to the accomplishment of those other ends. It would obviously be absurd to let pursuit of a goal valued merely as a means to get in the way of pursuit of the ends it is valued as a means toward.

We may, then, have grounds for weak paternalism in overriding the judgments of people who irrationally profess no interest at all in their health, or who risk unnecessary harm to it in pursuit of their other goals. We have no grounds, however, for overriding the judgment of people who suppose that there are pleasures—mountain climbing, racing, skiing, smoking, or whatever—worth risking their health to pursue. As the official representative of the U.K. Department of Health and Social Security put it to the European Community Council of Ministers, when they were considering new tobacco regulations, "individuals should be free to choose their own method of death—whether from high-tar cigarettes or from throwing themselves in front of the airport bus."[31]

The short way around the microeconomic "willingness to pay" argument is thus blocked. We are obliged to take a longer path instead. One such path starts from the standard observation that cigarette sales are substantially price inelastic. Estimates of just how inelastic vary.[32] But much evidence suggests that even rather large

31. Lord Skelmersdale, quoted by Robin Cook in *Hansard's Parliamentary Debates* (Commons), ser. 6, vol. 140 (1988), col. 831. See similarly Dworkin 1972/1983, p. 33 and Wikler 1978/1983, p. 41 for more careful statements of this proposition, common in incohate form in libertarian defenses of smoking such as Machan 1986, p. 51 and Tollison and Wagner 1988, p. 114.

32. In Maynard and Kennan's (1981, p. 39) survey, they vary from zero to −1.8919, with the majority of estimates falling in the −0.35 to −0.80 range. In Britain, H.M. Treasury (1980, p. 106) employs an official estimate of −0.46. Atkinson, Gormulka, and Stern (1984, p. 53), examining patterns in the British Family Expen-

increases in the price of the product (induced, e.g., by increased excise taxes) result in only slight decreases in sales, at least among adult consumers.

From that fact, we might infer either of two conclusions. One would be that there is an enormous "consumer's surplus"—that is, subjective benefit, net of subjective cost—that smokers enjoy, and that even hefty taxes would not extinguish. Price inelasticity would then be taken as evidence that there are substantial subjective gains to consumers from smoking, which ought to be set off against the calculated social costs in any utilitarian decision procedure. Which would predominate we cannot say in advance. But other things being equal, utilitarians ought be more inclined to allow smoking the more satisfaction consumers derive from it.

Alternatively, we might infer from price inelasticity that people are indeed addicted to the product (Atkinson 1974; Wikler 1978/1983, p. 18; Woodfield 1984, p. 120)—and that they are somehow objectively, and not just subjectively, hooked (cf. Schwartz 1989). Present users will pay any price for cigarettes for the same reason they will pay any price for heroin: they cannot help themselves. Most of them, when asked, report getting relatively little subjective pleasure from smoking (Kozlowski et al. 1989). Most of them would rather not smoke, surveys show. Most wish they were not hooked, but they backslide almost every time they try to get un-hooked. In that case, "the willingness of people to buy cigarettes does not genuinely reflect the value they place upon cigarettes" (cf. Tollison and Wagner 1988, p. 38).

Admittedly, there is a bit of a problem in determining what should count as a "benefit" to addicts. In one sense, they benefit from having their habits serviced—certainly they would suffer in some obvious sense otherwise. So in a way, the implication of the addiction interpretation would be much the same as that of the consumer surplus interpretation, that is, present users benefit, as indicated by their willingness to pay, from smoking. In another way, however, they would benefit—even in terms of subjective preferences—if they were to stop. In the same terms, others would benefit if they were never to start.

---

diture Survey for the period 1970–80, find that the price elasticity for the "typical" household is −0.60, dropping only a little (−0.46) for wealthier and higher status households and rising only slightly (−0.66) for poorer and lower status ones. Age seems to make much more difference than class. Lewit, Coate, and Grossman (1981) find that price elasticities are dramatically higher for younger smokers (−1.40 for twelve- to seventeen-year-olds; −0.89 for twenty- to twenty-five-year-olds) than for older, more established smokers (−0.45 to −0.47 for other age groups).

The point, here, is simply that addictive substances are not ordinary economic goods. Ordinarily, cultivating new tastes (acquiring a taste for fine foods, e.g.) is thought to make you better off, in the sense of being able to derive more pleasure, or whatever, than before. With addictions, however, you are worse off, even in your own eyes, than before (Stigler and Becker 1977); whatever momentary pleasures you derive from servicing the addiction, you would prefer to stop but find that you cannot. Thus, we should do whatever we can to prevent new addicts, who would be subjectively worse off once addicted than they were before (Sunstein 1986, pp. 1158–61, 1170; 1988, pp. 282, 290).

As regards existing addicts, the most we can say is that there may be a humanitarian-cum-utilitarian case to be made for continuing to service their addictions (Oken 1985; Lundberg and Knoll 1986). Even they would be subjectively better off in the long run, though, if they could be helped to break the addiction (Schelling 1986a, p. 552). We know that simply because that is how addiction is here defined: as trying to break the addiction, and failing. And we know, from the empirical evidence cited in section 2.2.2 above, that most smokers are addicts in this sense.

2.3.3   The "Overestimate of Net Social Cost" Rejoinder

The first "willingness to pay" rejoinder to utilitarian arguments for curbing smoking alleges, in effect, that those arguments underestimate the benefits consumers derive from smoking. A second sort of rejoinder alleges that those utilitarian arguments for curbing smoking overestimate the net costs that accrue to society from people's smoking.

The less interesting versions of this argument point to the tobacco industry's contribution to the national economy. Estimates of the annual contribution of the tobacco industry to the U.S. gross national product (GNP) vary wildly, from 3.3 billion (Gray and Walter 1986, p. 254) to 31.5 billion (Chase Econometrics 1985). The latter estimate, in a report commissioned by the Tobacco Institute from Chase Econometrics, is particularly suspect, for as its authors themselves say "without the tobacco industry, the expenditure on, and resources devoted to the production of tobacco products would simply be shifted elsewhere in the economy. . . . The compensatory responses that would occur automatically within the economy and within the Chase Econometric U.S. Macroeconomic Model in a total impact-type of study were [deliberately] constrained from taking place in this analysis" (quoted in Warner 1987, p. 2083). Still, even on that high estimate, the tobacco industry contributes only $31.5 billion to the U.S. GNP. Set off against the $52–$62 billion cost estimates described above, that still leaves the industry's account well in the red.

A more interesting version of this argument alleges that the above procedures overstate true social costs. As regards the narrow question of health care costs, everyone dies of something sooner or later. For an accurate assessment of the medical costs of smoking-related diseases, then, we must deduct the costs that would have been incurred had the people killed by smoking died of something else later (Wikler 1978/1983, p. 46). In terms of hospital-bed days and overall medical expenditure, over the course of their lives as a whole, there is some evidence to suggest that there may be no significant difference between smokers and nonsmokers (Leu and Schaub 1983; Weinkam, Rosenbaum, and Sterling 1987; cf. Rice et al. 1986, pp. 502–4).

Similarly, perhaps we need not worry too much about externalities, in the sense of the unfair imposition of burdens on others. Smokers could be refused treatment in public hospital beds and made to pay their own way. They could be required to carry complete insurance against smoking-related diseases; and to avoid unfairness to coinsureds, we could further require that risks to smokers be pooled only with those of other smokers (Wikler 1978/1983, p. 49), as is increasingly done by insurance companies for purely commercial reasons anyway. Alternatively, we might correct unfair external costs that smokers impose upon society at large by imposing a special tax on tobacco products. The basic idea here would be for "users of cigarettes . . . to pay an excise tax, the proceeds of which would cover the costs of treatment for lung cancer and other resulting illnesses" (Wikler 1978/1983, p. 49; see also Garner 1977; and Gewirth 1980, p. 125; Feinberg 1984, p. 25).

In a certain very narrow sense, it might be said that smokers already "pay their own way." A special "excise tax" is presently levied on tobacco, and substantial sums are generated in that way. In the United Kingdom, the cigarette tax annually accounts for 4–5 percent of total tax revenue, down from 8 percent in 1965, but nonetheless a hefty sum (Godfrey and Maynard 1988, p. 342; Preston 1971). Such sums go a long way toward reimbursing society for the costs of smoking. It has been estimated that in Ontario it takes only 8 percent of tobacco tax revenues to pay for all public health care expenditure on smoking-related disease (Stoddart et al. 1986). Even in the United States, if we count only the share of health care costs borne by the federal government, that is almost exactly counterbalanced by the federal excise tax on cigarettes (U.S. OTA 1985).

Those calculations work on a very narrow base. Perhaps the tobacco tax typically pays all the medical expenses borne by the government. Those are not the only costs to society from smoking, though; and the tobacco tax would not come nearly so close to covering the external costs of smoking if we were to include all of them (e.g., lost productivity) in that account. In principle, the solution here is straight-forward: simply raise the excise tax however much it takes to meet the bill. In practice, of course, that may prove politically difficult.

Beyond all that is the larger question of whether a mere excise tax is, even in principle, capable of addressing fully the issues of external cost that matter to utilitarians. Suppose the tax is high enough to generate sums sufficient to cover the full external costs to society from people's smoking. Then it certainly is true that society as a whole will be no worse off, in global terms, as a result of smoking. With ordinary excise taxes, though, there is no guarantee that the monies collected through the tax will be used to put right the damage done by smoking. Typically, excise tax revenues are just dumped into the government's general funds, without being earmarked to be spend for any purpose in particular. (An interesting exception is the Australian state of Victoria, where under sec. 32 of the Tobacco Act of 1987 a 5 percent levy on tobacco sales is paid into a trust fund earmarked for health promotion [Gray 1989]; in a 1989 referendum, California voters approved a twenty-five-cent increase in the cigarette tax, to be similarly earmarked for health promotion [*International Herald-Tribune*, November 10, 1989, p. 2].) We justified the collection of those tobacco taxes on the grounds that smoking increases demand for cancer wards in hospitals. But, in the absence of earmarking, we might end up spending the monies collected on sports stadia or aircraft carriers (U.S. DHHS 1989, pp. 536–39).

Joel Feinberg (1984, p. 25) thinks it does not matter. "Even if the tax revenues extracted from smokers go into a general fund, the effects would be almost the same as if they were earmarked for costs directly connected with smoking, for more funds would be available from the general fund for those special purposes" of remedying the harms caused by smoking. But to say that more funds would be available for those other smoking-related problems is not, of course, to say that they will necessarily be spent on solving those problems.

So far as Treasury economists are concerned, this is as it should be. They standardly boast of the efficiency of general fund financing. What they mean by saying that is simply that it allows funds to be shifted to the most urgent needs, as required. And, on certain narrow understandings of what utilitarianism is all about, efficiency of this sort is all that ought matter in those terms.

There is no reason to take quite so narrow a view of what utilitarianism requires, however. There is no reason, in utilitarian logic or anywhere else, for supposing that people (and hence societies made up of those people) either do or should have any simple form of utility function. They may derive satisfaction not only from their overall utility score but also from its composition. They may want not only to maximize utility but also to derive their utility from diverse sources and amusements, for example. Or, for another example more pertinent to the smoking issue, they may want certain funds to be spent in certain ways, regardless of the inefficiency that that might entail. It is perfectly possible that people have a richer texture to their utility functions in all these ways (Sen 1977; Goodin 1989). Insofar as they do, earmarked excise taxes may be required to maximize utility. As individuals, we care not only about the size of our income but also about how it is spent. So too, as a society, we care not only that enough money comes in through taxes to cover costs; we also care how that money is spent.

Specifically, we might think that if any special tax is to be levied against a particular product on account of damage it does, those who have been damaged by that product ought be the ones to benefit from the tax monies thus raised. One way to phrase the point would be in terms of fairness: it is unfair for people to impose external costs on others; by the same token, it is unfair to recoup those external costs but then not recompense those who suffered them. Now, "fairness" may not in and of itself be a utilitarian concern. (That is arguable both ways, but let us leave that problem to one side here.) The point here is simply that if people do internalize that standard of fairness for one purpose, the strain of consistency would press them to internalize it for both purposes. If they do, then to maximize their utility we must earmark tobacco excise taxes for use by the health services.

Economists are generally implacably opposed to earmarking taxes. Sometimes, however, they can be reconciled to it, when it serves as a surrogate for "user fees" for public services. The prime example is the gasoline tax, collected from road users, being earmarked for building and repairing the roads that they use. The point of imposing earmarked taxes, recall, is to overcome the problem of external costs. To avoid the opposite problem—that of imposing taxes-cum-user-fees on people in excess of the costs of the services used—those taxes must pass various tests. All users of the publicly provided service, and only users of that service, must pay the tax; the tax that they pay must be proportional to the amount of the service that they use; their benefits from the service must be proportional to the sacrifices entailed for them by the tax; and so on.

Some taxes-cum-user-fees come tolerably close to passing all those tests. The gasoline tax is a classic case in point.[33] The earmark-

---

33. Virtually all drivers of motorized vehicles consume gasoline; and, with certain exceptions (primarily drivers of off-road vehicles, like farm tractors and snowmobiles), only they consume the taxed gasoline. There is some variation in fuel efficiency between different vehicles, but broadly speaking drivers pay gasoline tax roughly in proportion to the number of road miles driven. Those who drive less fuel-efficient luxury sedans are, by and large, richer people whose time is worth more to them and

ing of tobacco taxes would not, however. To a large extent, the treatment of smoking-related diseases is not a publicly provided service at all, in certain places: in the United States, for example, it would be primarily for those old enough for Medicare or poor enough for Medicaid or some equivalent state program; others, generally, would have to finance treatment from private sources. Even where health care is a public responsibility (as under the British National Health Service), smokers are not the only ones to use lung cancer wards, and users of those cancer wards are only a subset of all those who smoke. Furthermore, some smokers pay the taxes without ever using the service, while others use the service having paid the same (or perhaps less) in taxes.

In part, this latter disparity can be rationalized by reconceptualizing the "service" in question as "medical insurance" rather than "treatment in cancer wards." Even then, there is no reason to believe that those who smoke the most, and hence pay the most in tobacco excise taxes, are also those who are the most averse to taking risks. That is what would be required, if we are to equate the benefit they derive from the insurance with the sacrifice they have made in paying the taxes. But, if anything, the opposite is more likely to be true: those who smoke most, and hence pay the most in tobacco taxes, are probably the most insensitive to risks, and hence value insurance least.

Friends of the tobacco industry seem to welcome the conclusion that earmarked taxes on tobacco consumption are unacceptable (Tollison and Wagner 1988, pp. 56–61). Yet that is curious. For if we object to the unfairness of external costs imposed by smoking, and if we cannot remedy that unfairness by any technical gimmick like earmarked taxes on tobacco, then we have no recourse but to try to reduce the unfairness by reducing tobacco consumption itself.

Decidedly the most interesting variation on the general theme that smoking costs society less than we think, though, is one that argues that smokers save us money by dying early. Just think: "smoking tends to cause few problems during a person's productive years and then to kill the individual before the need to provide years of social security and pension payments. From this perspective, the truly burdensome individual may be the unreasonably fit senior citizen who lives on for thirty years after retirement, contributing to the bankruptcy of the social security system, and using up savings

---

hence who would benefit most from faster roads; so those who are charged disproportionately more for use of the roads are those who benefit disproportionately (and, incidentally, those to whom any given dollar's tax would constitute less of a sacrifice, assuming the marginal dollar means less to the rich than to the poor).

that would have reverted to the public purse via inheritance taxes, had an immoderate life-style brought an early death" (Wikler 1978/1983, p. 46; see also Warner 1987b; Gori, Richter, and Yu 1984; cf. Schelling 1986a, pp. 556–57). And lest this proposition be regarded as altogether frivolous, I hasten to add that these considerations were taken very seriously indeed in the 1971 report of an interdepartmental committee of U.K. civil servants assigned to draft a smoking policy (Philips 1980); they figure from time to time in letters to the editor of the *New York Times* (quoted in Troyer and Markle 1983, p. vi); and so on.

In the eyes of many, however, this argument will appear to be a reductio ad absurdum. What it seems to suggest is nothing less than a thinly veiled form of not-altogether-voluntary euthanasia. Many suppose it is unjust, if not necessarily uneconomic, to encourage people to die off promptly upon their ceasing to be productive members of the work force (cf. Battin 1987).

What this is a reductio of, however, is not the utilitarian calculus but, rather, an economic calculus that serves as such a poor proxy for it. Most people who are already retired would wish to enjoy a long and happy retirement; most people still in the work force would wish the same for themselves and, indeed, for their elders. Those preferences, too, must be factored into any proper calculus of social utility. Once they are, early deaths induced by smoking are almost certain to turn out to be costs rather than benefits in the broader social scale of values.

Indeed, in light of those preferences, perhaps what we should regard as an external social cost is not being *able* to pay pensions to the prematurely deceased rather than having to pay pensions to those who live to a ripe old age. In the slightly purple prose of Schelling (1986a, p. 557), "We do not hope that 60-year-old fishermen die at sea, that 60-year-olds neglect seat belts and die in their automobiles, or that 60-year-old marital difficulties lead to suicide or homicide. . . . That people who die at retirement age bequeath more than they cost" is irrelevant to our assessment of their deaths as tragedies, and so too with smokers. "We would not be true to our own values if we . . . excused [their] smoking and let them die to our benefit. That is simply not the attitude that we take toward untimely death."

2.4 POLICY OPTIONS

Insofar as we are impressed with the case sketched above against smoking, in terms of harms to smokers themselves, the goal of social policy ought be to curtail smoking altogether. We have six broad policy options available to us for doing so.

2.4.1   Self-regulation

Tobacco companies could be encouraged to restrict voluntarily their own activities, refraining from advertising in certain ways and from selling to certain people (e.g., children). This, of course, is the companies' preferred option; and it is one that is still relied upon, albeit decreasingly (or as a precursor to legislation), in over a third of the Organisation for Economic Co-operation and Development (OECD) and in many other countries around the world (Cox and Smith 1984; Roemer 1986). Self-regulation is elevated to an art form in Britain and Australia, particularly, where most advertising and promotion of tobacco products is restricted by no more than a set of "voluntary agreements" between the industry and the government. In Britain, even warning labels are the subject of mere voluntary agreements (Taylor 1985, chap. 5; Baggott 1986).

These strategies are doubly flawed. First, it is doubtful that the agreements in question are fully voluntary. Typically they are—and apparently can only be—extracted from the industry under threat of legislation compelling compliance with government wishes, if "voluntary" agreement is not forthcoming. Tobacco companies in the United States announced a "voluntary code" to regulate their advertising only after the U.S. Federal Trade Commission had already published in the *Federal Register* its own rule on the matter, to take effect in six months' time (Fritschler 1969, p. 99). Similarly, successive British health ministers have been perfectly frank about the threat of legislation as the only mechanism that is really effective in securing voluntary agreements. David Owen, in his days in that post, went so far as to have the threat printed in *Hansard* in a written reply to a parliamentary enquiry, explaining later, "A minister needs to know before he goes into negotiations, and the industry needs to know it too, that he has the power to legislate. Then you can have a serious discussion" (quoted in Goodin 1986, p. 440).

Agreements extracted under duress, however, are not voluntary in any sense that contributes to the moral legitimacy of their enforcement. That is a standing rule of contract law, for example. And friends of the tobacco industry are quick to draw the parallel to the case of "voluntary agreements" extracted from it through such coercive threats. In a 1976 parliamentary debate, for example, one pro-tobacco Member of Parliament argued:

> I do not believe that the agreement with the tobacco industry is entirely voluntary. When a Minister goes to an industry and says that he wants an understanding, that he wants some progress, he knows, and the industry knows, that he has in his pocket proposals for legislation, or rules, or regulations, which, in

effect, say that if the industry does not do what the Government want, the result will be achieved by the use of compulsory powers. . . . I do not think in this case that my hon. Friend can claim to have a voluntary agreement with the tobacco industry. He has its reluctant consent, but no more than that. [Quoted in Goodin 1986, p. 442]

The point seems to me a perfectly fair one. Agreements concluded under duress just do not count, morally.

It would be wrong to conclude from that, however, that governments have no right to regulate the tobacco industry. The proper inference is merely that "voluntary agreements," concluded under threat of legislative compulsion if agreement is not forthcoming, do not add anything to the moral legitimacy of such regulations. Either it is morally permissible for governments to legislate along those lines, or it is not. If it is impermissible for them to legislate, then it is not permissible for them to threaten to legislate in order to extract "voluntary agreements," either; and any agreements extracted in this way are null and void. For it to be permissible for governments to threaten legislation in order to extract voluntary agreements, it must antecedently have been permissible for governments to legislate such regulations even in the absence of agreement. In short, voluntary agreements extracted in this fashion are morally superfluous. If a government has moral authority to extract agreements in this fashion, it has no need for such agreements: it has had the moral authority to impose the regulations without the industry's agreement, all along (Goodin 1986).

There is a second and more practical flaw with self-regulation strategies. That is simply that self-regulation is, to a large extent, tantamount to no regulation. There is anecdotal evidence aplenty to support this conclusion. Frequent and flagrant violations of the spirit—and sometimes even the letter—of voluntary agreements are reported, with little apparent effect, in both Britain (Taylor 1985, chaps. 6–8; Roberts 1986; Wilkinson 1986, chap. 10; Sherman 1988) and Australia (Coleman 1985). Despite a voluntary agreement on sports sponsorship in Britain, for example, televised coverage of tobacco-sponsored sporting events referred to the sponsoring companies, verbally or visually, on average once every three minutes (Lazarus 1989). And so on.

This outcome is unsurprising. Those charged with monitoring compliance with voluntary agreements with the tobacco industry find themselves involved in a continuing relationship with a very few firms in a single industry. Naturally, no one wants to rile those with whom he must continue to deal. In their study of 101 agencies regulating

Australian business, Grabosky and Braithwaite (1986, chap. 15) found
that it was precisely these conditions that made regulators reluctant to
seek criminal sanctions against firms, even when they were empow-
ered by law to do so. This combines with the institutional structure
characteristic of "voluntary agreement" regimes to inhibit serious
enforcement: one cannot help suspecting that the complacent tone of
the British report of the Committee for Monitoring Agreements on
Tobacco Advertising and Sponsorship owes at least as much to the
fact that the committee was half composed of representatives of the
tobacco industry as it does to the fact that it could confirm "only"
forty-one of the 462 breaches in the voluntary agreements alleged in
complaints to it (Lazarus 1988, pp. 2, 5).

The policy goal specified at the outset of section 2.4 was straight-
forward: curtailing tobacco consumption. In this connection, it is
particularly important to note the results of a systematic comparison
of fifteen OECD countries' experience, showing that those countries
relying upon legislation have reduced tobacco consumption by almost
consistently twice as much as have those relying upon self-regulation
and voluntary agreements alone. The explanation seems to be that
"the countries which have adopted a legislative approach to smoking
control not only tend to have implemented a wider range of measures
than their voluntary counterparts, but these measures are usually
enforced much more stringently" (Cox and Smith 1984, p. 578).

In short, it seems to be both bad morality and bad policy to rely
upon voluntary agreements to regulate any important aspects of the
tobacco industry. Self-regulation by the industry itself is simply
unreliable and, morally, there is no reason we should have to rely
upon it.

2.4.2   *Torts*

Paralleling self-regulation on the part of the tobacco industry would
be a policy of self-help on the part of those injured by that industry.
After all, tobacco companies—like all other members of the
community—are responsible, legally, for any damage that they do to
others. Such legal liability has nothing to do with recent legislation. It
derives, instead, from ancient principles of that branch of common
law known as "tort law."

Tort suits against cigarette manufacturers, demanding compensatory damage payments for wrongful death and injury done to
smokers of their products, grew increasingly common through the
1970s and 1980s. It was long thought that these suits were on solid
legal ground. It was standardly said to be only a matter of time before
one succeeded. It was widely expected that, once one such suit
succeeded, countless other victories would follow in fairly short order.

At that point, "cigarette makers may be held accountable for an estimated $80 billion a year in smoking, . . . saving millions from premature death" (Tribe 1986, p.788).

Naturally, such perceptions and predictions were common currency among attorneys active in litigation against tobacco companies on behalf of victims of smoking (Garner 1980; Edell and Gisser 1985; AMA 1986; Daynard, Popper, and Gruzalski 1986; Daynard 1988). But they are biased. Perhaps a better (because more impartial) measure of the widely perceived likelihood of large numbers of successful tort suits is the discount that financial markets have been applying to tobacco company stocks in recent years. In 1987, they seem to have been valued over 35 percent less than they should have been worth, on the basis of the companies' profit/earnings ratio alone (Cohen 1987, p. 5).

Now the landmark has been established, in the case of *Cipollone v. Liggett Group, Inc.*[34] In their June 1988 verdict, the trial jury in that case awarded $400,000 in damages to Antonio Cipollone, whose wife, Rose Cipollone, died of lung cancer in 1985, aged fifty-eight. This case has dragged on for five years already; with the defendants threatening to appeal, it may well drag on for a fair while longer before the final decision is rendered. Still, this victory will give heart to other victims of smoking-related diseases to bring yet more suits, in addition to the hundred or so pending at the time of the *Cipollone* decision. Hence we can expect an increasing barrage of tort liability suits against tobacco companies in the coming years, whichever way Liggett's appeal eventually goes.

It is obviously desirable that those who have been harmed should recover damages from those who have harmed them, wherever possible. Tort litigation is a very imperfect as a general solution to the problem of smoking, however. The problems that plaintiffs have heretofore experienced serve to indicate something of the limits that will continue to plague this as an overall strategy, even after a legal beachhead has finally been firmly established (Garner 1980; Daynard 1988).

Central to a tort claim is proof of causation. Even under the sternest rules of liability, plaintiffs can recover against someone only if they can prove that that agent caused the harm that they suffered. Typically, cancers admit of multiple causes and arise only after long latency periods. Any given cancer might have been caused by smoking, by workplace contaminants, by genetic endowment, or by some

---

34. Civil Action no. 83–2864, U.S. District Court for the District of New Jersey. For reports of the verdict, see Janson (1988) and Cipollone v. Liggett Group, Inc., 693 F. Supp. 208, 210 (D.N.J. 1988).

combination of all of these. In tort law, of course, the standard of proof is merely "more probable than not"; so plaintiffs do not have to prove "beyond a reasonable doubt" that cigarettes caused their cancer. But proving that they are twice as likely as anything else to have caused it (which is what the 50 percent rule often comes down to) might be almost as arduous.[35]

What we should be doing, of course, is apportioning blame among all causal factors, and assessing fractional liability to each. If there are four things that contributed 25 percent each to a plaintiff's cancer, each defendant should be required to pay 25 percent of the award that the plaintiff would have secured had there been but a single cause. Similarly, if it is 25 percent likely that smoking caused a plaintiff's cancer, the plaintiff should recover 25 percent of damages from the tobacco company regardless of the relative probabilities of other causes (Rosenberg 1984; Thomson 1986, chap. 12).

Moves toward some such model of "attributable risk" and "assigned share" are now afoot. A powerful "tort reform" counterrevolution is also afoot to upset them (Schuck 1988). In any case, this model may not prove to be a very successful strategy for recovery by individual plaintiffs, who may find it founders on problems of inferring from aggregate data to facts about particular cases (Thomson 1986, chaps. 12 and 13). "Sure," defendants' counsel will say, "in general the statistics are as the plaintiff says; but we are not being sued by a statistical artifact but rather by a particular person. How are we to know that what is true in general is true of this person in particular?" Plaintiffs can go some way toward meeting demands for particularized evidence by factoring into the equation all their personal case histories (family background, work history, etc.). But this still falls somewhat short of ideally individualized evidence of person-to-person harm, of the sort paradigmatic in torts (e.g., in an auto crash) (Schuck 1988, pp. 103–4). Some juries, rightly or wrongly, will no doubt balk at such evidence, refusing to compensate some people whom statistically they should.

There are various ways around such problems (Garner 1977). One is to use aggregate-level statistical evidence to generate a "rebuttable presumption" that smokers' cancer is caused by their smoking, unless defendants can prove otherwise in any given case. (The Black Lung Benefits Act of 1972 imposed a similar rebuttable presumption

---

35. Even in the *Cipollone* case, which was straightforward as these go, "the jury heard a series of medical witnesses who disagreed on Mrs. Cipollone's cancer. The defense experts said it was a typical carcinoid, a form they said was not statistically associated with smoking. Mr. Cipollone's experts said it was small-cell cancer caused by cigarette smoking. They said smoking produced both types of cancer," in any case (Janson 1988, p. B4).

against mine owners.) A second alternative is to have victims of smoking-related diseases transfer their tort claims to welfare agencies bearing the costs (medical care, disability/survivors' benefits, etc.) of their illnesses; welfare agencies can then mount tort suits against manufacturers for the total aggregate harm done by smoking, and in such suits aggregate-level statistical proof is obviously relevant in a way it might not be in case-by-case adjudication. (The Social Security Amendments of 1974 similarly require deserted mothers receiving Aid to Families with Dependent Children [AFDC] to transfer their claims to child support to welfare agencies, who are then responsible for recovering payments from delinquent fathers.) How far either strategy can or will be applied against cigarette manufacturers remains to be seen, though.

Then there is the further matter of "negligence." Of course, we might argue that tobacco companies should be held strictly liable for anything that happens when people consume their products. They had the capacity to test them in the laboratory, in a way that consumers could not have done. If using the product as intended kills 25 percent of its users then there is a case for considering it an "ultra-hazardous product," and for imposing strict liability in consequence (AMA 1986; cf. Anonymous 1986).[36]

Failing that, victims will be able to claim compensation only if they can prove that manufacturers were somehow negligent. Where the old-fashioned rule of "contributory negligence" still prevails, plaintiffs would also have to prove that they were not themselves negligent in any way—that they were not in any way responsible for the harm that befell them. That, obviously, is a tall order; increasingly, it has been seen as too tall an order, and states have shifted to a rule of "comparative negligence" instead. Still, in half the states, those new rules are written in such a way that, if the plaintiff is more negligent than the defendant, he cannot recover anything at all.[37] That law is ludicrous, in the same way (but only half as badly) as the "contrib-

36. Paradoxically, strict liability is imposed for "design defects" (failing to manufacture a product according to specifications) but not for defective designs. Surely the systematic infliction of damage is worse than the intermittent infliction of it, though (cf. Anonymous 1984).

37. Cohen 1987, p. 9. New Jersey is one such state, and the plaintiffs in *Cipollone* were caught in just this trap: while the deceased woman's husband was awarded $400,000 in damages, Rose Cipollone herself (through her estate) was awarded none. The jury found that she knew about the dangers of smoking "from reading and other notifications" to a sufficient extent that she could be said to have " 'unreasonably encountered a known danger' by insisting on smoking"; and they accordingly "assessed her 80 percent of the blame for her death and 20 percent to Liggett. Under the [New Jersey] law, she was not entitled to damages, unless the company had been found to be at least 50 percent to blame" (Janson 1988, p. B4).

utory negligence" rule it supplanted was ludicrous: it says that a plaintiff who bears 51 percent responsibility for harm that has befallen him must bear 100 percent of its costs, when the logic of the rule change should surely have led us to say he should bear merely 51 percent of the costs. Still, that is the law in half the states now.

To establish negligence on the part of cigarette manufacturers, plaintiffs will have to prove that there was information about health hazards of smoking that tobacco companies knew or should have known that would have led a reasonable man to take precautions in the manufacture and sale of the product (including, ultimately, withdrawing the product from the market). Such arguments might go a long way, just on the basis of what tobacco companies should have known about the hazards of smoking from the published scientific literature. Even more compelling, though, are arguments based on companies' own early in-house research showing the carcinogenic properties of tobacco smoke: it is very difficult for companies to claim that they did not know of the evidence, or that they gave it no credence, when it came from their own scientists. Much was made in *Cipollone,* for example, of a 1961 "confidential limited" report prepared by Arthur D. Little, Inc., who had done mouse-skin cancer experiments for Liggett and Meyers, that opened with the words: "1. There are biologically active materials present in cigarette tobacco. They are a) cancer causing b) cancer promoting c) poisonous d) stimulating, pleasurable, and flavorful."[38]

These internal company documents, obtained in the course of litigating *Cipollone,* are now in the public domain and are available for use by subsequent litigants in other cases. Subsequent juries might—in a way the *Cipollone* jury refused to do—construe them as evidence of "reckless disregard" for customer safety in the face of compelling evidence of probable harm. Then there would be grounds for a judgment of "intentional tort" and the award of punitive damages. (There might even be grounds for prosecution for criminal assault or manslaughter, although that day still seems fairly distant.) While the *Cipollone* jury did not buy this argument, the trial judge in that case refused the defendant's plea to quash it altogether. In his view, more than enough evidence had been produced from the company's files to show what he called "a callous, wanton, willful and reckless disregard" for the health of consumers and that tobacco companies had "entered into a sophisticated conspiracy . . . to refute, undermine and neutral-

38. "L&M—a Perspective Review," p. 1. This document was released in connection with litigation of Cipollone v. Liggett Group (U.S. District Court for the District of New Jersey, Civil Action no. 83–2864) as Plaintiff's Exhibit P-367. See, more generally, Bremner (1988), Gray (1988), Mintz (1988a; 1988b), and Janson (1988).

ize information coming from the scientific and medical community and to confuse and mislead the consuming public. . . . If the jury accepts the plaintiff's version . . . , it is difficult to envision a more compelling case for an award of punitive damages" (Sarokin 1988, 1492–93, 1500; Bremner 1988). The *Cipollone* jury itself rejected the plaintiff's claims on the conspiracy and fraudulent misrepresentation issues. It is too early to say whether others, looking at the same documents, will do likewise. This first indication is not encouraging, however (Shipp 1988).

What the *Cipollone* case turned on, in the jury's mind, seems to have been merely "failure to warn" and "warranty" aspects of the case. When Rose Cipollone started smoking in 1942, she chose the brand that was then being widely advertised under the headline: "Play safe—smoke Chesterfields." She switched in the 1950s to L&Ms, then advertised as "just what the doctor ordered." Such advertisements seem to have constituted a manufacturer's warranty guaranteeing the safety of the product. It was breach of this warranty, and failure to warn, instead of their products' dangers, that lost the case for Liggett (Rothenberg 1988; Janson 1988, p. B4).

What bodes worse still for the prospect of widespread litigation, the *Cipollone* jury was allowed to consider the adequacy of company warnings only prior to 1966. At that point, government-mandated health warnings began appearing on cigarette packets. They were very weak warnings, arguably wholly inadequate to convey the full sense of the risks involved. But under the U.S. Constitution, federal law "preempts" state law—tort law, among it—in cases of conflict (U.S. Constitution, article 6, sec. 2). Thus, if the U.S. Congress, in mandating the printings of health warnings, had intended to exempt cigarette manufacturers from any further liability for failure to warn of risks, then tort claims under state common law arising from the inadequacy of post-1966 warnings would be constitutionally precluded. Whether or not that was the intention of Congress is indeed questionable, but the current run of court of appeals opinions (yet to be tested, as eventually they will be, in the Supreme Court) seems to favor the "preemption" defense protecting tobacco companies from post-1966 claims.[39]

---

39. The legislative history suggests that, while Congress intended to prohibit states from requiring any further warnings, it did not prohibit companies from printing them voluntarily—nor did it intend to relieve them of ordinary tort liability if they did not do so, when reasonable people would have done (Garner 1980, pp. 1453–54; Edell and Gisser 1985; Tribe 1986). The "preemption" argument has been accepted by three circuits of the U.S. Court of Appeal, however, including the circuit in which *Cipollone* was tried: Cipollone v. Liggett Group, Inc., 789 F.2d 181 (3rd Cir. 1987); Stephen v. American Brands, 825 F.2d 312 (11th Cir. 1987); Palmer v. Liggett Group Inc., 825 F.2d 620 (1st Cir. 1987).

In short, the products liability approach to controlling smoking through the tort law is perfectly laudable. But it is a very imperfect solution to the overall problem. There are not enough people who have well-documented cancers of the right kind to stand up in court. There are not enough of them whose cancer can convincingly be traced to pre-1966 smoking patterns. Finally, the damage awards are not large enough really to scare tobacco companies, judging from the *Cipollone* precedent. As one financial analyst put it, "Industry earnings hit a record of $3.45 billion in 1985, the last year for which industry figures are available. . . . If they are only going to be hit with awards of $400,000, the impact of these cases is not going to be very significant" (Eichenwald 1988).[40]

2.4.3   *Taxation*

Taxing tobacco is a particularly popular way of controlling smoking overall, in the United States, Britain, and elsewhere. Judging from the evidence (summarized in section 2.3.2 above) about the price inelasticity of cigarettes, tax-induced price rises alone may do little to curb smoking among existing adult users. Of course, it is dangerous to estimate the effects of large-scale changes by extrapolating from the effects of small-scale variations.[41] But the order of magnitude of probable effects of dramatically increased taxation is effectively indicated by British calculations, assuming an elasticity around -0.5, that it would take more than a 50 percent increase in cigarette prices to reduce cigarette sales by even 20 percent (Atkinson and Townsend 1977, p. 492).[42]

40. Daynard (1988, p. 9) argues that the costs of defending such actions might in and of itself force up the price of cigarettes, and hence reduce consumption; he points to a successful defense of a single smokeless tobacco products liability case in 1986 estimated to have cost $15 million, which swamps the mere $400,000 awarded to Antonio Cipollone in damages. But that argument cuts both ways. The plaintiff's attorneys in *Cipollone*, who took the case on a contingency fee basis, are estimated to have spent $2 million in lawyers' time and expenses over the course of the five years it took to bring the case to trial, with a share in the $400,000 damage award as their recompense. Although they can reuse much of the material prepared for that trial in subsequent litigation, the firm will have to win quite a few $400,000 verdicts to recoup such expenses.

41. The standard methodological worry is that the relationship might not be linear, very much higher prices having either much larger or much smaller effects on consumption, penny-for-penny, than only marginally higher ones. So, too, might the political reaction vary according to the size of the price rise. Cox and Smith's (1984, p. 578) fifteen-nation study of income and price elasticities confirms our fears that "a 'pricing-out' strategy towards smoking control will meet with increasing resistance amongst established smokers."

42. Of course, publicity attendant upon increases in tax levies might indirectly serve to remind people of health risks, and in that way, too, reduce smoking. That is

What tax-induced price rises might do is make the habit substantially less attractive to teenagers not yet addicted to the drug. Precisely the same people whom we most want, on grounds of "informed consent," to prevent from starting to smoke are those who are least able to afford more expensive cigarettes. This a priori expectation is borne out by evidence that demand for cigarettes among teenagers is more than three times as elastic as among adults, on average; and any given price increase is almost six times more likely to make teenagers stop or never start smoking than it would adults (Lewit, Coate, and Grossman 1981). By such reckoning, it has been calculated that leaving the U.S. federal excise tax on cigarettes at sixteen cents, rather than letting it revert to eight cents as previously planned for 1985, has resulted in 1.9 million fewer people smoking in the United States, "including more than a million fewer under age 25" (U.S. CEA 1987, p. 185).

Morally, the issue is presumably whether it is permissible to use the instrument of taxation for purposes of reducing consumption of a good in such ways. After all, the purpose of taxation is to raise revenue. Some would say that using the instrument for any other purpose is simply inappropriate. At most, they would say, it might be a happy coincidence if as a by-product of raising revenue by taxing drugs their consumption falls.[43]

Certainly it is true that taxation always needs to be justified. The power to tax is the power to destroy, after all. It is also true that the state's need for revenue to pursue its legitimate purposes provides one such justification. It is not the only possible justification, though.

Mill (1859/1975, p. 123) says that "to tax stimulants for the sole purpose of making them more difficult to be obtained, is a measure

---

how Leu (1984) explains his interesting finding that smokers' behavior reacted strongly to nominal increases in Swiss cigarette prices induced by tax hikes, even though in inflation-adjusted terms they constituted little or no real increase in prices.

43. Mill (1859/1975, pp. 123–24), thus, writes: "It must be remembered that taxation for fiscal purposes is absolutely inevitable; that in most countries it is necessary that a considerable part of that taxation should be indirect; that the State, therefore, cannot help imposing penalties, which to some persons may be prohibitory, on the use of some articles of consumption. It is hence the duty of the State to consider, in the imposition of taxes, what commodities the consumers can best spare; and *a fortiori*, to select in preference those of which it deems the use, beyond a very moderate quantity, to be positively injurious. Taxation, therefore, of stimulants, up to the point which produces the largest amount of revenue (supposing that the State needs all the revenue which it yields) is not only admissible, but to be approved of." Wikler (1987, pp. 334–35) offers a similar, albeit less subtle, double-effect argument designed to show that taxing tobacco to raise revenue is not coercive whereas taxing it to reduce consumption is, even if both taxes have the identical effect of reducing consumption by raising the price.

differing only in degree from their entire prohibition; and would be justifiable only if that were justifiable."[44] Strictly speaking, that proposition is not quite right. The difference of degree might matter. We might be morally justified in partly destroying something, without being justified in destroying it completely.

The larger point, however, is that sometimes we *are* justified in destroying, in whole or in part, some sort of product or activity. The arguments in the previous sections of this chapter suggest that this is the case with smoking, in particular. The same arguments that justify us in restricting the activity in general justify us in doing so through swingeing taxes, in particular.

The problems with the taxation strategy are political, not moral. Through it, we give one powerful bureaucratic actor—the Treasury— a substantial interest in continuingly large volumes of cigarette sales. There is a risk, which has become a reality intermittently from the time of King James I onward (Harrison 1986), of financial considerations dominating health ones in the counsels of state (Breslow 1982, pp. 130–31; Taylor 1985, chap. 8; Wilkinson 1986, chap. 8).

In a way, there is no reason for the Treasury to mind, and much reason for it to welcome, increased tobacco taxes. "As long as the price elasticity is less than one"—and the U.K. Treasury's official estimate, recall, is -0.46 (U.K. Her Majesty's [HM] Treasury 1980, p. 106)—"the revenue will certainly increase when the tax goes up" because "the fall in consumption is more than offset by the extra tax paid by those who continue to smoke" (Atkinson and Townsend 1977, p. 492; see also Townsend 1987, p. 364; and Godfrey and Maynard 1988, p. 342). Thus it is estimated, by H.M. Treasury itself in Britain, that a 10 percent increase in the tobacco tax would yield an extra £ 178 million in net revenue, even after taking into account substitution effects, income effects and other second-round economic effects (U.K. HM Treasury 1980, p. 99).

Of course, that is not quite the whole story. If the effect of the increased tobacco tax is to prevent recruitment of new smokers, the long-term effects might be a reduction in tobacco tax revenues, as existing smokers eventually die off. For that reason, a Treasury operating with a very long-time horizon may oppose increases in the tobacco tax. And, of course, the tax revenues it receives from tobacco

44. The passage continues: "Every increase of cost is a prohibition, to those whose means do not come up to the augmented price; and to those who do, it is a penalty laid on them for gratifying a particular taste. Their choice of pleasures, and their mode of expending their income, after satisfying their legal and moral obligations to the State and to individuals, are their own concern, and must rest with their own judgment" (Mill 1859/1975, p. 123).

would give the Treasury a strong incentive to oppose reductions in tobacco consumption accomplished through any means other than increased tobacco taxes. But, at least when operating on the short-term logic that drives most treasury departments, there is really no good reason why they should oppose increases—even very sharp increases—in tobacco taxes.

I conclude, therefore, that dramatically increased taxation of tobacco might form one useful component in an overall smoking control strategy. It would be particularly useful in preventing the recruitment of new smokers, in their early teens. It would be less useful, however, in causing existing smokers to abandon the practice. For that, something else is probably required.

2.4.4   *Publicity*

Mandatory health warnings on cigarette packages and advertise-ments, and health education and health promotion campaigns more generally, are another popular government response to smoking. Some thirty-eight countries now require printed warnings on pack-ages and advertisements, of one form or another (Roemer 1986, pp. 7–8). And there has been a trend toward requiring stronger and more explicit warnings, in recent years.

Among the more important reasons for the popularity of this strategy is that health warnings and health education campaigns are seen as the least paternalistic forms of government intervention.[45] Mill (1859/1975, p. 118) himself holds that "labelling [a] drug with some word expressive of its dangerous character, may be enforced without violation of liberty," since presumably "the buyer cannot wish not to know that the thing he possesses has poisonous qualities." In this judgment, Mill has been followed by a whole host of more recent commentators.[46]

No doubt publicizing health risks reduces smoking. Publication of the two great official reports—by the Royal College of Physicians in 1962 and the surgeon general in 1964—produced long-term drops in cigarette consumption standardly estimated at 7–14 percent (Atkin-son and Skegg 1973; Leventhal and Cleary 1980, p. 381; Warner 1981). The antismoking television advertisements, broadcast under the Fairness Doctrine in the United States until cigarette advertising

---

45. Some, though, protest the paternalistic bossiness of health education cam-paigns run by medics in the habit of issuing orders and demanding obedience (Meenan 1976).

46. See, e.g.; Feinberg 1971/1983, p. 11; Wikler 1978/1983, pp. 52–53; Littlechild and Wiseman 1984, p. 66; Buchanan 1970, p. 72; Daniels 1985, p. 158; and Littlechild 1986, pp. 275–76.

itself was banned from television in 1970, seemed to have had an effect almost twice as strong (Hamilton 1972, p. 406).[47]

There are reasons to believe that health campaigns cannot work in isolation from other policy initiatives, though. Specifically, allowing cigarette advertising undercuts health messages by inducing newspapers and magazines to engage in self-censorship of health reports that might offend their tobacco sponsors (Smith 1978; Warner 1985; Warner et al. 1986). Thus, a publicity campaign might not really succeed unless coupled with something stronger: an advertising ban. Otherwise the message simply might not get carried effectively.

2.4.5   Bans

There are, in fact, various different regulatory options under this general heading. Most modestly, we might ban cigarette advertising, either in particular settings (e.g., on television) or in general. More dramatically, we might ban sales of cigarettes, either to a certain group (e.g., children) or in general. Most dramatically, we might ban use of tobacco, either in particular settings (e.g., where there is a particular fire hazard, as in elevators, theaters, and subways, or where there are synergistic effects with other substances in the immediate vicinity, such as asbestos) or in general.

These are separable policy options, any one of which can be pursued independently of any other. From 1975, Norway has banned advertising but not sale of cigarettes. Similarly, we can ban sale without banning consumption. (Most states allow you to eat game birds and fish you shoot or catch yourself but not to sell them.) Though there is no modern experience of a general ban on sale or use of tobacco, advertising bans are reasonably common: fifteen countries have total bans, and another twelve have strong partial bans (Roemer 1986, pp. 7–8).

Advertising bans can be particularly helpful in reducing cigarette consumption among adolescents, with whom we should be especially concerned on grounds of "informed consent." There is good evidence that cigarette advertising in general, and sport sponsorship in particular, appeals to children (Aitken, Leather and O'Hagan 1985; Aitken et al. 1987; Chapman and Fitzgerald 1982; Ledwith 1984; Warner et al. 1986). Conversely, banning advertising of cigarettes in Norway in

47. Schneider, Klein, and Murphy (1981) argue that models used to generate those results are misspecified; on their revised estimates, the cumulative effects of the 1953 American Cancer Society and 1964 surgeon general reports were to reduce tobacco consumption by 25 percent and antismoking commercials by another 5 percent. Note that their dependent variable—tobacco consumption—can be reduced by shifts to filter cigarettes (as happened especially in the post-1953 period) as well as by reductions in cigarette consumption per se.

1975 led to a sharp decline in the percentage of teenagers who subsequently have become daily smokers (Chapman 1985, pp. 16–18; 1986, pp. 39–40; British Medical Association [BMA] 1986; Warner et al. 1986, p. 372; White 1988, p. 159). Of course, it is perfectly true that tobacco consumption, particularly among the young, might be reduced even more by cleverly crafted antismoking commercials as appeared on television in the United States before 1970 (Hamilton 1972, p. 406; Miller 1985; U.S. CEA 1987, p. 186). But if the products are genuinely dangerous, we could perfectly well run commercials advising against their use without being obliged, in fairness, to allow commercials advocating their use.

Against bans on the use or sale of tobacco, the Prohibition analogy is standardly urged.[48] Already we have evidence of substantial "bootlegging" (or "buttlegging") of cigarettes between states with low cigarette taxes and those with high ones (Manchester 1976; U.S. Advisory Commission on Intergovernmental Relations [ACIR] 1977). Any more serious ban on sale or use of tobacco would no doubt lead to even more illicit activity of this sort. Even accepting such slippage, however, this strategy is still bound to reduce smoking substantially. Whether more would be lost in terms of respect for the law than would be gained in terms of public health remains an open question.

2.4.6   *Medicalization*

If nicotine is an addictive substance, as argued in section 2.2.2 above, then perhaps a medical rather than legal or economic response to its consumption, via smoking tobacco, is indicated. The idea here would be to make tobacco a prescription drug, available to registered users only.[49] Methadone maintenance programs for heroin addicts might serve as a model.

---

48.   Mill 1859/1975, pp. 108–10; Schelling 1980, p. 110; Breslow 1982, p. 140; Littlechild and Wiseman 1984, p. 64; Lundberg and Knoll 1986. The analogy has more historical warrant than those employing it realize; see sec. 4.9 below for details.

49.   If this seems like a bizarre proposal, it is worth recalling how recent an innovation compulsory drug prescriptions is. "Before 1938, the only drugs for which prescriptions were needed were certain narcotics specified in the Harrison Anti-Narcotics Act of 1914. Any other drug could be obtained by walking into a pharmacy and buying it" (Temin 1979, p. 91). Ironically enough, nicotine-containing chewing gum is in many places—the United States, the United Kingdom, Canada, Sweden—available only on prescription, whereas the most closely analogous tobacco product (the currently favored form of chewing tobacco, "wet snuff") is freely available over the counter to adult purchasers, although its nicotine content per "dose" is twice as great (Kozlowski et al. 1982). Perhaps as a first step in the "medicalization" direction I am here considering, Czechoslovakia now requires consumers of twenty or more cigarettes per day to register with the medical service that monitors respiratory diseases there (*Daily Express*, London [February 17, 1986]).

The aim in making tobacco a prescription drug would be to respond humanely to the needs of present addicts, while discouraging new users. Again, it would be impossible to stop all new users. They can always smoke the cigarettes of registered users illicitly (unless, following the methadone-maintenance model, we require registered users to smoke only in the clinics). But, again, such a policy would have a strong tendency in the desired direction.[50]

2.4.7 *A Composite Policy Package for Smoking Control*

Reflecting just upon the harm that smokers do to themselves, in light of various moral doctrines, led us to set as our policy goal the curtailment of smoking as such. Making tobacco a prescription drug is clearly the most appropriate method of doing so, given the way in which I argued for that goal in the first place. The reason that people cannot meaningfully consent to the risks of smoking is that they are addicted; and the way we cope with addictive drugs is to put them on prescription. The only reason, utilitarian or otherwise, for allowing smoking to continue at all is out of compassion for existing addicts; putting tobacco on prescription would get it into their hands but (virtually) no others.

That is a novel proposal, however. I have few illusions about its practical political prospects, at least in the short term. As a second-best stopgap, I therefore propose a package of more familiar policy options. It would start with more serious enforcement of laws already on the books against selling cigarettes to minors or (what typically amounts to the same thing) breaking packs and selling single cigarettes. The centerpiece of my reform proposals would be a swingeing tax on tobacco products—again designed primarily to stop people in their early teens from starting to smoke in the first place. That would be combined with a stringent ban on tobacco advertising in all its forms (especially sponsorship of sporting, cultural, and other events that tends to make smoking attractive in the eyes of youngsters, again).[51] With those policies in place, health education campaigns—particularly antismoking advertisements of the pre-1970 form—could then serve as useful supplements to discourage smoking. That package is not ideal, leaving many existing addicts without any very strong inducement to stop. Still, it may be the best that, politically, we can do.

---

50. Peltzman (1987), using admittedly thin data, finds that making certain medicines available by prescription only has not had the desired effects of reducing overdoses or suicides using them. More worryingly for the tobacco application, he finds that putting drugs on prescription actually increases demand for them. But presumably the reason is one that has no analogue in the tobacco case: putting a therapeutic drug on prescription constitutes a guarantee of its usefulness in curing disease.

51.   This combines with a ban on smoking in public, justified in sec. 3.5.5 below in terms of harms to others.

3   Harm to Others

If protecting smokers from harms that they do to themselves when smoking is the most obvious reason for restricting smoking, protecting nonsmokers from harms that they suffer at the hands of smokers has proven politically the most compelling in contemporary debates. This chapter opens with a brief statement of what is known about the extent of those risks (Sec. 3.1).

Whether those risks can ground ethical justifications for restrictions on smoking in public is the subject of subsequent sections. Some arguments juxtapose a putative "right to smoke" with the right to breathe clean air (Sec. 3.2), while others turn on the alleged voluntariness of passive smoking (Sec. 3.3) or the alleged disutility of preventing it (Sec. 3.4).

The upshot of all of those discussions is that the risk of damage to others from a person's smoking nearby is a real one, and in light of it we should strive to restrict smoking in public places. The closing section (3.5) surveys various policy options for promoting that goal. These range from self-restraint on the part of smokers, through reliance on market forces, to legislation banning or restricting smoking in public places. In the end, I conclude that the latter, more stringent measures will necessarily have a large role to play in any overall program to stop passive smoking.

3.1   THE NATURE OF THE RISKS

Broadly speaking, there are three classes of negative effects on others arising from a person's smoking nearby. The first two—harm to the fetus and harm to passive smokers—clearly are harms. The third—creation of offensive odors—is the first cousin of a "harm," if not exactly a harm in the classic sense.

3.1.1   *Harm to the Fetus*

First, there is the well-established harm to the fetus inflicted by the mother's smoking.[1] Maternal smoking is strongly associated with prematurity, low birth weight, stillbirth, and infant mortality. The extent of the effects are well known. The mechanisms by which they are produced is obvious (U.S. DHEW 1976, chap. 5; U.S. DHHS 1980, pp. 189–250; Cushner 1981).

The only real question, perhaps, is whether mother and fetus really are two separate people yet. The problem is particularly acute in the first trimester of pregnancy: that period is absolutely crucial to the fetus's proper development; but it is also the period during which we allow a woman to abort at will. Some would say that as long as a woman may legally abort the fetus, she cannot be legally or morally required to undergo medical treatment on the fetus's behalf (Fletcher 1981). That argument would presumably apply with particular force to especially "invasive" treatments that would seriously threaten the mother's bodily integrity. But it would presumably apply, with at least some force, to behavior modification therapies—like compulsory smoking cessation—for the sake of the health of the fetus.

There are various ways to try to counter the argument that if the mother may morally abort the fetus she may do anything short of aborting it, however. One would set up a conflict between rights: the mother's right to abort, along with all that it implies, and the fetus's right to life. The trick there, obviously, lies in showing that fetuses have a right to life, even before they have developed to the point where they would be viable outside the womb. A second, more promising strategy would be to set up a conflict between the mother's rights and the mother's duties. If, as I have argued elsewhere (Goodin 1985), we all have a particularly strong duty to protect the interests of those who are particularly vulnerable to our actions and choices, then one implication would be that the mother has a strong duty to protect the health of the fetus she is carrying. Its dependency on her, after all, is absolute: it has no option but to share her blood; it is hardly in a position to leave her womb. The duty that the mother has by virtue of those facts must be set off against any rights she might have to harm it, deriving from her right to abort it altogether, though. Which would prevail—the right or the duty—is an open question.

There is another, more conclusive counter to the argument that if the mother may morally abort the fetus she may do anything short

---

1.   Recent evidence also suggests that the fetus is harmed by the father's smoking, through the pregnant woman's breathing environmental tobacco smoke he has generated (Martin and Bracken 1986). But that is just a special case of harm to passive smokers, to be discussed in Sec. 3.1.2 below.

of aborting it, including damaging its health by smoking during pregnancy. This counterargument takes its cue from our standard response to another, parallel argument—dating from the earliest social contract theorists (Grotius 1625, 3.4.10; Hobbes 1651, chap. 20; Locke 1690, sec. 85), used to justify slavery. In a just war, you have a right to kill your opponents. From that it follows that you have a right to do anything short of killing them, including enslaving them.

Now, we may well want to qualify, or to deny outright, the first of those premises—just as, in the smoking application, we may care to qualify or deny the mother's right to abort the fetus. But even if that first premise is granted in precisely the form stated, the second proposition simply does not follow from it. Saying that we may kill a person during a war does not imply that we may kill him after the war is over. Saying that we may inflict harms on him short of death during a war does not imply that we may inflict similar damage on him once peace is at hand.[2] If you failed to take advantage of your rights to inflict harm on him during the war, your rights simply pass into oblivion at war's end.

We should respond similarly to the version of this argument that would license parental despotism. Since children owe their very existence to a supererogatory act on the part of their parents, they have no right to complain about their parents' treatment of them, just as long as that treatment is not so bad as to make the children wish they were never born.[3] It is certainly true that parents had every right not to conceive and, having conceived, every right to abort and, having delivered a baby, every right to put it up for adoption. But having failed to avail themselves of any of those rights when they had them, now it is too late. They cannot appeal to legitimate options that they let pass them by to justify their present child abuse (Thomson 1971, p. 65).

2. In the course of combat, we might permissibly inflict injuries that have continuing consequences for the person after the war is over. But there is obviously a difference between the continuing consequences of a past action (hobbling a man through force of arms in a past fight) and a continuing practice (hobbling a man daily, by chaining his legs). The distinction is poorly masked by the legal fiction that "enslavement" is a change in the person's status that, like the war wound, occurred once-and-for-all at some time in the past.

3. Sidgwick (1907, p. 347) notes this paradoxical consequence of claims like Pufendorf's (1672, bk. 2, chap. 2, sec. 12) that the benefits parents bestowed upon children by giving them life are incalculable, so the child's debt "can never be cancelled or repaid." For a more subtle modern version of such arguments, see Parfit (1984, chap. 16). Tollison and Wagner (1988, pp. 73–74) come perilously close to embracing this position in arguing that it should be up to the parents to determine the appropriate levels of tobacco smoke exposure suffered by their own children.

The same is true of child abuse during pregnancy. It is perfectly true, let us stipulate, that a woman has every right to abort a fetus during the first trimester of her pregnancy. If, however, she forgoes that right and continues to carry that child, then so long as she is carrying the child she has obligations to provide it with a safe and healthy environment in her womb (Mathieu 1985, p. 37). The fact that she could have aborted—or even that she could still abort—the fetus does nothing to lessen her obligations to care for it, so long as she fails to abort it.

How, exactly, to characterize the beneficiary of that duty is unclear. We might analyze it as an obligation owed to "the person presently within her," if we regard the fetus as a person already. We might, alternatively, analyze it as an obligation owed to "the person that the unaborted fetus will become," although the we are going to face difficulties in analyzing harms to the fetus so severe as to prevent its being born at all (Feinberg 1984, p. 96). Or, yet again, we might analyze the obligation as one owed to "the society that takes an interest in the future of the fetus."

On these issues, commentators will inevitably differ. But those differences do not matter for present purposes. It is clear enough that there is an obligation, however we describe it, to care for the unaborted fetus, until and unless it is aborted.

3.1.2   *Harm to Passive Smokers*

Second, there is the harm to others arising from "passive smoking." That term refers to the inhalation of "sidestream" smoke from the burning tip of lit cigarettes and of smoke exhaled by smokers nearby.

The technical literature on this subject, though less overwhelming in sheer bulk weight than that on the direct effects of smoking on smokers, is nonetheless voluminous and increasingly compelling in its conclusions. Again, the best guide to the settled scientific view are official reports, both dated from 1986, from the U.S. National Academy of Sciences and the U.S. surgeon general.[4]

The evidence contained therein is essentially of two forms. The first is essentially a matter of chemistry. Analysis of the chemical composition of sidestream smoke shows it to be richer in known carcinogens than is the smoke that smokers themselves inhale (U.S. DHHS 1986, pp. 134–37); and chemical analysis of urine samples of

---

4. The official British report—Froggatt 1988—presents similar findings, albeit more briefly and less conclusively. Perhaps the best short statement of the scientific consensus is Wald et al. 1986. For a useful gloss on these findings written by one of the pioneering researchers in this field expressly for a philosophical audience, see Repace 1985.

nonsmokers living with active smokers, examining concentrations of metabolites of nicotine (which are virtually unique to tobacco) as an indicator of their uptake of environmental tobacco smoke, reveals that these passive smokers have concentrations that would be characteristic of people who were themselves light smokers (U.S. DHHS 1986, chap. 4). The second sort of evidence is essentially epidemiological in nature. It involves studies of nonsmokers in prolonged exposure to secondhand smoke ("environmental tobacco smoke," in the jargon). These studies—typically, of the health of nonsmoking wives with smoking husbands—show that passive smokers run something like a 34 percent greater risk of lung cancer than do nonsmokers not exposed for protracted periods to environmental tobacco smoke (U.S. National Academy of Sciences [NAS] 1986b, p. 231; U.S. DHHS 1986, chap. 2). Lest those findings be thought not to generalize outside the home, it should be noted that the daily dose of environmental tobacco smoke the average person receives at work—where he shares his airspace with more people and hence more smokers—is calculated to be nearly four times the dose received at home (Repace and Lowrey 1985, pp. 4–5 and apps.; see, similarly, U.S. DHHS 1986, pp. 146–64).

That precise a number, 34 percent, has a certain spurious precision about it. Though both the National Academy of Sciences and surgeon general settle on that number as their "best estimate," it is also true that studies regarded by the academy as perfectly respectable have estimated the risk as between 14 percent and 66 percent (U.S. NAS 1986b, p. 47). It would be wrong to let such marginal disagreements over the precise coefficient obscure the larger point, though. As the surgeon general is at pains to emphasize, the question is not whether passive smoking causes cancer. On that, the epidemiological evidence is clear. The question is, as the surgeon general says, merely one of how much cancer it causes (U.S. DHHS 1986, p. 10; see, similarly, Froggatt 1988, par. 68).

Statistical purists, here as before, might question the practice of basing causal assertions on merely epidemiological evidence (Burch 1986). Correlation does not prove causation of lung cancer any more in the case of passive smoking than it does in the case of active smoking, they would say. What made that criticism particularly biting in the case of active smoking, recall, was the fact that these critics could offer a hypothesis that was at least superficially plausible—the "genetic constitutional hypothesis"—to explain how the observed correlation might be spurious.

In the case of passive smoking, there is no such hypothesis that is even superficially plausible to explain away the apparent link between passive smoking and lung cancer. Repace and Lowrey (1986) rightly scoff at the utter absurdity of any suggestion that the apparent link between passive smoking and lung cancer might arise because non-smokers who are prone to lung cancer are biologically driven to marry smokers, while nonsmokers who are resistant to cancer are led to marry nonsmokers. Or, again, self-reports of smoking behavior might be unreliable. But there is no reason to suppose that spouses of smokers would be differentially prone to underreport or deny their smoking, as compared to spouses of nonsmokers. If anything, the reverse seems more likely. That would lead, in turn, to an underestimate rather than an overestimate of the true effects of passive smoking. Our conclusion must be that, while accepting the force of the general point that correlation does not prove causation, there is no plausible alternative in the present case to the hypothesis that passive smoking increases a nonsmoker's risk of lung cancer by something like 34 percent.

Of course, that is a relatively large increase on a relatively small initial probability. Hence the absolute numbers of people who on that reckoning die annually from passive smoking is rather small: any-thing from several hundred to a few thousand, depending upon how many nonsmokers actually suffer regular, protracted exposure to smoke-filled environments. At the absolute outside, 4,700 Americans might die annually from passive smoking (Repace and Lowrey 1985). According to more official sources, "passive smoking results in an estimated 2,500 fatal cancers per year" in the United States (U.S. CEA 1987, p. 185).

Compared to the more than 300,000 people estimated to die annually in the United States from their own smoking, such numbers are undeniably small. But they should be seen, in the words of the official British report, as "small but not negligible" (Froggatt 1988, par. 69). Even by that modest count, passive smoking still kills more people than all airborne pollutants regulated by the U.S. Environ-mental Protection Agency, asbestos excepted (Repace and Lowrey 1985, p. 12). And the only reason asbestos kills more people, come to that, is that more people are exposed to it for prolonged periods. Per person exposed, "the calculated and observed excess of lung cancer produced by passive smoking is some 50 times greater than that estimated to be the effect of 40 hours a week exposure to asbestos in an asbestos-containing building" (Sir Richard Doll, quoted in Jenkins et al. 1987, p. 36).

Another way to look at the health hazard posed by passive smoking is to consider the annual per capita risk of death it entails, compared to that posed by other activities that we think should be regulated in the interests of public health. Put in those terms, the risk of death from passive smoking—of the order of magnitude of one chance in ten thousand—is small. But it is nonetheless one-hundred times greater than the level of risk that the Environmental Protection Agency would regard as adequate to justify the regulation of carcinogenic air pollutants or the Nuclear Regulatory Commission would use in guidelines for acceptable cancer mortality risks from reactor accidents. And it is ten-thousand times greater than the threshold the Food and Drug Administration requires before deeming carcinogenic residues in foods as "virtually safe" (Repace 1985, p. 23). It may well be true that some of those other regulatory thresholds are excessive, of course. The point, however, remains that the risks of passive smoking exceeds those other standards of "acceptable risk" by several (two to four) orders of magnitude. So if those other regulatory regimes are anywhere near right, we ought by the same logic impose similar restrictions on passive smoking.

Most emphasis, both in my discussion here and in the scientific literature upon which it is based, has been on the tendency of passive smoking to cause lung cancer. Besides that, however, passive smoking also aggravates a number of other conditions: bronchitis, asthma, and emphysema (U.S. DHHS 1986, pp. 60–65), angina and ischemic heart disease (Garland et al. 1985); and allergies. It also causes irritation of the eyes, nose, and throat of most of those exposed (U.S. NAS 1986b, pp. 176, 214; U.S. DHHS 1986, chap. 2); and the effects can be particularly severe in the 3 percent of the population that is hypersensitive to tobacco smoke (Repace 1985, pp. 5–6). Once again, then, when referring in shorthand fashion to "cancer" as the risk of passive smoking in my subsequent discussion, I am in no way intending to minimize these other perfectly palpable health risks that also result from it.

3.1.3   *Offensive Nuisances*

Both of those first two effects are "real harms," in the sense of genuine health hazards imposed on one person by another's smoking nearby. Beyond all that, however, is a third category more akin to "sheer disamenities" that nonsmokers experience when breathing others' smoke.

The surgeon general's report on passive smoking offers convincing evidence that a great majority of nonsmokers are genuinely annoyed by others' smoke (U.S. DHHS 1986, pp. 229–38). It is hard to say what, exactly, we should make of that fact for policy purposes, though. Some, such as the Royal College of Physicians (1983, p. 79), might argue that, whether or not passive smoking actually damages health, "there is already sufficient evidence as to the discomfort and annoyance that breathing other people's smoke can cause. Nonsmokers at work and play, in transport and in public places, should

have the right not to be so exposed." Friends of the tobacco industry
retort: "There are many habits others have which are offensive to me,
yet I am not justified in prohibiting indulgence in them. Mere
offensiveness clearly cannot constitute actionable conduct" (Machan
1986, p. 51). Or, again, "Obviously, some nonsmokers find tobacco
smoke annoying. But by the same token, some non-sports fans find
sports annoying, some nonvegetarians find vegetables annoying, and
so on. Freedom of choice implies freedom to do things that others
may dislike" (Tollison and Wagner 1988, p. 66).

Such retorts proceed too quickly, however. For there are some
forms of annoyance, perfectly analogous to nonsmokers' annoyance
at the smell of tobacco smoke, that are actionable by law. Emitting
offensive odors, when done by a factory, is subject to public regulation. In Malaysia, it is illegal to carry the evil-smelling durian fruit on
public transportation. Many nonsmokers (especially ex-smokers) find
the smell of burning tobacco similarly offensive. Perhaps burning it in
their presence might be banned on similar grounds.

Curiously enough, Mill (1859/1975, p. 120) himself can be en-
listed in support of such an argument. "There are," he writes, "many
acts which, being directly injurious only to the agents themselves,
ought not to be legally interdicted, but which, if done publicly, are a
violation of good manners, and coming thus within the category of
offences against others, may rightfully be prohibited." Primary
among the examples Mill has in mind here are "offences against
decency"—sin, blasphemy, and such like. But he goes on to say that
the moral case against offensive behavior in public is "equally strong"
even where (as is presumably the case with smoking) the "actions [are]
not in themselves condemnable, nor supposed to be so."

What makes arguments of that sort hard to swallow is just this:
our standard moral and legal justifications for social regulations are
essentially harm-based rationales; and "giving offense" is simply not
the same as "causing harm," in any of the standard senses of "harm."
That fact makes "offensiveness" a notoriously tricky notion to fit into
those standard rationales for social regulation of conduct (Feinberg
1985; Jones 1980).

Of course, it is perfectly true to say that "offensiveness" shares
many of the same characteristics of a standard harm.[5] We might
therefore deem offensiveness a harm, in some extenuated sense. But

5. Certainly those offended are subjectively worse off—their utility is reduced,
their welfare compromised, their preferences disappointed—as a result of the offense.
Hence, offensiveness is clearly harmful, at least in the denuded terminology of
microeconomics. Thus, Tollison and Wagner (1988, p. 66) are being untrue to the
central tenets of their own discipline when writing, "The argument about [passive
smoking] is *not* an argument about whether or not some nonsmokers dislike tobacco.

then the issue becomes one of whether the sense in which offense is a harm is too attenuated for the standard justifications for social regulation to apply. No amount of staring at the dictionary is going to resolve that issue. We need examine instead the reasons we have for thinking that some sorts of offenses ought be immune from regulation and others subject to them, and then to consider which set of reasons apply better to the case of passive smoking.

On the one hand, given our essentially harm-based rationales for social regulation, we are ordinarily inclined to deem "harmless immoralities" perfectly permissible. We are particularly inclined in that direction when those immoralities touch upon values of free speech and expression (Jones 1980; Feinberg 1985, p. 44). The mere fact that others may be offended by such immoralities is, in those cases, clearly an insufficient basis for social prohibition. We have grievous qualms about letting the notion of "actionable offense" range so widely as to allow, on the basis of it, the banning of sexually explicit plays, pointed political protests, interracial marriage in the deep South, or deviant religious practices (Feinberg 1985, chap. 8).

On the other hand, we are perfectly comfortable in regulating, as "offensive nuisances," smelly or noisy factories. It may be perfectly true that they are "mere" nuisances, posing no real hazards to health. But showing that they do constitute genuine nuisances—showing, in other words, that a great many others suffer prolonged and intense disturbance by the sounds or smells—is more than enough to justify us in restricting what factory owners do and where they may do it, according to some larger balancing of social utility (Feinberg 1985, pp. 7–8, 35).

Smoking seems more nearly analogous to the smelly factory than to the political protestor. There is no larger social interest of free speech or any other to be served by allowing the activity. An increasingly large majority of the population are now nonsmokers (Helyar 1987), who suffer annoyance of a prolonged and often

---

Obviously, some nonsmokers find tobacco smoke annoying. But . . . the proper focus of the argument . . . is whether or not smokers impose involuntary costs (either health-related or not) on others." In ordinary economic parlance, being subjected to something you would prefer to avoid is a cost. In ordinary economic parlance, there is no other way of defining "cost." What lies behind Tollison and Wagner's argument is a libertarian presumption that there are certain sorts of costs that simply should not count for purposes of justifying coercive state interventions: it is none of the nonsmoker's business; if there are costs, they are his problem. But that is not to say that there are no costs, it is merely to say that social policy should respond to rights rather than costs—or even to harms, come to that. It takes more than a smuggled-in presumption to establish that case.

intense sort when forced to share confined quarters for protracted periods with smokers. Smokers can easily enough avoid giving such offense, simply by stepping outside to smoke, And so on. By all the ordinary standards (Feinberg 1985, p. 35), smoking seems just the sort of offensive nuisance that any reasonable balancing of social interests would justify us in regulating. It is, in all those respects, perfectly on a par with regulation of smelly factories as a public nuisance.

Showing a "real harm" to health is always a stronger argument for such regulation, of course. There is evidence of that, too, as shown in Sections 3.1.1 and 3.1.2 above. The point here is just that that might not be strictly necessary. The nuisance argument might in itself suffice.

3.2   THE RIGHT TO SMOKE
AND THE RIGHT TO BREATHE

The argument for restricting smoking in enclosed public spaces is characteristically couched in deontological terms of rights and duties. It is the right of nonsmokers to breathe clean air, and the duty of smokers not to pollute the atmosphere that others must breathe. In the language of a recent World Health Organization resolution, "Passive, enforced or involuntary smoking violates the right to health of non-smokers, who must be protected against this noxious form of environmental pollution" (WHO 1986; see, similarly, U.S. DHHS 1986, p. xii). Or, in the more florid terms of the turn-of-the-century Non-Smokers' Protective League president, "The right of each person to breathe and enjoy fresh and pure air—air uncontaminated by unhealthful or disagreeable odors and fumes—is a constitutional right, and cannot be taken away by legislatures or courts, much less by individuals pursuing their own thoughtless or selfish indulgence" (Pease 1911, quoted in Troyer and Markle 1983, p.39).

The issue has been joined on this high deontological plane from the other side, too. The less interesting version of this argument is Machan's (1986, p. 51) libertarian lament, tracing the right to allow smoking to rights of private property. "Few people now advocate banning smoking in people's homes," Machan writes. "Why do they believe that they are entitled to non-smoking sections in restaurants or aeroplanes, when these do not belong to them? . . . Whoever owns the area . . . ought to have the right to say whether [smoking] is permitted" in it.

By an analogous standard, restaurant owners ought presumably be allowed to refuse to serve whoever they like, discriminating against blacks or women, for example. Or, again, restaurant owners should, by this analogous standard, be allowed to serve unsanitary food to any customers who (having been duly warned, perhaps) choose to partake of it.

Surely no policymakers are prepared to take this general proposition at all seriously. If you open your establishment to the public, and profit from trade with the public, then the public has a right to determine certain conditions upon which you may conduct that trade (Berle 1952, p. 943). That right follows simply from the act of public trading itself, conducted as it necessarily is under state charter. Even writers such as Tollison and Wagner (1988, p. 77, n. 7) are prepared to concede as much.

The more interesting version of the deontological defense of smoking turns not on the property owner's right to allow smoking on his premises but instead on the rights of the smokers themselves. The tobacco industry's U.K. pressure group, the Tobacco Advisory Council (TAC) maintains that just as nonsmokers have rights, so too do smokers have a "right to smoke" (TAC 1987). And one U.S. court has been prepared to concede, at least for the sake of argument, "that there is a liberty interest within the fourteenth amendment that protects the right of firefighters to smoke cigarettes when off duty" (Barrett 1987, p. 543).

The Tobacco Advisory Council leaflet goes on to say that "neither group"—neither smokers nor nonsmokers—"has any absolute right to dictate to the other," since each has rights at play in the matter (TAC 1987). As the French version of this advertising campaign has it, "for smokers and non-smokers, liberty is reciprocal" (Jacobson 1989). I take it that that is simply untrue, and that the matter can be settled (presumptively, at least) in favor of the nonsmoker (Wikler 1987, p. 354).

In the words of the familiar old adage, your rights and your freedoms stop at the end of my nose. In the case of environmental tobacco smoke, your smoke obviously transgresses the privacy of my nasal passages. "Just as my bodily integrity is violated by a punch in the nose, so too is it threatened by toxins and carcinogens others place in the environment. . . Just as I have a rights claim against those who would punch me in the nose, so too I have one against those who would batter my lungs" (Daniels 1985, p. 151; see also Gibson 1985). The surgeon general has rightly concluded, "The right of smokers to smoke ends where their behavior affects the health and well-being of others; . . . the choice to smoke cannot interfere with the non-smoker's right to breathe air free of tobacco smoke" (U.S. DHHS 1986, p. xii).

In this way, we can break down the apparent symmetry between the loss that would be suffered by the smoker, denied the pleasures of tobacco to spare the nonsmoker, and that which would be suffered by the nonsmoker, denied the pleasures of clean air to indulge the smoker. "Each interferes with the other," it is true. But the nonsmoker "merely wishes to breathe unpolluted air and, in the pursuit thereof, and unlike the smoker, does not reduce the amenity of others" in so doing (Mishan 1967, p. 280).[6]

The symmetry suggested by the "right to smoke vs. the right to clean air" formulation is, thus, illusory. The crucial asymmetry is just this. The smoker would be neither better nor worse off if the nonsmoker did not exist. The nonsmoker would definitely be better off if the smoker did not exist.[7]

At root, the grounds for assigning priority to the right to breathe clean air are simply that everyone—smoker and nonsmoker alike—needs this right in order to flourish. The point is effectively evoked by a fanciful example offered by James Repace (1985, p. 27): "Suppose that individual nonsmokers, in defense of their asserted right to breathe tobacco-smoke-free indoor air, were to release a gas into indoor spaces where they were forced to breathe tobacco smoke. Suppose further that when sucked through the burning cone of a cigarette, pipe, or cigar this gas decomposed into irritating byproducts which cause moderate to intense discomfort to the smoker, much the way ambient tobacco smoke affects the nonsmoker. Would smokers feel that they had the inalienable right to gas-free air?" If so, they must concede that nonsmokers have a right to smoke-free air, a right which takes priority over their right to smoke.

Some might say that the analogy is not a perfect one. For example, it might be argued that, unlike the antismoker gas bomber, the smoker is not intentionally harming anyone. The gas bomber actually intends to discomfort anyone who lights up a cigarette in the room. The discomfort caused to others by smokers' smoking is regarded, even by smokers themselves, as an unfortunate by-product of their smoking; they would happily remove that side effect if they could do so, without undue cost or discomfort to themselves.

To this claim, the antismoker gas bomber might reply that he does not intend to harm anyone, either. Smokers will be discomforted by his gas only if they smoke. If they refrain from smoking, they will not be harmed in the slightest. Furthermore, the gas bomber might

6. Mishan (1967, p. 280) continues, "The conflict of interest does not arise from *reciprocal* effects and does not imply equal culpability. The conflict arises from the damage inflicted by one of the parties on the other."

7. Or, more precisely, if the person who smokes did not smoke. The more familiar case—equally ill-formulated as a conflict of rights—of the mugger and his victim is just a more extreme case of this pattern. Not only would the victim be better off if the mugger (qua mugger) did not exist, but the mugger would actually be worse off if his victim did not exist to be robbed (cf. Kelman 1979, p. 791).

continue, if they do smoke then nonsmokers would have been analogously discomforted. The gas bomb can thus be construed as an act of self-defense which, though preemptive, has the endearing property of harming potential aggressors only if and when they turn into actual ones.

Some such argument might establish a presumptive priority of the right to clean air over the right to smoke. Like all presumptions, however, this one can always be overcome—in this case, in either of two ways.[8] One is to show that nonsmokers have voluntarily consented to others' smoking. The other is to show, through a calculation of costs and benefits, that the losses to smokers who are stopped from smoking would far exceed the losses to nonsmokers who are exposed to environmental tobacco smoke. Each of these possibilities will be considered and rejected, in turn, in Sections 3.3 and 3.4 below.

If, as I shall argue, the presumptive priority of the right of clean air cannot be overcome in either of those ways, then the upshot is that the rights of nonsmokers should prevail over the rights of smokers to smoke, in cases of conflict. Put another way: nonsmokers should have a right to veto others' smoking in the airspace that they must share. In framing smoking policies, the right rule is indeed that "the preferences of both smokers and non-smokers will be respected, but when these conflict, the preferences of the non-smoker will prevail" (Jenkins et al. 1987, p. 11).

3.3   THE VOLUNTARINESS OF PASSIVE SMOKING

In the case of the smoker himself, it could plausibly (but wrongly, as we have seen in Sec. 2.2.2 above) be argued that the risks of smoking were somehow voluntarily incurred. In the case of the passive smoker, that argument would be far harder to sustain. Passive smokers do not themselves light up. They merely breathe. You can voluntarily choose to do something only if you can, realistically, choose not to do it; and no one can choose not to breathe. Since passive smoking "generally occurs as an unavoidable consequence of being in proximity to

---

8.   Both are in play in the contrasting case of the automobile driver. Nondrivers in a congested city are forced to breathe noxious fumes emitted as the by-products of others' driving, just as nonsmokers in an enclosed space are forced to breathe noxious fumes emitted as the by-products of others' smoking. In both cases, the by-products are unintended and undesired by the perpetrators; in both cases, they would happily remove them if they could do so costlessly. Yet we are not nearly so tempted to ban or restrict driving as we are to ban or restrict smoking. The reason is that cars are a necessary part of commerce which is necessary, in turn, for the well-being of all; cigarettes are not. In the first instance, that argument works in cost-benefit terms. But since people might reasonably be presumed to consent to arrangements that are so clearly beneficial to them, it might serve to ground a consent-based argument, as well.

smokers, particularly in enclosed indoor environments," the surgeon general prefers simply to define passive smoking as "involuntary smoking" (U.S. DHHS 1986, p. 6).

Smokers sometimes might—as Miss Manners (Martin 1983, p. 637) says that they should—have sought and been granted the permission of all nonsmokers in the vicinity for them to light up. Assuming that that consent was given freely (i.e., that it was not a tyrannical boss "asking" permission of a secretary) and that it was based on full information about the hazards of passive smoking, nonsmokers' exposure to environmental tobacco smoke would indeed then be voluntary. Given the dangers of duress and of fraudulent claims that rights have been waived, we may prefer to treat the right to clean air as if it were as inalienable as the right to life itself (Rose-Ackerman 1985).

Be all that as it may, this whole voluntary waiver scenario is plausible only among moderately small groups of people. It is fine for a dinner party. But in an ordinary-sized restaurant or a busy airport terminal, it is simply unreasonable to expect that the issue should be resolved by those who wish to smoke going around and securing the permission of each other person who would be affected before lighting up.

Among larger and more anonymous groups, the only sense in which passive smoking might be thought to be voluntary would be insofar as people voluntarily enter environments they knew were or would become smoky. Thus, it might be argued that if people do not want to breathe other people's smoke, they should not go into notoriously smoky places like English pubs.

For a particularly forceful statement of this position, consider the words of Tollison and Wagner (1988, pp. 75–76). "In the days of the military draft, it might have been accurate to speak of nonsmoking draftees 'being exposed' to ETS [environmental tobacco smoke]. But as a general rule in a free society, people 'expose themselves to' ETS." After all, unlike the microbes against which standard public health programs protect us, "tobacco smoke is clearly visible and gives off a noticeable odor, and lit cigarettes are obvious." People can hardly expose themselves to this hazard without knowing it. Furthermore, "individuals will frequently find it to their advantage to have dealings with those whose personal characteristics—whether they involve table manners, personal appearance, bathing habits, or smoking habits— are not entirely pleasing to them. If individuals continue to interact with others who have disagreeable personal characteristics, it must be true that they perceive themselves better off by doing so" (Tollison and Wagner 1988, p. 75). From this pair of propositions, Tollison and Wagner (1988, p. 76) draw the inference that "people may become exposed to smallpox or polio involuntarily and without their knowledge, but prolonged exposure to ETS cannot be anything but the result of *voluntary choice*."

Just how voluntary a choice this is, however, depends upon just what range of choices is being offered to the nonsmoker. There is, of course, the larger question of why nonsmokers should banish themselves from certain sorts of places to protect their lungs, rather than smokers banishing themselves to certain sorts of places to abuse theirs.

But in any case there is a range of places that it would be simply unreasonable to expect people to avoid going, just in order to avoid exposure to other people's smoke (Gibson 1985, pp. 156–57). Among them are the workplace, public transportation, public buildings, and perhaps public entertainments (restaurants, theaters, etc.). The free choice that people have in voluntarily choosing whether or not to go to work or to appear in court when summoned is, in the recent words of a judge in quite another context, "akin to the free choice of coming up for air after being underwater" (Brown 1987, p. 627).

(There is indeed an important place for a public/private distinction here. If people who have chartered an aircraft privately want to allow smoking, that is rightly regarded as their prerogative under the new U.S. regulations. Similarly, the government ought to hesitate to apply smoking restrictions to genuinely private clubs, even if they provide their members with entertainment facilities—restaurants, theaters, and so on—that would otherwise fall under such restrictions. The difference, in both cases, lies in what it is to participate fully in the life of the community. It would be unreasonable—it would unduly restrict people in their participation in social life—to tell people who do not like others' smoking that they should refrain from riding city buses, or going into the city hall, or going to the public cinema. Private activities are truly optional, by contrast. No one needs to ride a chartered airplane or to dine in a private club to participate fully as a member of our society.)[9]

---

9. Smoking in the privacy of one's own home is more problematic, in a way. Spouses have no grounds for complaint. They are undeniably harmed by breathing their partner's smoke, to be sure—virtually all the studies used to establish the health risks of passive smoking relate to the lung cancer rate of nonsmoking wives of smoking husbands, after all. But since smoking habits are generally established in early adolescence, well before marriage, spouses generally know what they are letting themselves in for ahead of marriage; and, in any case, they can always withdraw from the union if they are all that bothered by their partner's smoking. Those responses are not altogether satisfactory, even in the case of spouses. (Nonsmokers marrying smokers in the 1950s, e.g., might have had no idea what health risks they were courting; nonsmoking wives who have sacrificed their career prospects to the marriage, and

If people have no reasonable choice but to go to work, and to get there by public transportation, they then cannot reasonably be said to have voluntarily chosen to subject themselves to such tobacco smoke as they find in those places. It does not matter how, exactly, we flesh out the argument at this point. Some would say that it is not a choice at all, if you could not have chosen otherwise; others would say that, though a choice, it is not a free or fully voluntary one under such circumstances; still others, conceding that it is a voluntary choice, would nonetheless appeal to Hume's doctrine ("no consent without the possibility of withholding consent") to claim that such a choice, however voluntary, still does not constitute consent to the risks of passive smoking in those environments. Whichever way we run the argument at that point, the conclusion is the same. At least for those areas where we cannot reasonably expect people to refrain from going, just to avoid environmental tobacco smoke, their going there cannot constitute consent to the attendant risks of passive smoking in those places.

Beyond all that is the further question of whether people should be asked (or even allowed) to consent at all to the risks of passive smoking. Consider the parallel case of the testing of experimental drugs on human subjects. Certainly we insist that people's participation in such experiments be fully voluntary, based upon completely informed consent, if those experiments are to count as morally permissible. But voluntary consent is a necessary rather than a sufficient condition. Before we allow experimental trials involving humans at all, we insist that there be some evidence (based on animal studies, e.g.) that the drugs are safe and effective to use as intended. We regard it as morally impermissible to subject humans to experiments ahead of that—even if they consent (or even demand) to be used in such ways. Perhaps being subjected to other people's smoke is,

---

would be encumbered with dependent children making them substantially less remarriagable if they were to divorce, might not be able to withdraw from the health-threatening union all that easily.) But it is the children who are forced to breathe their parents' smoke that pose the more difficult case. They have been shown to suffer significantly impaired respiratory function in consequence of their parents' smoking (U.S. NAS 1986b, pp. 216–17, 269–72; U.S. DHHS 1986, pp. 38–59; Froggatt 1988, pars. 70, 71). In a way, that might be considered a case of "child abuse." Still, as libertarians take great pleasure in pointing out, "few people now advocate banning smoking in people's homes" in consequence (Machan 1986, p. 51; see, similarly, Tollison and Wagner 1988, pp. 72–74). This, however, should be seen as a manifestation of our more general reluctance to interfere with who has children and how they choose to raise them, rather than as a manifestation of any reluctance to interfere with people's smoking even though it harms others.

likewise, something that ought not to be done to people, even with their consent.

The drug testing case suggests that a crucial element in determining whether consent is relevant is whether there is some prospect that the people involved might conceivably benefit from the practice to which they are giving their consent. Tobacco industry apologists insist that there is, in the case of passive smoking. It is not a benefit that is intrinsic to breathing other people's smoke as such, of course. Instead, it is an extrinsic (e,g., commercial) benefit derived from consorting people who happen to be inveterate smokers (Tollison and Wagner 1988, pp. 75–76).

The difference between an intrinsic and an extrinsic benefit is likely to be crucial here, however. If the benefit were an intrinsic one, then you cannot enjoy the benefit without taking the risk: in the case of the experimental drug, the benefit is intrinsic in this way. If the benefit is merely an extrinsic one, as in the case of passive smoking, that is not true. Breathing other people's smoke, and the health hazards that that brings, is an *unnecessary* by-product of work, play, and so on. Those activities could perfectly well take place without anyone smoking—or, pari pasu, passively smoking—in the course of them. The risks of passive smoking are, therefore, utterly gratuitous ones. Just as we do not allow people to court gratuitous risks in the case of testing experimental drugs, taking drugs we have no reason to believe will work, so too should we not allow them to court gratuitous risks in the case of passive smoking. Just as their consent is irrelevant in the former case, so too perhaps ought it be in the latter.[10]

3.4   COSTS AND BENEFITS

Even if we suppose that the issue is properly couched in terms of rights—and especially if we do not—a calculation of the costs and benefits to all interested parties under all policy options is nonetheless relevant. Some rights violations matter more than others, after all. It would be a violation of bodily integrity for someone else to force smoke into your lungs. It would equally be a violation of bodily integrity for someone else to brush against your arm, yet few courts would take cognizance of that invasion. Technically, it might count as

10.   This argument would, e.g., support the policy developed by a U.K. subsidiary of Johnson and Johnson requiring "meetings of two people or more held in private offices are to be non-smoking occasions, unless *all* present are smokers. Non-smoker(s) must not be allowed to waive the right to a smoke-free environment in such circumstances" (Ethicon Ltd. Standard Personnel Practice no. F3 (A), reproduced in Jenkins et al. 1987, p. 28).

a case of assault, but the law does not deal in trifles, as the saying goes. Neither should public policy.

When deciding which rights violations matter most, we tend to employ a rough-and-ready utilitarian calculus of a sort, taking into account both costs to the violated and benefits to the violator. In that calculus, the former weighs particularly heavily. If rights holders have suffered serious harm, then rights violators have wronged them, almost regardless of whatever benefits the rights violators themselves stood to gain (or losses to avert). Thus, insofar as the case against passive smoking can be made in terms of increased lung cancer and other potentially grave illnesses, the deontological case is once again quickly closed. But insofar as the stakes are more modest—offensive odors and watery eyes—we would have to take seriously into account costs and benefits to both parties, on the model of nuisance law for example (Feinberg 1985, chap. 8).

Dealing in straight utilitarian terms, the case against passive smoking is necessarily less strong than that against direct smoking. That is simply because the passive smoker gets only a small fraction of the dose of poisonous substances that is received by the active smoker. A smoker's chances of lung cancer are increased by 980 percent, a passive smoker's by only 34 percent; and so on. Since the costs of passive smoking are necessarily lower than those of active smoking, there is more of a chance that the benefits there might outweigh the costs, in a utilitarian calculus.

As before, one easy way to meet this challenge is to conceptualize "benefits" in terms of interests rather than of preferences. However much smokers might want to smoke, it is not in their interests to do so. We are doing them a favor—conferring upon them an objective health benefit—by stopping them from smoking, even for a little while (Repace 1985, p. 27). But such arguments are subject, once again, to the rejoinders found devestating in section 2.3.2 above.

If dealing in preference-based terms, we must take account of the severity of the characteristic reactions involved: of smokers, forced to suffer withdrawal for the period of time they would be constrained from smoking, on the one hand; of nonsmokers forced to suffer environmental tobacco smoke for the period of time they would be closeted with it, on the other. Of course, variable physiology on both sides means that some people will suffer more than others. Not all smokers would suffer withdrawal during a two-hour flight, on the one hand; not all nonsmokers would mind the smoke all that much, on the other. At the other extreme, most smokers probably would suffer some withdrawal symptoms over the course of a whole day at work; yet surveys show that most nonsmokers suffer at least eye, nose, and throat irritation from being subjected to day-long smoking in an enclosed office, and prolonged exposure of just this sort is what has been shown to increase nonsmokers' risks of lung cancer by a third. Fine-grained interpersonal utility comparisons are notoriously difficult, of course. But, in rough-and-ready terms, it would seem that the severity of the characteristic reactions of smokers and nonsmokers are approximately on a par pretty much across the range of possible exposures.

Our naive expectation, I suspect, is that, if anything, smokers might characteristically be bothered marginally (but probably only marginally) more by no-smoking rules, even once they have made all the adjustments to them that they can, than nonsmokers were by rules permitting smoking.[11] That supposition is contrary to the considered judgment of the U.S. National Academy of Sciences (U.S. NAS 1986b, pp. 151–52), however. In recommending a ban on smoking on all domestic commercial airline flights, it acknowledges that "some habitual smokers might experience nicotine deprivation on flights longer than three hours. However, in the judgment of the Committee, the potential health effects of passive smoking are of more concern than the discomfort of withdrawal, and more people are at risk."

For what it is worth, we can also consider the result of one admittedly very casual piece of experimental economics. Benham (1981, p. 572–73) reports that "when faced with the prospect of actually paying (or being paid) for the property rights to the air during classroom lectures over a semester, nonsmoker students in my classes at Washington University have always placed a larger aggregate value on the air rights than smokers. Nonsmokers in these classes have generally been willing to pay from ten to 100 times as much as the smokers for air rights." Presumably the numbers involved in these experiments were small, and there was no guarantee that relevant extraneous factors (e.g., wealth) were properly controlled. Still, as a preliminary indication of the relative intensity of feelings on the two sides, this is an important observation.

There is another consideration to be entered on the "intensity" side of the basic utilitarian calculus. This concerns the magnitude of

---

11. In the transitional period, of course, smokers may well experience much more discomfort that nonsmokers did, when they were used to taking evasive action to avoid others' smoke. In the long term, though, smokers' costs will decline as they get used to shifting their smoking patterns or as they give up the practice altogether. Transition costs are not to be discounted. But since transitions are short-lived, their costs are contained. Their impact on any utilitarian calculus ought not, therefore, be exaggerated.

possible suffering, should worse come to worst, that might be experienced by parties on each side.[12] At worst, the smoker prevented from smoking suffers discomfort. The nonsmoker exposed to environmental tobacco smoke might, at worst, suffer lung cancer or other debilitating diseases (Gibson 1985, p. 155; U.S. NAS 1986a, pp. 151–52). That is not the most common outcome, by a long stretch. But in light of other less risky airborne contaminants that the Environmental Protection Agency does regulate, it certainly is a common enough outcome to take seriously in framing policies.

In other words, our calculations should weigh especially heavily on the interests of individuals who are hypersensitive or otherwise particularly vulnerable to the hazards of passive smoking—asthmatics, pregnant women, and so on. This conclusion would follow from my arguments, developed elsewhere (Goodin 1985), that we have a strong moral duty to "protect the vulnerable" in general. In any case, the practice of being especially responsive to the interests of particularly sensitive and vulnerable people is already well-established in various other areas of social policy.

Consider, for example, the so-called egg shell skull rule in tort law. The rule there is that "tortfeasor . . . take[s] his victim as he finds him, no matter what his condition or susceptibility or how extraordinary its consequences" (Hart and Honore 1985, p. 274). Suppose you slap someone who, unbeknownst to you, has hemophilia or an egg shell skull, and you end up killing him with a blow that you intended (and reasonably expected) would only startle him; you are guilty of manslaughter nonetheless (Feinberg 1970, p. 213).

Or consider, again, the sorts of limits we quite properly put on the operation of majoritarianism in democratic theory. We might, as Barry (1965, p. 312) suggests, be perfectly happy to let smoking rules be determined by majority vote of those riding in a particular carriage, especially where the carriage has been left unmarked and where no inference can be drawn either way from the absence of markings. But as Barry himself says in a subsequent auto-critique, if one among them were asthmatic, we think that person ought to be given veto rights on smoking in the carriage (Barry 1979, pp. 170–71).

12.   Another thing, perhaps, is the relative voluntariness of the harms. The risks to the nonsmoker are almost wholly involuntary; the risks to the smoker are widely, albeit wrongly (cf. Sec. 2.2.2 above), perceived to have been voluntarily incurred. This distinction is principally of deontological force. But it may have utilitarian bearing, as well, given that the social acceptability of risk studies show that people are prepared to accept voluntary risks one thousand times greater than involuntary ones (Starr 1969).

This rule is, on its face, quite different from one of giving nonsmokers veto rights on smoking in a confined public space, whether they are asthmatics or not. But much turns on how we define "hypersensitive" and on how we operationalize it. To some (e.g., microeconomists), the best way of defining a "hypersensitive individual" would simply be as one who objects strongly to breathing others' smoke; then anyone who chooses to exercise a veto, against strong social pressure from smokers, would qualify. Or, again, we might as a matter of operational practice prefer to accept people's self-nominations for the status of "hypersensitive individuals"—we may think it unnecessarily stigmatizing to require them to produce a physician's note testifying to their infirmities, when those infirmities would in no way compromise their job performance in an ordinary smoke-free workplace. In either of those two cases, the rule of giving hypersensitive individuals a veto would, in practice, amount to a rule of giving any nonsmoker a veto.

Allowing smoking unless some self-identified hypersensitive individual vetoes it will work, however, only insofar as hypersensitive individuals know who they are. Sometimes we can be reasonably sure that they do: asthmatics, for example, cannot help noticing their condition or the way that others' smoking aggravates it. But there are other instances in which we cannot be nearly so sure of this. People might be particularly at risk of ischemic heart disease or lung cancer (because, perhaps, of previous exposures to carcinogens) without their realizing it. And such people might, similarly, have no immediate indicator, equivalent to the asthmatic's coughing fit, to signal the ways in which others' smoking nearby aggravates those other conditions. If substantial numbers of those who are genuinely hypersensitive to environmental tobacco smoke do not realize it, then we cannot count on them protecting themselves through the exercise of veto rights. Instead of counting on hypersensitive individuals to veto smoking when it bothers them, we must instead ban smoking altogether in confined spaces in which they are likely to find themselves.

All this is offered as one possible variation on a utilitarian theme. Of course, the appeal of this more general principle of "protecting the vulnerable" need not be exclusively utilitarian: other sorts of philosopher might find it attractive, as well. But this principle certainly does have a utilitarian side, among others. By protecting those whose interests are particularly vulnerable to our actions and choices, we would be promoting their welfare and, thereby, overall social utility.

There is a second crucial element—so far undiscussed—in any classically Benthamite utilitarian calculation. This is the number of people affected each way. In principle, this should be relatively straightforward. Whereas getting inside people's heads to measure the intensity of their reactions poses difficult methodological problems, assessing the number of people affected each way should in principle be merely a matter of counting. In practice, it is slightly more tricky.

Certainly it is true that nonsmokers now outnumber smokers in the United States by a ratio of almost three to one (Helyar 1987). On the face of it, that statistic would seem to have obvious implications for a utilitarian assessment of smoking policies. So long as each smoker would lose something less than twice the value of what each non-smoker would gain from a ban on smoking in public, the fact that there are more than twice as many nonsmokers would seem to imply that the utility gained from the ban exceeds the utility lost from it, across the whole society. Although rarely spelled out quite so completely, some such logic seems to underlie many arguments for restricting smoking in public places (U.S. NAS 1986a, pp. 151–52).

That argument moves rather too quickly, however. In effect, it invites us to consider the two classes—smokers and nonsmokers—as homogeneous groups, with everyone in each group having the same experiences and reactions as everyone else in the group. In fact, of course, not all nonsmokers are equally exposed to others' smoke; nor do all nonsmokers suffer identical reactions to identical exposures. Nor, come to that, are all smokers alike. So the argument as stated is obviously not altogether satisfactory.

There are some diseases, such as lung cancer, that seem (on present evidence, at least) to be caused only by protracted exposure to environmental tobacco smoke.[13] We need to know—in a way that we do not yet know (U.S. DHHS 1986, p. 10; Froggatt 1988, par. 69)—how many people suffer, either at home or at work, such protracted exposure before we can assess the full utilitarian implications of those risks. There are some other diseases, such as bronchitis, emphysema, and asthma, that are clearly aggravated by even brief, intermittent exposures to environmental tobacco smoke. We need to know the number of sufferers from such diseases to assess the full utilitarian implications of passive smoking, in that respect.

The upshot seems to be this. As regards serious health hazards, all nonsmokers are affected by others' smoke only in some cases (i.e.,

---

13.   Since, as has been well established in the case of direct smoking, there is "no safe level"—any amount of smoking will pose some risk of lung cancer—it is only reasonable to suspect that there is no absolutely safe level of exposure to second-hand environmental tobacco smoke, either. But since protracted exposure only increases lung cancer risks of nonsmokers by something like 34 percent, the level of added risk from brief or intermittent exposure might reasonably be suspected to be miniscule.

cases of protracted exposure) and only some nonsmokers (e.g., asthmatics, etc.) are affected by it in all cases of exposure. The three-to-one numerical advantage that nonsmokers enjoy over smokers is thus reduced, perhaps dramatically, when we are talking of serious health hazards to those who fall in one or the other of these special cases.

Here, however, we need to start factoring the "'intensity" variable back into our utilitarian equation. Even if it turns out that there are fewer nonsmokers suffering serious health risks than there are smokers inflicting them, the damage that nonsmokers risk is so much greater than the pleasures that smokers enjoy that the utilitarian calculus still decides matters in nonsmokers' favor. Conversely, the small pleasures that smokers enjoy from smoking is quite nearly matched, person-for-person, by the annoyance to eyes, nose, and throat that nonsmokers experience when subjected to their smoke in confined quarters; and the fact that nonsmokers outnumber smokers by three-to-one means that, even if their annoyance is marginally less than smokers would suffer from having to step outside to smoke, the nonsmokers' case will prevail in a utilitarian calculus.

Thus, at least at the level of national aggregates, numbers do indeed seem to conspire with considerations of intensity in arguing for policies to restrict smoking in confined public places. The only question that then remains is whether we should be looking at these overall sums (the total number of smokers and nonsmokers in the society as a whole) and framing a uniform, nationwide policy on the basis of them. Overall utility for the whole society might be better promoted by a more flexible, localized policy, wherein smoking rules for each subpopulation are set according to the distribution of smokers and nonsmokers within them. A uniform, nationwide ban on smoking in public places would, for example, have the effect of banning needlessly (in terms of the risks of passive smoking, anyway) smoking in an office shared only by smokers. Social utility—understood as satisfaction of social preferences, anyway—would be better promoted by allowing smoking in such circumstances.

The utilitarian case against localized arrangements of this sort—like utilitarian arguments in general—is wholly pragmatic. I shall say more about these considerations when discussing market-based strategies for controlling passive smoking in Section 3.5.4 below. But the basic problem lies in the enormous costs of negotiating and renegotiating new smoking rules, every time a new user enters the public place. Imagine the costs of negotiating with all other diners in even a small restaurant whether smoking would be allowed or not; imagine, next, the costs of moving to some other restaurant down the street when, in the middle of your entrée, a large group of smokers comes in and upsets the previous utility balance. Were transactions costless and mobility likewise, it might be plausible that more situation-specific smoking policies might be utility maximizing. Since both are far from costless, a more uniform policy is almost certainly to be preferred, even on purely utilitarian grounds.

3.5   POLICY OPTIONS

The arguments and counterarguments considered in previous sections of this chapter lead us to adopt, as our policy goal, the minimization of involuntary passive smoking. That, in turn, entails the goal of minimizing environmental tobacco smoke in confined public areas. This goal is of particular importance with respect to those areas into which people have no reasonable choice but to go for protracted periods; but it is not without relevance for all public places in general, as several of the above arguments have shown. Here again, there are several possible policies for pursuing that goal.

3.5.1   *Reduce Smoking*

First and foremost, notice that anything done to reduce smoking will also, simultaneously, reduce the indirect consequences of smoking, among them passive smoking. If no one is smoking then no one is passively smoking, either. Hence, all the options outlined in Section 2.4 for curtailing smoking are also relevant to the goal of reducing passive smoking.

3.5.2   *Self-restraint/Courtesy*

The individual-level analogue to industry self-regulation would amount to self- restraint among smokers to curb the passive smoking that they inflict upon those around them. Ideally, "common sense and natural courtesy" should solve the problem (Littlechild and Wiseman 1984, pp. 60, 66; see, similarly, Littlechild 1986, p. 283; and Machan 1986, p. 51). That has "long been the best approach to solving the occasional difference of opinion between smoking and non-smoking employees," according to the tobacco industry's pamphlet on workplace smoking policies (TAC 1987). Or, again, a recent R. J. Reynolds advertising campaign offered "common courtesy" as the solution to the problem of smoking in public: "Smokers and non-smokers have to talk to one another. Not yell, preach, threaten, badger, or bully. Talk. . . . We continue to believe in the power of politeness to change the world" (quoted in White 1988, p. 172).

Ideally, smokers should of course ask others for permission before lighting up in confined quarters. Ideally, a polite request for them to cease should suffice. As Miss Manners instructs, "If you wish to smoke in the presence of clean people, you must ask their permission and be prepared to accept their refusal to grant it" (Martin 1983, p. 637).

For those smokers who are considerate in such ways, self-restraint is indeed ideal. Not all are, however. Given the nature of addictions, internal sanctions of shame at discourtesy will often be overcome by internal compulsions of nicotine cravings; and, as an example of the theory of cognitive dissonance in action, surveys show that smokers when asked grossly underestimate the extent to which they think nonsmokers find their smoking behavior discourteous (Bleda and Sandman 1977).

It is to curb the smoking of those who are unwilling or unable to abide by the canons of common courtesy that we need formal policies about where and when people can smoke. Consider, here, the analogy with "children's rights." Ideally, children (or social workers, on their behalf) should never have to claim such rights. But in the nonideal world in which such rights need to be pressed, it is an indisputably good thing that they are there.

In any case, the strategy of "polite requests" is more plausible in intimate company than in larger groups. No one presumes that one-to-one requests would be the appropriate way to regulate behavior in large, open-plan offices, on airplanes, or in restaurants.

Another form of self-restraint would be for smokers to shift over to using "smokeless" forms of tobacco: snuff, chewing tobacco, tobacco pouches, etc. The new "smokeless cigarette" recently being test marketed by R. J. Reynolds under the advertising slogan "the cleaner smoke" may or may not be another example (Helyar 1988).[14] There is no reason to suppose that any of these products pose fewer health hazards to users themselves, of course. But they do at least promise to avoid inflicting similar hazards on others around them.

Disposal of chewing tobacco or tobacco pouches might pose public health problems of other sorts, of course. There is also some doubt that tobacco pouches are a lifelong substitute for smoking: once youngsters have become addicted to nicotine through using them, they will shift over to smoking as a way of servicing that habit whenever their personal circumstances change (through marriage, employment, etc.) in such a way as to make the use of tobacco pouches

---

14. There is some thought that this cigarette might just emit smaller particles of smoke which, while harder to see, contain much the same carcinogens (Helyar 1987). In a prepared statement announcing the launch of the new product, the president of R. J. Reynolds Development Co. pointedly said: "Because almost no smoke comes off the lit end after the first few puffs, and because the exhaled smoke dissipates quickly, people have mistakenly called Premier a 'smokeless' cigarette" (Steyer 1988, p. 14). In the end, the product failed to find a market and has now been withdrawn; a better-tasting version might be reintroduced (Morris and Waldman 1989).

inconvenient or socially unacceptable. If that speculation is correct, then these alternatives to smoking do not avoid the problem of passive smoking but merely postpone it for a few years.

3.5.3   *Technological Fixes (Improved Ventilation, Air Filters, Etc.)*

Passive smoking, notice, is a problem that arises principally in relatively close, confined spaces. If windows can be opened without problems (of undue heat gain/loss, etc.), then that is one easy solution. But there are some places—airplanes, increasingly trains, and modern office blocks—where the windows do not open. In such places, we must rely instead upon technological fixes: air filters and such like.

In practice, those models presently available for commercial use are both costly and inadequate. They are incapable of removing small particles and gases contained in cigarette smoke; typically, they serve merely to recirculate smoky air (Repace and Lowery 1980; U.S. DHHS 1986, p. 11; Jenkins et al. 1987, app. C). Even air systems on aircraft—presumably the most controlled, self-contained environments most of us regularly experience—fail to eliminate cigarette smoke from the air adequately, and according to the U.S. National Academy of Science (1986a, p. 151) increasing ventilation so that it is adequate to do so "is not technically feasible on existing aircraft." The next generation of aircraft—because they rely more heavily on recirculated air—is expected to be worse, if anything, in this respect (Mattson et al. 1989).

Of course, we should not rule out the possibility of some technological breakthrough. We might yet find some way to clean the air of tobacco smoke very cheaply and very effectively. Obviously, however, we should not frame our policies in a way that relies upon a discovery not yet made, either. At most, we should make our plans in a way that is open to the possibility of a breakthrough. That might amount to no more than saying that we will provisionally ban smoking in public places, but that we are prepared to reconsider that ban upon production of solid evidence that some new technology will allow smoking in confined spaces without subjecting nonsmokers to unacceptable levels of environmental tobacco smoke.

3.5.4   *Market Forces*

To some extent, perfectly ordinary market forces might take care of the passive smoking problem. If people want nonsmoking provision, then they should be willing to pay for it: they should patronize establishments offering it, in preference to ones that do not; and so on. Airlines will win more flyers, restaurants more diners, and businesses more employees and customers if they cater to such demand. Insofar as this happens naturally, no government intervention would be required (Littlechild and Wiseman 1984, pp. 60,66; Littlechild 1986, pp. 280–81; Buchanan 1986; Machan 1986, p. 51; Shughart and Tollison 1986; Tollison and Wagner 1988, p. 71).

Certainly much of this is already under way. Many restaurants provide nonsmoking areas for their patrons, even where state law does not require them to do so, out of purely commercial motives. Northwest Orient airlines went beyond the mandatory ban on smoking on flights of less than two hours' duration to ban smoking on all its flights, whatever their duration. Spokesmen for the tobacco industry sneered at this as a desperate measure on the part of a failing company, but that they can win customers in this way is precisely the point that advocates of the market strategy are making.

There are also familiar limits to the extent to which market strategies may be relied upon, however. They presuppose, first, that people are perfectly informed, in all sorts of way. They must be perfectly informed about the risks of passive smoking; given that a nontrivial minority is still not very well informed about the effects of direct smoking, fully two decades after the surgeon general's first report (see Sec. 2.2.2 above), we have reason to doubt that people are universally well informed about the risks of this newer hazard. Even if people are perfectly informed of the risks of environmental tobacco smoke, they may not know where to look for a nonsmoking establishment if they decide that they want one. Search and information costs of this more mundane sort, too, might lead to higher levels of passive smoking than optimal if its regulation were left to market forces alone.

Market strategies presuppose, second, perfect competition. They presuppose that, if there is unsatisfied consumer demand, some adventuresome entrepreneur will seek out and exploit that marketing opportunity. In practice, we tend to find something much more akin to "price leadership" even within highly fragmented markets (e.g., restaurants), when it comes to smoking policies. Proprietors not only know little about their customers' preferences as regards provision of nonsmoking areas; they are also characteristically reluctant to be seen to be doing something very different from their competitors in that regard, for fear of losing customers. That is not the way a genuine market is supposed to work, of course. But that is how the market as we know it tends to work, in these matters at least.

Market strategies presuppose, third, that transactions are costless. They suppose that whenever something is more valuable to you than to me—and hence that there is a "gain from trade" to be had—that that trade will in fact take place. But the follies of this assumption have been discussed above, in Section 3.4. As any housebuyer knows, the costs of concluding the transaction may eat deeply into the profits—so deeply, sometimes, as to make an otherwise mutually advantageous trade simply not profitable at all.

Economists are fond of the famous Coase (1960) theorem, and Tollison and Wagner (1988) appeal explicitly to it in justification of a market-based approach to passive smoking. That theorem purports to show that it does not matter how you assign property rights in the first instance—whether, for example, you give nonsmokers the right to a smoke-free environment or whether you give smokers the right to smoke. Either way, Coase claims, the ultimate outcome would (under certain ideal conditions) be the same, provided we are prepared to allow a little bit of bargaining.[15] Suppose it is worth $20 to a nonsmoker to have a certain area free of smoke, and $15 to a smoker to smoke there, and that those are the only two people using the area. Then no matter who is given the original say in the matter, the ultimate outcome will be no smoking. If the smoker was given the right to smoke, the nonsmoker would be prepared to pay his asking price of $15 (he would actually have been prepared to pay up to $20) to bribe him to waive that right. If the nonsmoker was given a right to clean air, he would not sell it for the $15 that the smoker is prepared to offer (his firm price being $20). Thus, the same socially optimal outcome will emerge, however we assigned the initial rights, just so long as we allow bargaining and a market in those rights to emerge. Or so Coase, and various economists following him, would argue.

There are two things wrong with that argument, though. One, alluded to before, is that it assumes—explicitly—that transactions are costless. If the bargaining eats into the gains from trade, then Coase would be the first to concede that the outcome may well depend more upon how the initial rights were set than upon who values the rights the most. In such cases, Coase suggests that social policymakers simply try to anticipate the outcome of an ideal market in rights, assigning the rights to those to whom they mean the most. As argued in Section 3.4 above, that would mean assigning rights to nonsmokers to a smoke-free environment.

A second flaw in Coase's and all other arguments for a free market in rights is that market outcomes depend upon the initial distribution of resources, in the widest sense. Those who are richer can afford to pay more for something, even if in utility terms it means less to them, than can the poor. (Imagine, if you will, a rich, cigar-

---

15. We are not always prepared to allow people to bargain away their rights, though. Property rights serve poorly, in that respect, as a general model; they typically can be bought and sold. There are other rights we consider to be nonfungible and inalienable, however (see Sec. 3.3 above). The right to a healthy environment, like the right to life and liberty, might be among them.

chomping boss bribing his secretary to permit him to smoke in her presence: the $5,000 per annum he pays her for the privilege constitutes merely a hundredth of his annual income but a quarter of hers.) Unless we have some antecedent guarantee of the justice of the initial distribution, of resources, therefore, our allowing people to bargain away their rights might result in the perpetuation of unjust advantage on the one side and of unjust disadvantage on the other.[16]

I do not want to denegrate the considerable accomplishments that have already been made through purely market forces toward an end to involuntary passive smoking. To a very large extent, nonsmokers want not to be exposed to environmental tobacco smoke, and are prepared to spend a good deal of time and money to avoid doing so. My point is merely that we cannot expect market forces to provide a complete solution to this problem, for much the same reasons we cannot expect it to provide a complete solution to so many others.

Notice, finally, that there is something ironic in people who see the political world as a market, much like any other, refusing to respect the outcomes of the market in political pressure. It is an article of faith in the "public choice" school that economic and political markets differ, fundamentally, only in the currencies that they use—money in the former, votes in the latter. Assuming votes can be traded just like anything else, those currencies in turn differ fundamentally only in their distribution—money's being unequal, votes' being (much more nearly) equal. Thus, though the standard objection to political intervention in markets is that it is motivated by dishonorable "distributional" rather than honorable "efficiency" considerations (Shughart and Tollison 1986; Buchanan 1986), the same may be true of that objection, as well.

Minimally, advocates of markets over politics must explain what makes money—and efficiency defined in terms of it—so decisively superior to the currency of votes and efficiency defined in terms of voter satisfaction. In their reply to this challenge, advocates of the economic market over the political one dare not appeal to the universal fungibility of money (i.e., the fact you can buy anything in

16. A perfectly analogous distributional problem would arise, of course, if it were a poor smoker trying to bribe a rich nonsmoker—which, given the fact that smoking is concentrated among the poor (Townsend 1987), might be more common. Notice that the problem arises principally when parties of unequal wealth are involved, and one therefore enjoys a distributional advantage over the other in bargaining. Where—as often happens—smokers and nonsmokers in their proximity are of roughly equal socioeconomic status, the problem is less pressing. Still, the combination of a richer smoker and poorer nonsmoker in the same air space occurs often enough (especially in large, open-plan offices accommodating workers of very unequal status) to be of a real concern.

exchange for it); that would invite the rejoinder that we should completely politicize everything in society, so everything and anything could be bought through votes. Similarly, they dare not appeal to the economic market's requiring unanimous consent for changes to the status quo, since the status quo does not itself enjoy unanimous consent in the first place (Rae 1975).

3.5.5   *Litigation*

Under tort law, everyone has a duty not to harm anyone else. Insofar as one person's smoking causes another harm, the latter has a legal claim against the former at law. In addition to that general duty not to harm others, there are certain classes of people who have traditionally been held to owe a special "duty of care" to certain others (Bohlen 1908; Kirchheimer 1942). Among these are:

1.   public transport operators;
2.   inn keepers;
3.   employers, at least where it is impossible for workers to protect themselves from the hazard;
4.   jailers; and
5.   heads of households.

In all of these circumstances, nonsmokers might legally merit special protection. And, to a greater or lesser extent, they are increasingly seeking—and increasingly winning—it, under each of these headings.[17]

Many of the most interesting cases along these lines arise out of workplace exposure to environmental tobacco smoke, and tend to be handled by the workmen's compensation system that has supplanted the tort system in that setting. In 1985 a Swedish insurance court of appeal upheld the decision of a regional court that "a case of lung cancer in a non-smoker should be classified as an occupational injury due to passive smoking in the workplace" and compensated accordingly (Jenkins et al. 1987, p. 5; Mosey 1985). A series of Australian cases have similarly awarded workmen's compensation on the order of A\$20,000 to A\$40,000 to nonsmokers suffering illnesses traceable to

---

17.   To a surprising extent, they are already receiving it. Developments under headings 1–3 are relatively familiar. But suits have also recently been brought to require provision of smoking and nonsmoking cells in jail (Ellis v. Director, Texas Department of Corrections, USDC TX) and by a wife with respiratory disease to enjoin her husband not to smoke in her presence (Reade v. Reade, Ontario Dist. Ct.); both are reported in the *Tobacco Products Litigation Reporter*, vol. 2, no. 7 (July/August 1987). In a similar case in New York, state supreme court Justice Ralph Diamond ordered Elizabeth Roofeh not to smoke in front of her estranged husband, who is particularly sensitive to tobacco smoke, or their children; she was further ordered to confine her smoking to one room of their house (*New York Times* [February 24, 1988], p. B3).

environmental tobacco smoke in the workplace (Jenkins et al. 1987, p. 6); and a nonsmoking Melbourne bus driver with lung cancer recently reached an out-of-court settlement, after a three-day administrative appeals tribunal hearing, consisting of A$30,000 in workmen's compensation and A$35,000 as a common law settlement for negligent exposure to tobacco on his company's buses and in their lunch room (Anonymous 1988).

The trouble with litigation as a strategy for controlling passive smoking is the same as the trouble with it as a strategy for controlling direct smoking, only magnified. Since the linkage is less strong, causation will usually be even harder to prove to the satisfaction of law courts. Since the awards are less large, there is less incentive for nonsmokers to pursue such claims and less disincentive for owners and managers of public premises to restrict smoking for fear of them. Again, such litigation is wholly laudable, in its own right. We simply must not count on it as a complete solution to the problem of passive smoking.

3.5.6   *Legislative Bans on Smoking in Public Places*

The most efficient, certain way to prevent people from being subjected involuntarily to environmental tobacco smoke is simply to legislate bans or restrictions on smoking in confined public places. On the basis of the evidence and arguments offered in this chapter, it seems especially important to curtail smoking in certain sorts of places. These include:

1. Confined quarters generally. Enclosed spaces, if poorly ventilated, magnify the effects of environmental tobacco smoke, both on the health and on the comfort of nonsmokers in the vicinity.
2. Places where a special "duty of care" is owed to others who might be harmed, especially where the service is provided directly by the government (e.g., city buses, public jails) or where it operates under license from the government (e.g., hotels and restaurants, airlines).
3. Places where people cannot reasonably be expected to avoid going.

If self-contained, separately ventilated areas are available, then designating them as "smoking rooms" and restricting smoking to those places might suffice to accomplish these goals.[18] But absent some

18. If there are extra costs entailed in providing such quarters for smokers (because, e.g., separate ventilation has to be installed specially), then there might be a further question as to whether smokers ought be subsidized in these ways. Such arguments were deployed with particular force by Peter Wilenski in support of a total

separately ventilated room, "the simple separation of smokers and non-smokers within the same air space"—assigning smokers to one end of a large, open-plan office and nonsmokers to the other end, for example—"does not eliminate the exposure of non-smokers to environmental tobacco smoke" (U.S. DHHS 1986, p. 13). So if no self-contained quarters are available for designation as smoking rooms, a total ban on smoking in the whole area might be required. Such bans or restrictions on smoking in public places are now in force in four-fifths of the American states and in forty-seven countries of the world (Roemer 1986, p. 17; U.S. DHHS 1986, p. 267; U.S. DHHS 1989, pp. 552–73).

3.5.7   *A Composite Policy Package for Passive Smoking Control*

Reflecting upon the harm that smokers do to others through passive smoking imposed upon them, in light of various moral doctrines, led us to set as our policy goal minimization of environmental tobacco smoke in confined areas, especially those into which people have no reasonable choice but to go for prolonged periods. Legislation banning smoking in those areas, or confining it to independently ventilated portions of those areas, is far and away the most appropriate means of pursuing that goal. Just how necessary legislation is depends upon just how successful other control strategies—that are proceeding independently, in any case—prove to be. If enough people give up smoking altogether, or are courteous enough not to smoke in front of nonsmokers, or if technology is developed to allow smoking without a build-up of environmental tobacco smoke, or if market forces work to ensure broad provision of smoke-free areas, then legislation will to those extents prove less necessary. But those developments would not be hindered, and might be hastened, by legislation of the sort here in view; and, judging from the discussion in Sections 3.2, 3.3, and 3.4 above, legislation would not infringe any morally important values in this case. I conclude that a legislative ban on smoking in confined public spaces can only help and never hinder pursuit of the goal that our moral theories set for us in relation to the control of passive smoking.

---

ban on smoking in all Australian public service offices. It is hard to see how the provision of smoking rooms is different in kind from any other job "benefit" (e.g., a gymnasium) that is in principle available to all employees but in practice used by only some of them.

4　　Issues Arising

In the previous two chapters, I have been addressing standard moral principles, as they apply to smoking policies, in relatively standard ways. I hope nonetheless to have said something morally interesting, novel, and policy-relevant in those chapters. Still, in preparing such ethical background papers for policymakers, there is inevitably the sense of something akin to "writing to a formula." The accepted format—so standard by now as to be de rigueur—is to start by asking what are the facts of the matter, how we know them, and how sure we can be in our assessment of them. Then proceed to ask what each of the main moral positions (utilitarian and Kantian, most typically) would make of those facts. Finish by cataloging policy options and assessing how well each of them stands up to the demands of the moral philosophies discussed.

There is nothing particularly wrong with that formula. It points us to questions that may well be the first ones that any policymaker should ask of an ethical advisor. But sticking to those routine questions to the exclusion of all else would blind us to some interesting and morally important side issues that arise in the course of discussing any particular policy puzzle.

It is not idle curiosity alone that should lead us to go off the main moral track and explore some of these side issues. Sometimes, owing to peculiarities of the particular case at hand, some nonstandard "side issue" might turn out to be so morally central that it ought to dominate our policy decision. Indeed, sometimes exploration of "side issues" suggested by some particular case might even lead us to add a whole new set of questions to our standard protocol.

In what follows, I address a range of just such "side issues" that arise from discussions of smoking policies. They are arranged in no particular order (and certainly not in order of their moral importance, either ascending or descending). Each arises with particular poignancy from discussions of smoking policy. But each also has broader relevance to a whole (and often large) class of analogous policy problems. While none of them seems to suggest an entirely new moral theory, several of them do seem to suggest a serious reorientation of the way we think about various aspects of public policy in light of the requirements of morality.

4.1   FAIRNESS TO PEOPLE AND FAIRNESS TO PRODUCTS

Tobacco companies still refuse to accept that their product kills 25 percent of its users, arguing that all that has been shown is a "merely statistical" connection. This echoes, in some ways, lawyers' worries about "trial by mathematics" (Tribe 1971; see also Thomson 1986, chaps. 12–13; Schoeman 1987). The sort of scenario they fear goes something like this. Suppose a black man and white woman held up a store, driving away in a 1954 Buick with Idaho plates; suppose that, though no one can identify the criminals (they wore masks), a couple exactly fitting this description has been apprehended for speeding nearby; and suppose that, statistically, the chance of this particular combination of characteristics in that town were one in one million. Is that statistical evidence enough to convict? If "beyond a reasonable doubt" means 95 percent certainty of guilt, it seems so.[1] Yet we have a lingering sense of unfairness here—of "trial by mathematics" rather than of trial by evidence directly pertaining to those particular individuals.

Of course, in a sense, all evidence is essentially probabilistic. Suppose an eyewitness identifies the couple in court as being, without doubt, the pair that perpetrated the crime. The jury is still left with the question of how much credence to give to that identification, which comes down to a question about their view of the probability that the eyewitness has made an accurate identification. But that probabilistic judgment feels importantly different from the other one. Judging the probable validity of evidence definitely connecting the couple to the crime is somehow different from judging on the basis of evidence probably connecting them to the crime—even if the probability number in both cases is the same. The sense of unfairness in the latter case still lingers.

---

1.   That is the interpretation suggested by the .05 confidence interval standardly demanded in statistical decision theory, at least. Blackstone's (1783, bk. 4, chap. 27) maxim that it is better that ten guilty persons escape than that one innocent person should be punished suggests that 90 percent certainly might be good enough; Sir Matthew Hale's (1694, chap. 39) five-to-one ratio suggests that 80 percent certainty might be. Tribe's (1971) complaint is not, of course, with any of these being the wrong number; rather, it is that this is the wrong way to think about these issues altogether. Probability of guilt miscasts the question, he would say.

Can cigarette manufacturers claim regulatory relief on the basis of this same notion of unfairness? I think not, on several grounds. First and most obviously, a different standard of proof is (and should be) required for regulatory and criminal proceedings. Before we incarcerate a person, we want evidence that he is guilty beyond a reasonable doubt. That is in part because of the "expressive" function served by criminal trials (Tribe 1971). Regulatory policy, in contrast, is purely instrumental. There, we are perfectly prepared to keep products off the market if it is merely "more likely than not" (or maybe even if there is just "some reason to believe") that they cause serious harms.

In part, that is merely to say that we would require a different level of probability in the two cases: a 50 percent (or perhaps just a nonzero) likelihood is enough to regulate a product, whereas a 95 percent certainty is required to convict people of crimes. But it is not merely a matter of different probability levels. Along with that less demanding standard of proof, we are also intuitively much more inclined to accept less rigorous forms of proof in support of regulatory policies, among them probability numbers and statistical evidence.

The standard of evidence required is different in kind, not just in quantity. In criminal proceedings, we may need particularized evidence; in regulatory proceedings, we do not. One reason has to do with the very different implications of convicting people and of convicting products. Capital punishment, for example, clearly means something very different in the two cases.

Second, notice that regulation designed to prevent harm ex ante is importantly different from ex post actions (be they punitive or compensatory) for remedying harms once they have happened. When making people pay for what they have done, we may need particularized evidence that they really were the ones who did it (cf. sec. 2.4.2 above). When trying to prevent harms through regulatory policy, we do not. Even in the case of crime prevention, it seem permissible to patrol some (e.g., inner city) areas more intensively than others, on the basis of clearly convincing albeit "merely" statistical evidence about the relative frequency of crimes in those areas. For purposes of cancer prevention, it seems permissible to regulate certain classes of chemicals more closely than others on the basis of merely statistical evidence, likewise.

Third and perhaps most tellingly, statistical evidence is more directly relevant where products than where petty thieves are concerned. With the case of the thieving couple, we are forced to talk in terms of probabilities because we are uncertain which of the few dozen couples in the country meeting that description actually perpetrated the robbery. Our fear of unfairness, in using statistical evidence to indict one of those couples, is that we may thereby be blaming one couple for the crime of another in that larger group. With the case of cigarettes, in contrast, we are forced to talk in terms of probabilities merely because we do not know which 25 percent of their users they will kill. In short, with the thieving couple we are uncertain of the culprits, whereas with tobacco we are uncertain only of the victims.[2] For purposes of justifying regulatory policies, that makes all the difference.

We know that tobacco kills 25 percent of its users. All we do not know is, ex ante, which 25 percent it will be who die. But why should that matter? A gunman who fired a shotgun into a crowd, killing only 25 percent of its members, would not be exonerated. Why should we seriously consider a similar claim on behalf of tobacco?

Note, further, that evidence can be both "direct" and "particularized" without involving a detailed tracing of causal connections (cf. Thomson 1986, pp. 222–23, 230 ff.). Suppose that we were dealing with a murderer who gassed his victims rather than shooting them. Suppose the defendant's attorney, quizzing the coroner, asked, "But how, *exactly*, does this gas kill the 25 percent of those whom you say will invariably die if exposed to it?" Suppose that with this gas, as with so much else, our knowledge is somewhat incomplete. (At some level, we do not know *exactly* how many of even the most familiar poisons work.) So under such scrutiny, a coroner simply has to throw up his or her hands and say, "Look, I have long experience in these matters, and we have a vast literature on the effects of this poison; believe me, in those doses it is somehow or another fatal in a quarter of cases." Surely that is an adequate answer in ordinary poisoning cases. Surely the same sort of answer should be adequate in the case of tobacco.

4.2   CONCEPTS OF CAUSATION FOR POLICYMAKING

Both philosophers and lawyers have come to see increasingly vast difficulties with the concept of causation in general (Sosa 1975; Hart and Honoré 1985). In a world of multiple, interacting causal factors, it proves frustratingly difficult to disentangle the contributions of each and assign in any meaningful sense each its "true" share of causal responsibility. That complicates the lives of medical statisticians trying to apportion responsibility for a particular disease among various

---

2. Of course, it is also true that there are many carcinogens besides tobacco smoke, many of which any given individual might also have experienced. But by controlling those other factors statistically, we can say with confidence how much of a contribution tobacco makes to the causation of any given disease in general (though not, of course, in that particular individual's case).

interacting causal factors (Doll and Peto 1981, p. 1219). It similarly complicates the lives of lawyers, trying to apportion liability for a particular outcome among various contributory factors.

Philosophers and lawyers have now come to appreciate how, to a surprisingly large extent, what we should regard as "the" cause of something depends upon the reasons we have for asking questions about causation in the first place. In tort litigation, we are in the business of assigning liability for harm that has already been done. There, we might want to pick out, among those multiple factors whose causal contributions cannot be easily disentangled, as "the" cause the actions of whomever can bear the cost most easily or of whomever had the last or cheapest opportunity to avert the harm (Calabresi 1970; Hart and Honoré 1985; Anonymous 1986, pp. 818–26). But the crucial thing about those judgments is that they are necessarily retrospective, coming after the harm has already been done.

In making public policy generally—and regulatory policy, more particularly—our focus is prospective, instead. Our aim there is to choose policies that will shape the future in desired ways, rather than just allocating blame for what is past. Given that aim, we ought adopt Collingwood's doctrine of looking for "causal conditions which have a handle on them which we can grasp and manipulate," regarding "causal generalizations . . . as 'recipes' for cooking up desired effects" (quoted in Feinberg 1970, p. 144; cf. Hart and Honoré 1985, pp. 36–37). That is to say, we should isolate, for policy purposes at least, those causes that are best within the policymaker's capacity to control.

From that point of view, it is gratifying rather than frustrating that there are often many interacting causal factors at work. Suppose "two different factors are each responsible for 75 percent of all cancers that occur at a particular site, in the sense that appropriate modification of either would result in a reduction in the incidence of the disease to a quarter of its previous level." Then "we have a choice between two lines of action for preventing most cases, one of which may be simpler, quicker acting, or more acceptable than the other." And "in this situation, the additional effort required to modify both factors may have little absolute additional effect" (Doll and Peto 1981, pp. 1219–20).

For an application of this principle that we should be looking for causal factors with handles on them, consider education policy. Genes and early childhood experiences might, in some sense, make more of a contribution than school facilities or curricula to a child's ultimate educational attainment. But the latter factors are within the control of educational policymakers in a way that the former (in our society, at least) are not. The latter, therefore, ought be regarded for policy purposes as the causes of educational accomplishment among children (Cain and Watts 1970, p. 230; Hanushek and Kain 1972).

Similarly with smoking, many factors may contribute to lung cancer and other smoking-related diseases. Many of them are environmental contaminants like asbestos, which are also controllable by policymakers. In many of these cases, though, controlling smoking instead will even there prove the most cost-efficient strategy for preventing the onset of the disease. Consider the interaction between smoking and gaseous radon, emitted in the course of the decay of particles of uranium, that can concentrate in buildings. It is estimated that some 13,000 Americans die annually as a result of this radon exposure; and, given the well-established synergism between radon exposure and smoking in producing lung cancer, some 11,000 of these deaths are thought to be smoking-related (Kerr 1988). But to detect the radon, and to prevent it seeping into buildings, is an expensive business. Thus, one member of the National Academy of Sciences committee reporting these findings concludes that, "perhaps ironically, the most direct method of reducing the lung cancer burden in the general population due to radon exposure in the home would be to stop smoking" (Jay Lubin, quoted in Kerr 1988, p. 607).

Furthermore, many of the other factors contributing to lung cancer and other smoking-related diseases—genetic or fundamental personality factors, for example—are not even remotely controllable by policymakers, in a way that smoking clearly is. Were the connection between smoking and cancer *wholly* an artifact of a connection both have to genotype, then of course there would be nothing that policymakers could do to reduce cancer short of genetic engineering. That is not what the evidence seems to suggest, though: even archadvocates of the "genetic constitution" model concede that there is also an independent causal path running from smoking to cancer (Burch 1978); and that path can be cut by antismoking policies.

Many studies purporting to show that both smoking and cancer are linked to genetic constitution, either directly or indirectly (through personality), fail to map conclusively the path of causation. Which way the arrows run matters. The correlation would be wholly spurious—and wholly outside the control of social policymakers— only if the arrows ran one from genes/personality to smoking and the other from genes/personality to cancer. But the evidence is usually equally consistent with the hypothesis that, at least to a large extent, there is one arrow running from genes/personality to smoking and quite another arrow running from smoking to cancer.

Insofar as that is true, the cancer can be prevented by breaking that last link—through antismoking policies, for example. Notably, Eysenck's (1986, p. 52) twin studies conclude that genes are important in the maintenance but not in the origin of smoking habits. The implications of that finding are enormous. If smoking policies can curb the sociological influences (peer pressure, etc.) that initiate smokers into the habit, the causal chain can be broken, even if elsewhere there is an unbreakable genetic element in the chain.

Thus, when the surgeon general calls smoking the largest preventable and chief avoidable cause of cancer death in our society, his words are particularly apt (U.S. DHHS 1982, preface; 1986, pp. 5–6). It is precisely that avoidability and preventability that makes it—for policy purposes, at least—causally preeminent.

4.3   BAD HABITS AND ADDICTIONS

Many who oppose government regulation of smoking designed to protect smokers from themselves implicitly or explicitly treat it as nothing more than a bad habit (Littlechild and Wiseman 1984, p. 65). "Assumption of individual responsibility for one's own health" is, in these terms, far preferable to treating "sloth, gluttony, alcoholic overuse, reckless driving, sexual intemperance, and smoking" as "a national, not an individual responsibility" (Knowles 1977, p. 59; see, similarly, Wildavsky 1977, pp. 105, 122–23; and Wikler 1987).

In many ways, these writers have a point. Presumably it is perfectly true that we expect people to alter their own bad habits—or anyway not to complain when harms befall them in consequence of the practice of their own bad habits. After all, they could have altered their ways. Addictions are otherwise. They may, in the very first instance, have been self-induced. Once induced, however, they are not (easily) remediable thereafter, through any simple act of will. Indeed, that is one of the primary criteria used diagnostically to distinguish "drug dependence" from merely "habitual behaviors" (U.S. DHHS 1988, pp. 7–8).

Thus, the habit versus addiction issue can be cast as an issue about responsibility, but it comes out rather differently than "responsibility for self" theorists suppose. People may bear responsibility for their own bad habits and for whatever follows from them. They bear responsibility for having become addicted to drugs. Once addicted, though, they ought no longer be considered responsible for their addiction-driven actions.[3] For that reason, the addiction evidence is

3.   The law, presumably in a desperate effort to deter, tends to take a harder line on this matter. The Model Penal Code, e.g., suggests that (with very few exceptions indeed) people should be held fully responsible for actions committed while intoxicated (American Law Institute [ALI] 1974, sec. 2.08). But that rule sits uneasily with the basic logic of the criminal code. Insofar as those acting under the influence of a drug are in some deep sense no longer "in control" of themselves, their actions do not manifest the

crucial in making the case for governmental action on smoking in several respects.[4]

Some theorists—especially economists—might nonetheless resist these conclusions, insisting that the distinction between addictions and mere bad habits is meaningless. Essentially, there are three bases for grounding this distinction. Economists often remain unimpressed by all of them.[5]

The first basis for the addiction-habit distinction has to do with the way in which, with addictive substances, the more you have consumed of them in the past the more you want to consume of them in the future. But that is merely to say that present preferences over those goods are a positive function of past consumption; and, put that way, there is nothing particularly unique about addictive as against all sorts of other goods (Stigler and Becker 1977).[6] One particularly blunt way of putting the point is to say that "there is, of course, a large degree of habituation in all consumption, in the sense that people seek to repeat activities they enjoy. How," ecomomists ask, "is being 'habituated' to cigarettes any different from being habituated to chewing gum, ice cream, television, jogging, or swimming?" (Tollison and Wagner 1988, p. 39; see similarly Schwartz 1989). There is nothing wrong with habituation per se. Some habits are bad; others are good, in the sense that you are better off objectively as well as subjectively for having cultivated them (Stigler and Becker 1977;

---

sort of mens rea or evil intent that we ordinarily regard as the defining feature of criminality. Such logic has led a variety of legal philosophers to conclude that those acting "under the influence," and no longer capable of distinguishing right from wrong for that reason, ought not be responsible for their actions as such; what they should be responsible for, instead, is putting themselves in such a position that they might lose control of themselves in a way that would involve the "reckless endangering" of others (Hall 1944; Fitzgerald 1961; Fletcher 1978, pp. 846–52; Brandt 1985, pp. 109–92).

4.   Ranging from publicly sponsored smoking-cessation programs to restricting or banning the sale of tobacco (see, generally, U.S. DHHS 1988, esp. chap. 7).

5.   See, generally, Kelman 1979. Cf. Sunstein (1986, pp. 1161–64), who agrees that the two are analogous but would on that account be prepared to regulate both, unlike economists who would be prepared to regulate neither.

6.   One criterion—which even Stigler and Becker (1977) would recognize—is the tendency for an addict's tolerance to grow, the more of the substance he has taken. With ordinary goods (like olives, say) that are "acquired tastes," the more of the good you have consumed in the past the more pleasure you get out of each subsequent unit of consumption. With addictive substances (like heroin, say), this is not true: it takes increasingly large doses to produce the same subjective effects as before, thanks to increasing tolerance. This is a characteristic which nicotine dependence shares with all other addictions, however (Winsten 1986; U.S. DHHS 1988). That this phenomenon "tops out" sooner (at around twenty—or, given 50 percent underreporting of smoking behavior, perhaps thirty— cigarettes a day for most addicts) rather than later (as with heroin) is surely irrelevant for purposes of classifying a substance as addictive.

Littlechild and Wiseman 1984, p. 65). On that score, economists are absolutely right.

The second basis for a distinction between addiction and habit rests on essentially physiological evidence. Receptors in the brain have now been identified for the pharmacologically active substances in tobacco smoke; and partly on the basis of that discovery the American Psychiatric Association and the World Health Organization have deemed nicotine addictive. Yet, as economists are quick to add, there are presumably "pleasure centers" in the brain that are stimulated by ordinary consumption goods, too. Where, exactly, those centers are and how, exactly, consumption stimulates them we do not yet know in any detail. But there is no reason to believe that the neurochemical processes involved there are radically different than those involved in the relationship between nicotine and its receptors in the brain.

The third and most important basis for the addiction-habit distinction has to do with the addict's wanting to stop but being unable to do so. This is the central element in the APA/WHO diagnostic criteria used to class nicotine as addictive.

Economists critical of the habit-addiction distinction have a quick retort, here too. They say, "There are, of course, many overeaters who claim they want to lose weight but do not," also (Tollison and Wagner 1988, p. 39). They go on to say, "It is clear that many smokers say they would like to stop. . . . And it is equally clear that for most of them, the intensity of that wish is weak, as judged by the observation that they continue to smoke. Should we therefore say that the demand for cigarettes is somehow fraudulent? Perhaps, alternatively, it is the professed desire to stop smoking that is misleading" (Tollison and Wagner 1988, p. 39).

The central point in this economistic attempt to collapse the addiction-habit distinction is the claim that all temptations are resistable and all addictions curable, at a cost.[7] To quote Tollison and Wagner (1988, p. 39) yet again: "We know that people can change their habits if they truly want to . . . . It surely makes less sense to say that those who do not lose weight are habituated to food . . . than to say that some people value losing weight more highly than others, and are thus willing to pay a higher price to overcome their eating "habit." And the same, they would say, is true of smoking: "There are many ex-smokers, so we know that people can stop smoking, just as they can stop overeating, if they are willing to pay the price—that is, if they

---

7. Economists are not alone in this claim. Feinberg (1970, p. 282), e.g., also remarks—to rather different purpose—that "no impulse is irresistible; for every case of giving in to a desire, I would argue, it would be true that, if the person had tried harder he would have resisted it successfully."

value more highly the benefits they think they will derive from reducing their eating or from stopping their smoking than they value the continuation of their present eating or smoking practices" (Tollison and Wagner 1988, p. 39).

Thus, to the economist, the pain of withdrawal is just the cost that an addict has to pay for the good of a "clean" life. In that respect, it is formally analogous to the cost that anyone pays (also in terms of pain, or discomfort anyway) in breaking a bad habit (cf. Kelman 1979, pp. 783–84). Neither, furthermore, is there any reason to suppose that the cost of breaking the one (breaking a weak addiction, e.g.) would necessarily always exceed that of breaking the other (breaking a long-standing, well-entrenched bad habit, e.g.). If people are not prepared to pay the price of stopping, then they surely must not mind smoking all that much after all. Or so the economist's logic would hold (Schwartz 1989).

What this comes down to is an issue of whether addicts really are subjectively worse off smoking, or not. Their words may suggest that they are, but their actions suggest that they are not; and the latter is what counts most heavily in contemporary microeconomists' crassly behavioral concept of preference (Sen 1973). There is no need to follow them in those conceptual rigidities, however. At least sometimes, what a person says is a better indicator of the true state of his mind than is what he does. Such would clearly be the case if he were physically restrained, in a way that rendered him simply unable to do what he said he wanted to do. We may well question the practical relevance of a preference for doing what he is unable to do. But we could hardly question, in those circumstances, that his true preference is to do as he says; and we would be quite wrong to infer from the fact that he does not do it that he does not really want to do it, after all. Similarly, if a person is physiologically restrained (by a drug dependence, defined inter alia in terms of the state of certain receptors in his brain), we might also say that he was simply unable to do what he truly wants to do, better revealed once again through his statements than through his actions.

If economists insist upon a more behavioral way of putting this point, we can employ a hypothetical-choice formulation: would the people involved have chosen otherwise, if they had it to do over again (Kelman 1979)? If not, then their initial choice can unambiguously be said to have promoted their welfare; if so, it can unambiguously be said to have ill-served it. Where people plainly "regret" previous choices, and would choose differently next time, that is clear enough. In cases of addiction, matters are only a little more complicated. Once addicted, people would choose the same addictive good next time as last; but if given a chance to choose over whether or not to begin consuming the addictive substance in the first place, they would choose not to do so. (That is how "addiction" is here defined and how it is operationalized in the studies demonstrating the addictiveness of nicotine.) Stopping people from becoming addicts by stopping them from beginning to consume tobacco in the first place would thus be justified in terms of their own self-assessed welfare, defined in terms of their own (hypothetical) choices.[8]

Of course, it is highly desirable that people should take charge of their own lives in both respects, breaking bad habits and addictions alike. Of necessity, that must be primarily a task for individuals themselves. But there are some things that governments can do to help—such as making practices people wish to abandon more expensive (through excise taxes) or restricting the number of hours or number of places in which they can engage in them. Such assistance can be justified on the grounds that, far from imposing paternalist policies on people, we are merely helping them enforce rules of their own choosing upon themselves (Schelling 1980, 1983, 1984b, 1985; Crain et al. 1977). That rationale works equally well, whether it is a mere bad habit or an actual addiction that is involved.

Whether or not that argument is convincing in showing that smokers themselves would be subjectively better off if prevented from smoking, it is decisive in establishing another even stronger rationale for public policies against smoking. That has not so much to do with protecting present addicts from themselves as it has to do with preventing future addicts from becoming addicted. Addictions are unambiguously bad, from the point of view of the person addicted.[9] Being defined in terms of a desire to quit coupled with an inability to quit, addictions necessarily would make the addict worse-off; and, on the evidence of section 2.2 above, a vast majority of those who do smoke will become addicted in this way. Once they are addicted, they face a high price to pay in overcoming the addiction, and we cannot be absolutely sure whether their health is worth that price to them.

8. The formulation is only pseudo-behavioral, of course, insofar as the choices in view are hypothetical rather than real, and the test is cast in terms of counterfactual rather than actual states. But economists are used to that: "opportunity cost" is defined in some such terms, as indeed is "causation" itself, come to that. In any case, much the same sorts of tests must presumably be used in the vast majority of welfare judgments that policymakers are required to impute to people, inferring from the choices they make in one set of circumstances what they would prefer in other circumstances which by their nature cannot be brought into existence without relying upon those very welfare judgments at issue.

9. Stigler and Becker (1977) talk, unhelpfully, in terms of "beneficial addiction" in cases of good habits. Here I use the term "addiction" to refer to "bad addictions" only; this is implicit in the WHO/APA criteria set out above.

But we can be sure that those who are not yet addicted—just like those who already are—would much rather not have to face that choice. If they were to become addicted, they would almost certainly come to wish they had not. On the basis of that hypothetical choice that we can reasonably impute to people not yet addicted, we can justify public policies to prevent them from getting addicted.

The policy implications of a distinction between addictions and mere bad habits, couched in some such terms, are clear. Since habits are not necessarily bad, public policies discouraging them are not necessarily desirable (although it may of course be socially desirable to curtail the practice of those habits in public). Addictions, in contrast, are necessarily bad. Policies discouraging them are therefore always desirable. We might wish to show compassion toward present addicts. But clearly we should do what we can to prevent new addicts.

4.4   "GRANDFATHERING" HEALTH HAZARDS

All sorts of laws regulating conduct do not apply to those engaged in such conduct at the time of enactment of the legislation. Exemptions for "preexisting" conditions, practices, or usages are often written into a law, which explicitly regulates only "new" ones arising subsequent to its enactment. Such "grandfather clauses" are most common in zoning ordinances, perhaps. But they also find some application in public health contexts. The Food, Drug, and Cosmetic Act Amendments of 1958 required all new drugs to be subjected to careful screening, for example, but presumed all existing products to be safe. It is often (and rightly) said that if aspirin were invented today, it would not get past FDA testing on any plausible risk/benefit calculation. Yet because it has long been sold, we allow it to continue being sold. Perhaps tobacco might claim some regulatory relief under similar principles. Cigarettes, too, are a long-established product on the market.

What precise arguments can be offered for "grandfathering" public health hazards in such ways? I can imagine three.[10]

1. Maybe substances with which we have long experience should be subject to different and less demanding safety standards either
    (a) because that experience establishes, in Bayesian fashion, an indication of innocence, or
    (b) because the risks from that substance form part of the background risk by now.

---

10. Building on brief remarks in Breyer (1982, p. 154).

Tobacco can claim no exemption under principle 1*a*, however. We do have long experience of tobacco use. We also have long experience of cancer, increasing (in lagged fashion, as is the way with diseases with long latency periods) with increases in smoking. Bayes's rule works, if anything, to damn smoking.

Principle 1*b* is patently absurd. Surely we should reduce natural background risks of death if we can—by removing naturally-occurring carcinogens from drinking water or building materials, for example. Surely we should be no more relaxed about socially created contributions to the "normal" risk of death. If they can be removed cheaply and easily from our lives, surely they should be.

2. Maybe substances with which we have long experience have, by virtue of that experience, greater benefits (albeit no fewer risks).

All arguments for respecting long-standing traditions turn on some such point, and sometimes those arguments for respecting traditions might entail permitting continued use of dangerous products. Consider the case of lead additives in gasoline. No doubt they do great harm, but it is argued that since most of the tractors presently in use on family farms would not run without them we cannot eliminate leaded gas (in the short term, at least) without endangering that whole way of life (Owen 1987, p. 56).

Similarly, perhaps, with tobacco. Certainly farmers growing it are dependent upon the crop; at least in the short term and for a few people, radical changes in their lives would be necessitated by any great change in tobacco consumption.[11] More important, because potentially more widespread, the "smoking ritual" might play an important role in the way of life of several broad classes of people.[12] Insofar

11. Consider the various claims quoted in White (1988, chap. 3), e.g. It is worth recalling, however, that "the number of people who earn most of their living from growing tobacco is smaller than the number of people who are estimated to die annually as a result of the tobacco they smoke. [More than] one premature death per year is a pretty high social cost for keeping a tobacco [farmer and his] children from having to shift to another crop or another occupation" (Schelling 1986a, p. 650). Warner (1987b, p. 2086) supplies numbers taking account of the employment effects of tobacco more generally: "tobacco annually produces 710,000 jobs in the tobacco core sectors and supplier industries. Given that 350,000 people die each year as the result of using tobacco, each of whom loses an average of 15 years of life, tobacco in our society creates a year of employment for each of two people in exchange for a decade and a half of life for every person killed by tobacco use."

12. Machan (1986, p. 51), e.g., makes much of the fact that, "for some people smoking is an important part of their life-style. They know it involves risks, but so does scuba diving, jogging, flying, kissing, water skiing, playing baseball, and so on. Life is

as we find those ways of life valuable, and insofar as they truly cannot be sustained without the smoking ritual, perhaps we ought not discourage smoking (among those groups, at least).

But both those provisos are likely to go unsatisfied. Central though smoking may be, few whole ways of life would disappear without it. There are typically some less unhealthy substitutes that could take the place of smoking in those life-styles. Furthermore, it is principally people with very boring or very stressful life-styles who get hooked into these patterns of repetitive behavior (Leventhal and Cleary 1980; Spielberger 1986; U.S. DHHS 1988, pp. 397–412). Those are hardly aspects of those ways of life that we would care to see perpetuated (Spencer 1893, 214–15).

3.   Producers of well-established products might have a legitimate expectation, growing out of long tradition, of continuing in business.

The analogy here would be to Hume's theory of property rights, wherein rights grow out of expectations legitimated by long usage. Squatters, even though they originally have no right (and, indeed, originally may have been wronging someone) to squat, come to acquire rights if they carry on squatting long enough. Tobacco, being a long-established product, might give its producers similarly legitimate expectations of continued access to markets.[13]

What count as "legitimate expectations" has always been the tough question for this line of analysis, though. The best Humean defenders of property can do is to cash out "legitimate" in terms of "well-founded," and to point to the benefits the public at large derives from the increased productivity generated by secure expectations. In the tobacco case, such defenses would be unavailable. It is clear, from the evidence above, that the continued marketing of the product is counterproductive of public health. It has always been clear, with tobacco as with all other consumer products, that the product's continued access to markets was predicated on the assumption that it

---

full of risks, some attached to significant activities, some to merely pleasurable ones, some to trivial pursuits."

13.   Though not, of course, necessarily continuing high profits. Furthermore, all that those legitimate expectations would strictly speaking give rise to is a right to compensation should the state, in exercise of its police powers, upset such expectations. By analogy, when the opium trade is prohibited, we might be similarly obliged to give transitional support to traditional poppy growers to help them retool—but that is not to say we cannot prohibit the opium trade.

was "safe" for consumers to use as directed.[14] Cigarettes palpably are not.

4.5   THE ETHICS OF ADVERTISING AND THE ETHICS OF SELLING

One of the most standard policies for preventing children from becoming addicted to tobacco is to ban advertising of it on television and in magazines targeted at children and young adults. There are pressures to extend those bans to all cigarette advertising and promotion.[15]

Against such bans, tobacco spokesmen urge two propositions. First, elevating the issue to the plane of high constitutional principle, they claim that a ban on advertising would violate their "right to free speech" under the First Amendment to the U.S. Constitution. Such a claim is tenuous in several respects, however. First, there are problems about the status of the corporations whose free speech is being infringed. It is true that the law has a habit of regarding corporations as "persons" for a wide variety of purposes. But whether they ought rightly be regarded as persons for all purposes—and most especially whether they really should enjoy all the same constitutional protections as natural persons—is a genuinely open question (Berle 1952; Tushnet 1982, pp. 255–57).

In any case, commercial speech has long been regarded as importantly different from other form of speech, for First Amendment purposes. Traditionally (indeed, until 1976), it did not enjoy any First Amendment protection whatsoever. It is still very much a live issue how much protection, if any, it should enjoy. On that, neither commentators nor the court itself have come to any settled judgment (Jackson and Jeffries 1979; Cox 1980; Weinberg 1982; Miller 1985; Blasi and Monaghan 1986).

One thing, at least, is tolerably clear. That is simply that, whatever protection is due to commercial speech, it is much more heavily qualified than that due to other forms of speech (Blasi and Monaghan

14.   Compare the prospective ban on cigarette manufacturing and sale to that imposed on distillers and brewers by Prohibition: they were not compensated for the fact that their machinery was turned into useless junk by prohibition laws, and the U.S. Supreme Court held in Mugler v. Kansas, 123 US 623, 669 (1887) that there was no need for them to be; Ackerman (1977, p. 153) suggests an explicit extension of that rule to the case of a cigarette ban.

15.   The same rules ought obviously apply both to conventional commercial advertising and to "promotions" (sports sponsorships, etc.) which are just thinly veiled forms of advertising designed to evade advertising bans. They are in principle indistinguishable from advertising of the ordinary sort (Ledwith 1984).

1986). John Stuart Mill—the most famous philosophical champion of free speech—would himself concede that point happily.[16] And the U.S. Supreme Court seems firmly of the view that, at least where commercial speech is concerned, "false, deceptive, and misleading advertising can be prohibited, and even non-deceptive advertising can be banned where necessary to accomplish a substantial governmental purpose" (Blasi and Monaghan 1986, p. 503, summarizing *Central Hudson Gas & Electric Corp. v. Public Service Commission*, 447 U.S. 557, 566 [1980]). On the evidence surveyed in section 2.2.1 above, much cigarette advertising might be covered by the first clause; insofar as banning advertising of cigarettes is necessary to prevent the young from becoming addicted, it might be justified on the latter (Blasi and Monaghan 1986).

If tobacco companies want to hide behind the First Amendment, they can only try to cast their advertisements in an "op-ed controversy" format, hoping that they will be entitled to First Amendment protection as expressions of "opinion" even if, as the Federal Trade Commission complained in the case of the R. J. Reynolds ad "Of Cigarettes and Science," they deliberately misrepresent scientific findings (White 1988, pp. 172–82). How many judges will fall for the trick of "crafting promotional messages in the guise of an editorial" remains, too, an open question, legally. The morals of the matter, though, are surely pretty settled. Galbraith (1959) is surely right to protest at the perversion of the "fairness" doctrine which has publishers printing—as part of every news story on the results of yet another government-sponsored research project showing the harmful effects of smoking—a tobacco industry denial. Tobacco industry special pleading and scientific findings, Galbraith (1959) insists, simply should not be treated "with equal respect."

More interesting is the tobacco companies' second argument: if it is legal to sell a product, then it should be legal to advertise it (Boddewyn 1986; cf. Chapman 1985, pp. 7–8; and Warner 1987a). How, exactly, that logical entailment is meant to work remains something of a mystery. Perhaps the idea is that there can no more be "private trade" than a "private language"—trade, by its very nature, must be interpersonal (Den Uyl and Machan 1988, p. 26). True

---

16.   Mill (1859/1975, p. 121) is in general a staunch advocate of the rule that "whatever it is permitted to do, it must be permitted to advise to do." But he is the first to agree that the appropriateness of that rule "is doubtful . . . when the instigator derives a personal benefit [e.g., profits] from his advice." That makes the "expression of opinion" just a form of special pleading, thus undermining both the moral and the prudential arguments for allowing free expression (Galbraith 1959).

enough. There can, however, be such a thing as a "private sale," where the seller makes an offer to the particular buyer that has not been made to the public at large. There is nothing incoherent about the notion of such a sale, private though it may have been.

Those who say "if it is legal to sell it must be legal to advertise" must presumably be arguing that, if it is permissible to engage in practices which are by their nature public (i.e., interpersonal), then it must be permissible to publicize those practices. But that cannot be right. Just as it is permissible for us to talk about doing all sorts of things it would not be permissible for us actually to do, it is permissible for us to keep people from talking openly about all sorts of things it would be perfectly permissible for them actually to do quietly. Surely it is legitimate for us to permit various practices between consenting adults in private, while prohibiting (in the name of public decency) their being publicly flaunted. Maybe smoking, like sexual perversions, should be among them (Lundberg and Knoll 1986).

More plausibly, the argument might turn on the justifications for having markets at all, and on the presuppositions built into them. Markets can be shown to maximize social welfare, under certain ideal conditions. One of them is that consumers have perfect information. Insofar as information is what advertising provides, its justification is thus implicit in the justification for permitting a market in the product at all. That is the only really interesting sense, I think, in which it is right to deny that "economic activities can be divorced from communication and information about such activities" (Den Uyl and Machan 1988, p. 25).

That argument is going to do tobacco companies less good than they think, however. If what we have is simply an argument for the provision of pure information, what it would justify is no more than what is known in the trade as "tombstone advertising"—"no models, slogans, scenes or colors"; just a picture of the unadorned cigarette packet with information on price and on tar, nicotine, and carbon monoxide content printed in plain lettering (Warner et al. 1986, pp. 383–84). Interestingly enough, just such draconian limitations on tobacco advertising are currently under discussion within the European Community (Hencke 1989). It may well be that bare-minimum advertising of that "tombstone" sort might be logically implied in the activity of selling a product at all. But it is far from clear that anything like advertising as we know it is implicit in the logic of permitting sale of the product.

There are, of course, various other more direct responses to the argument that, if it is legal to sell cigarettes, then it should be legal to advertise them. One would be to grasp the nettle and ban cigarette-sales altogether.[17] Another would be to point out that cigarette sales to minors are already banned; and judging from past experience, tobacco companies are unwilling or unable to frame advertisements in such a way that they appeal to legal (adult) consumers without also appealing to illegal (child) consumers (Taylor 1985, chaps. 6–8; BMA 1986; Chapman 1986; Roberts 1986; Wilkinson 1986, chap. 10; Aitken et al. 1987). Banning advertising of cigarettes could then be justified as a corollary of our ban on their sales to minors (Warner 1987a).

Another response, yet again, would be to turn the slogan, "if it is legal to sell, it is legal to advertise" on its head. If it is morally and legally legitimate for us to ban sale of a product, then it is permissible for us to ban advertising of it. As the U.S. Supreme Court has recently held, "the greater power to completely ban" a product or activity from the market "necessarily includes the lesser power to ban advertising of it" (Rehnquist 1986, p. 283).[18]

Furthermore, what sort of advertising we should permit depends upon what sort of argument we have for allowing continued sale of the product. If the argument is that people are better off using the product than they were before ever using it, then advertising designed to attract new customers is permissible on welfarist grounds. If the rationale is instead "servicing an addiction" of people who would have been better off never to have used the product (but who would suffer withdrawal if they discontinued using it now) then advertising that attracts new users, by design or otherwise, is definitely ruled out on utilitarian-style "welfarist" grounds.

Methods of advertising that could be guaranteed to reach only existing addicts might still be permissible. (Perhaps the best strategy here might be to oblige manufacturers to allow other companies to buy advertising space on the back of their products' packets.) Insofar as cigarette advertising encourages brand switching among existing users—and there is little reason to suppose that it does that

17.   Over-the-counter sales, anyway. Even if cigarettes were available as a prescription drug, the only advertising that that would justify would be in medical journals, addressed to doctors responsible for writing out the prescriptions rather than to their patients.

18.   The issue in *Posadas* was casino advertising but in passing Rehnquist's majority opinion offered, as obiter dictum, the view that cigarette advertising could be similarly restricted without infringing First Amendment rights (Rehnquist 1986, p. 284). The issue continued to be queried by Justice Department lawyers to the end of the Reagan administration, though (Kmiec 1986).

exclusively[19]—there are (probably marginal) welfare gains to smokers from switching to a preferred brand that must be figured into the utilitarian calculus.

(Manufacturers also claim that advertising contributes to social welfare by communicating important health information about products—especially their tar and nicotine levels—to smokers. It seems likely that advertising has played a role in encouraging the shift to low tar and nicotine brands [Hamilton 1972; Boddewyn 1986]. But given the evidence about the way that these cigarettes are simply smoked more intensively to compensate for their lower nicotine yield, the health consequences of this shift may be nothing much [U.S. DHHS 1981, sec. 7].)

To a large extent, however, cigarette advertising appeals to non-users as well as to existing users. The appeal to children is especially worrying, given problems about informed consent raised in section 2.2 above; but for purposes of the argument being advanced in this section, there is no need to focus upon them exclusively. That appeal to nonusers is apparently inevitable. Judging from past practice, it certainly seems incorrigible, at least. Insofar as cigarette advertising would appeal to nonusers in such ways, to that extent we have a strong welfarist case for banning advertising of the product altogether.

4.6   DISCRIMINATION

One way of discouraging smoking is to put an extra tax on tobacco products. One way of preventing passive smoking is to segregate smokers physically in some self-contained room or compartment. A variation on that latter strategy is for firms to hire only nonsmokers. That practice was common at the turn of the century (Troyer and Markle 1983, p. 37) but is only now beginning to regain popularity. The surgeon general estimates that only 1 percent of businesses make a policy of hiring nonsmokers exclusively; only 5 percent give systematic preference, even, to nonsmokers in hiring decisions; but perhaps as many as 10 percent of businesses permit supervisors

---

19. The evidence standardly offered for supposing that cigarette advertising merely encourages brand switching rather than recruiting new smokers is the weak relationship between advertising and overall volume of tobacco sales (Hamilton 1972; Fujii 1980). Although that is true for the short run, there is evidence that the relationship might be much stronger (0.2 or so) in the long run, which is where the effect of advertising in attracting new customers would really be felt of course (McGuinness and Cowling 1975). In any case, given the rate at which smokers die and quit smoking, even a constant volume of cigarette sales would represent significant numbers of new smokers being recruited each year.

themselves to exercise a nonsmoking preference when they make hiring decisions (U.S. DHHS 1986, p. 301).

All such policies are sometimes said to involve discrimination. The discrimination is most directly against smokers themselves: they are denied jobs or the company of fellow workers, or they are made to bear a disproportionate share of the government's general expenditures (Tollison and Wagner 1988, chap. 1). Since smoking correlates strongly with race and class, these policies also discriminate indirectly against lower classes and certain racial minorities (Tollison and Wagner 1988, p. 100).

A tax that falls disproportionately upon the poor is regressive, and is generally deemed undesirable on account of that fact. Tobacco taxes certainly are regressive.[20] A 1981 U.S. survey shows that households in the lowest income quintile spend on average 2.3 percent of their income on tobacco, whereas those in the highest income quintile spend on average only 0.42 percent (U.S. Department of Labor 1983, p. 54). In Britain, the equivalent figures circa 1985 were 5.3 percent and 1.2 percent, respectively (U.K. Central Statistical Office 1987).

One historically favored response would be to outsmart the critics, by admitting the regressivity of the tax but by going on to say that that is a virtue rather than a defect in it. In 1604, King James I —himself an ardent antismoker—dramatically increased the tobacco tax originally levied at a very low rate by Elizabeth. His avowed intention in doing so was precisely "to price tobacco out of the reach of the lower classes, while leaving sufficient supplies for those of the 'better sort,' who would smoke in moderation" (Harrison 1986, p. 555). True though that proposition may be, such overt class bias is no longer regarded as morally acceptable, however, and criticisms of class discrimination must necessarily be taken seriously.[21]

There are, however, various other, more moderate responses that advocates of tobacco taxes can make to charges of regressivity. Not all are equally convincing, though. One singularly unsatisfactory argument would be to say that increases in the tobacco tax would not be all that regressive, because smokers in lower income classes are more likely to respond to real rises in cigarette prices by smoking less, whereas smokers in higher income classes are more likely to continue

20. For elaborations, see Atkinson, Gomulka, and Stern 1984; Savarese and Shughart 1986; Tollison and Wagner 1988, esp. chaps. 1, 2, 6; Townsend 1987.

21. Modern conspiracy theorists of the "public choice" school of economics suppose that antismoking ordinances in our own day are similarly designed to advance the interests of nonsmoking professional classes against those of lower-class smokers (Tollison and Wagner 1988, pp. 81–82, 100).

smoking the same as before and hence pay more of the taxes (Townsend 1987, p. 361). The statistics are perfectly correct, and in the narrowest possible economic sense that makes raising the tax "progressive": more of the extra tax revenue will come from the rich than the poor.

It is hard to see how we can take much comfort from that thought, though. The reason we worry about regressive taxes in the first place is that we fear that their impact on the poor is greater than their impact on the rich. Presumably abandoning altogether an activity they would prefer to continue is more of a sacrifice than merely paying more to continue as before. So in the sense that matters, raising the tobacco tax would be all the more regressive a move—in welfare if not in revenue-raising terms—for pricing the poor out of the market for tobacco. They might be better off in objective terms as a result, of course: smoking, after all, is unhealthy. But in the subjective preference terms within which economists standardly operate, the poor would be all the worse off for having been priced out of the market for tobacco that they would still like to buy, if only they could afford it.

A more satisfactory response to the critique of tobacco taxes as regressive picks up on the suggestion, in section 2.3.3 above, that that tax might be regarded as a kind of "user fee" designed to recoup from smokers the full cost that their smoking imposed upon society. Tort law requires everyone—rich and poor alike—to pay the full cost of any damage they do to others. Perhaps government taxation, conceived of as a user fee, should do likewise. On this account, it would be unacceptably regressive to charge the poor more for causing the same amount of damage. But if the poor cause more damage, then charging them the same price for it as we would charge the rich for causing similar damage is not regressive in the least.

That response is still not altogether satisfactory, however. For one thing, the model of tobacco taxes as user fees would simply be a lot more plausible if they were earmarked—as they hardly ever are earmarked—for paying the costs created by smoking. When these tax collections are simply despoited to general fund revenues, it looks rather as if poor smokers are being required to pay a disproportionate share of the general running expenses of the government. And in a certain way, they indisputably are. For the second thing to note about tobacco taxes is that they often exceed—often by a wide margin—any costs of smoking that are indisputably costs to others in society. The fact that these extra fees, over and above what is necessary to recoup costs, are being paid disproportionately by poor smokers makes the tobacco tax genuinely regressive in the standard sense.

In the end, then, the best response that advocates of the tobacco tax can make to the charges that such taxes are regressive is to say that that simply is a separate issue. If such taxes are unacceptably regressive, the government can always "mitigate the [distributional] effects by simultaneous support for low-income households" (Atkinson and Townsend 1977, p. 493). Most likely, this would come in the form of income supplements for poor households; it is barely conceivable that governments would allow rations of such patently unhealthy products as tobacco on food stamps, for example (although they historically have included cigarettes in rations for fighting troops at the front). There are various other compelling reasons for income supplements for the poor, too. Overcoming the distributional effects of the tobacco tax is just one other. The point here is simply that, through such familiar strategies, this distributional objection can be overcome.

Let us consider, next, problems of discrimination that arise from policies of segregation of smokers and nonsmokers. A policy of segregation, especially when its effects fall disproportionately upon historically discriminated-against racial minorities, is uncomfortably reminiscent of southern lunch counters in the age of Jim Crow (Victor 1987; Rothstein 1983). Some go so far as to call it "tobacco apartheid" (Tollison and Wagner 1988, p. 69). As one California assemblyman said in protesting against a ban on smoking on public transportation being considered there, "This is really a civil rights issue. First you say 'smokers get to the back of the bus,' and now you're telling smokers to get off the bus" altogether (quoted in Will 1987).

The Tobacco Institute also alleges "class discrimination" in smoking-at-work policies. The grounds for that allegation is that those with private offices are typically still allowed to smoke at their desks, whereas those with shared offices must go elsewhere (quoted in Wilkinson 1986, p. 138). But the class aspects of the issue seem not to resonate particularly well, politically. One reason may be that "many blue-collar workers, barred by tradition from smoking on the assembly line," simply "are not experiencing any new deprivation" (Freedman 1988).

One response to the more general allegations of discrimination would be to admit that the policies are discriminatory, but to go on to argue that the discrimination is against the behavior (smoking) and not the person (the smoker).[22] How powerful a move this will be

22. Similarly, it is one thing to punish an alcoholic for being an alcoholic, quite another to punish an alcoholic for drinking in public (Marshall 1968). Policies of preferential hiring might be unable to appeal to this distinction: they discriminate precisely against the person who smokes, no matter where or when. But segregating and taxing smoking are both policies arguably directed at the behavior rather than the person.

depends upon how much of a wedge can be driven between the behavior and the person. If smoking were no more than an annoying personal habit like chewing gum or whistling off-key, then discriminating against the behavior would not be discriminating against the person, necessarily, because the person could presumably always renounce the behavior and thus avoid the sanction. If smoking were regarded as an addiction that is to some extent beyond a person's power to alter, however, then to that extent the distinction between the person and the behavior is a distinction without a difference. Discriminating against the behavior, then, just is discriminating against the person.

On the evidence of section 2.2.2, most smokers are indeed addicted to nicotine, in the sense that they are unable to cease their intake of the substance even if they want to do so. It is precisely such an inability of people to alter discriminated-against characteristics that has come to define them as "suspect classes" in recent U.S. court cases arising under the Fourteenth Amendment to the Constitution (Anonymous 1981; Daniels 1985, pp. 201–3).[23] It is precisely the fact that drug addicts are incapable of altering their status as addicts that has led the U.S. Supreme Court to strike down penalties for being an addict per se as involving unconstitutionally "cruel and unusual punishment" (Stewart 1962; cf. Fingarette 1975).

Even those who are addicted, and who cannot (easily) alter *whether* or not they smoke, can nonetheless control *where* they smoke, however. Thus, insofar as the policy is merely one requiring smokers to step into another room to smoke and then return to their desks, it is a policy with which smokers can indeed comply without changing themselves in some almost impossible way. Insofar as it requires segregation of the smoker from nonsmoking workmates, the separation is brief and presumably inconsequential. There are all sorts of activities that we ask people to step out of the room to perform. Prostitution, where legalized, is characteristically confined to certain zones within the city (Yondorf 1979). No one protests that either form of segregation is unacceptably discriminatory.

Sometimes, as with preferential hiring policies favoring nonsmokers, genuine discrimination might be involved. Notice, however,

---

23. Specifically, they might claim that they are "handicapped" by their nicotine addiction and thus deserve whatever protection we offer other handicapped individuals. Ironically, it is hypersensitive nonsmokers who have met with more success in qualifying as handicapped or disabled in the eyes of U.S. courts. See, e.g., Vickers v. Veterans Administration, 549 F.Supp. 85 (W.D. Wash. 1982) and Parodi v. Merit Systems Protection Board, 690 F.2d 731 (9th Cir. 1982); see, more generally, Repace (1985, pp. 15–16).

that neither laws nor morals prohibit discrimination per se. All that is prohibited is arbitrary discrimination. If we are distinguishing between prospective employees on grounds clearly relevant to the task to be performed, then that is permissible; and it would remain so, even if at the end of the day more white men are hired than black women as a result.

A case can certainly be made on these grounds. Smoking clearly is detrimental to the performance of certain sorts of tasks; it damages equipment, slows workers' reaction times, and so on. Furthermore, insofar as smoking at work harms co-workers as well as smokers themselves, employers can hardly be held to be acting improperly if they display the same concern for their workers' health as for their own machinery.[24] In all these ways and more, it might be argued that discriminating against smokers is discriminating between people on grounds clearly relevant to the proper functioning of the business concerned.[25] To a large extent, problems of these sorts can be solved simply by prohibiting smoking on the job. But insofar as there are significant spillovers from off-duty smoking to on-the-job performance, as in the case of firefighters for example (Barrett 1987), a policy of restrictive hiring might be perfectly justifiable, on grounds there is a rational relation to performance of a legitimate public function in the case of government employees and on the grounds of "business necessity" in the case of private-sector employees (Daniels 1985, pp. 212–13).

4.7   NONSMOKING AS THE NORM

A standard slogan of the antismoking lobby is that "nonsmoking should be regarded as the norm," particularly "in enclosed areas

24. As a New Jersey judge recently remarked, in ruling that the employer's common-law duty of care with respect to its employees required New Jersey Bell to restrict smoking in working areas: "The company already has in effect a rule that cigarettes are not to be smoked around telephone equipment. The rationale behind the rule is that the machines are highly sensitive and can be damaged by smoke. Human beings are also very sensitive and can be damaged by tobacco smoke. . . . A company that has demonstrated such concerns for its mechanical components should have at least as much concern for its human beings" (Shimp v. New Jersey Bell Telephone Co., 368 A.2d 408, 145 N.J.S. 516 (1976), quoted in Jenkins et al. 1987, p. 5).

25. It is also true that smokers cost employers more (in terms of lost productivity, higher health insurance costs, higher maintenance and repair costs to equipment, etc.) than nonsmokers (Kristein 1983). The surgeon general describes as conservative the estimate that the annual cost to a firm per smoking employee run $300 to $600 (U.S. DHHS 1986, p. 305). That gives employers an incentive for hiring only nonsmokers, to be sure. But if nicotine addiction is classed as a handicap, then it is unclear whether merely marginally greater costs can count as a relevant reason for discriminating against smokers. After all, the U.S. Rehabilitation Act of 1973 requires employers to make "reasonable accommodation" for employees' handicaps, including moderately costly steps like building wheelchair ramps.

frequented by the public or employees" (Froggatt 1988, par. 74). In practice, what that slogan means is "special provision being made for smokers rather than vice-versa" (Froggatt 1988, par. 74).[26] Thus, instead of designating certain areas as "no smoking" and signposting them accordingly, we would signpost special areas where smoking is to be permitted. The presumption would be that you may not smoke, unless you see a notice giving you specific positive permission to do so in that area. This, in fact, is precisely what is stipulated in the 1975 Minnesota Clean Indoor Air Act and the various city and state legislation following in its wake (U.S. DHHS 1986, p. 267).

The slogan itself—"nonsmoking as the norm"—turns on something of a rhetorical trick. On the one hand, saying that something is "the norm" is to say that it is the statistically most common outcome—that that outcome is the "normal" one. On the other hand, saying that something is "the norm" is to say that it is the morally proper outcome—that that outcome is the "normatively correct" one.

We regularly side between notions of the statistically expected and the morally required for all sorts of purposes in moral and legal philosophy. One is in determining the sorts of actions for which people ought to be held morally and legally responsible: we hold them responsible for consequences of actions that deviate from the norm, in either a statistical or a moral sense of the term (Mackie 1955; Hart and Honoré 1985, chaps. 2–3). We define what counts as a morally unacceptable coercive threat (as opposed to a perfectly proper noncoercive offer) in similar terms: someone is said to be engaged in coercion if and only if he is proposing to deviate from the norm, in either sense (Nozick 1972, p. 112).

That the practice of sliding between these two senses is standard does not make it any less of a fudge to do so, however. It is a fudge, principally because of the familiar problems associated with the so-called naturalistic fallacy. You simply cannot, without further ado, slide from "is" to "ought." To say that something is (statistically) the case is not, necessarily, to say that it ought (morally) to be the case. Injustice that is truly systematic may well be statistically expected. But that fact does not make it morally correct. On the contrary, the very fact that injustice is systematic makes it all the worse, morally.

In the statistical sense, it is clear enough that nonsmoking is indeed the norm. In the United States, nonsmokers now outnumber smokers by almost three to one (Helyar 1987). The question is simply what moral significance to attach to that fact, and why.

---

26. That is to say, nonsmoking should be "the *rule* rather than the *exception,* so that smokers have the responsibility to restrict their smoking to where it can be permitted without risking harm or discomfort to others" (Jenkins et al. 1987, p. 11).

It is not as if literally nothing follows, morally, from the fact that nonsmoking is statistically the norm. In utilitarian calculations, for example, aggregate utility of society as a whole would clearly be better served by no-smoking rules the fewer smokers there were to suffer from such rules and the more nonsmokers there were to benefit from them. But some bridging principles—such as those provided, in this example, by utilitarian premises—are always required to close the gap between "is" and "ought" and to justify us in making nonsmoking the norm, morally as well as statistically. From what has already been said in this book, it will be clear that I think that various such moral bridging principles can indeed be found. My point here is just that they are needed. The slogan "nonsmoking as the norm" cannot do the whole job, all on its own.

Some commentators, influenced by Coase (1960), might argue that in principle it should not matter how we set the presumption. It should not matter whether we allow smoking only where designated (labeling certain railway carriages "smoking," as on old-fashioned trains, e.g.) or whether we prohibit smoking only where posted (labeling certain carriages "no smoking," as we tend to do today, e.g.).[27] The two cases, they would say, should in principle be perfectly symmetrical in their practical consequences—just so long as everyone knows which way the presumption runs and what inferences to draw therefore from the absence of signs either way.

Antismoking campaigners resist that argument. They say that the rule of prohibiting smoking only where posted prejudices the situation against the nonsmoker. It makes nonsmokers seem like the oddities, when in fact they enjoy a three to one majority in the population.

Practicality considerations might nonetheless seem to dictate that rule of permitting smoking except where it is explicitly prohibited. An argument along these lines would go something like this. Surely smoking can safely be permitted in the open air. By their very nature, though, it is impractical to post open spaces that have no natural

---

27. Of course, it is perfectly possible to have a general presumption against smoking unless you see a sign explicitly permitting it and to make a practice of posting "no smoking" signs in places (such as elevators, theaters, and storerooms containing flamable materials) where we especially want people to refrain from smoking. Nothing can be inferred from the fact that we do in practice post "no smoking" signs. Similarly, farmers post "no hunting" or "no trespassing" signs if they are particularly keen to keep hunters off of their property. But we do not infer from that fact that we have permission to shoot rabbits anywhere (or even on any farmland away from houses, tractors, etc.) that is not so posted. The posting of a sign in that case merely reinforces, emphatically, a standing prohibition against trespassing unless permission has been specifically granted.

perimeters with signs designating them as "smoking" areas. Hence, the argument would run, the presumption should be that you may smoke, except where you see a sign prohibiting it.

This is not a particularly compelling argument, though. For one thing, it is just as easy to post a "smoking permitted beyond this point" notice on doors leading out of buildings as is to post a "smoking prohibited except in designated areas" notice on doors leading into them. For an analogy, consider the way in which highway engineers post "resume normal speed" signs on the roads leading out of towns.

In any case, we could perfectly well have a presumption of no smoking in any enclosed space, absent specific permission to smoke in some designated area within that space. (What exactly counts as an "enclosed space" might not always be completely obvious, of course: stairways or escalators leading directly onto the street, or London Underground stations open to the sky three stories above, are ambiguous cases requiring specific posting, perhaps). This presumption could be reinforced by signs on the doors leading into the building, such as are now found on the doors to Florida airports, emphasizing that there is no smoking inside the building except in designated areas.

The advantages of this sort of rule have largely to do with how the precise way in which legal notices are phrased can help to socialize people into nonsmoking behavior. It is important (for reasons given in sec. 2.2.2 above) for children to be discouraged from taking up smoking. Norms requiring "no smoking" areas to be specifically posted suggest that smoking is a normal part of adult life, and that nonsmoking is a special case. Such norms encourage adolescents to take up smoking as part of joining the adult world. Norms that require "smoking" areas to be specifically posted carry the opposite implication: nonsmoking is normal, and there is no need for adolescents to take it up to become a full-fledged adult.

Or, again, it is important (for reasons given in Chap. 3 above) for smokers to be sensitive to the rights of nonsmokers who would prefer not to breathe their exhaust. Norms that make smokers look for a sign that permits them to smoke sensitizes them in that way. Norms that would make nonsmokers look for a sign that offers them protection from smoke would not do so, or at least would do so only much less strongly.

4.8 OTHER COUNTRIES

In my discussion so far, there has been a smattering of references to smoking and its control in Canada, Australia, and Western Europe. I have talked principally, however, about the case of the United States and, to a lesser extent, of Britain.

In part, that focus has been accidental. It merely reflects the countries in which, and about which, most of the previous research has been done. That focus has also been deliberate, in part. Those countries represent the principal intended audiences for whom this book is being written.

Any so narrow focus necessarily understates wildly the worldwide scope of the smoking problem, however. A World Health Organization Expert Committee on Smoking Control estimates that smoking "is now responsible for more than a million premature deaths each year" worldwide; other estimates run as high as 2.5 million (Chapman 1986, p. 11; Stebbins 1987, p. 523). No doubt the WHO experts exaggerate when they go on to say that the control of smoking "could do more to improve health and prolong life . . . than any other single action in the whole field of preventive medicine" (quoted in Chapman 1986, p. 11)—unless, perhaps, they are regarding the prevention of malnutrition as somehow outside the bounds of preventive medicine. Still, smoking is an indisputably serious problem in the wider world, just as it is in North America and Western Europe.

Furthermore, smoking is becoming more of a problem in the Third World at the same time as it is becoming less of one in the First World. As U.S. cigarette sales decline, "much of the future for world cigarette sales lies in finding a market away from home," as U.S. tobacco companies are the first to admit (Shelton 1984, p. 57). In this, they are making great strides. While U.S. cigarette sales dropped some 7 percent during the early 1980s, cigarette consumption was rising by some 33 percent in Africa and 24 percent in Latin America in the same period (Stebbins 1987, p. 523; see, similarly, Williamson 1986, p. 124). Overseas promotions have been so successful that, for all six major U.S. cigarette manufacturers, "foreign cigarette sales . . . now exceed the volume of domestic sales" (Stebbins 1987, p. 526).

In one way, smoking has traditionally been less of a health hazard for people of the Third World simply because they did not live long enough for it to catch up with them. The latency period of lung cancer, for example, would usually have exceeded their normal life expectancy. But "as the traditional killer diseases of developing countries (smallpox, yellow fever, malaria, etc.) are gradually brought under control and people live longer because of vaccination, better nutrition and medical services, millions of Third World smokers are beginning to incubate lung cancer, bronchitis and heart disease" (Taylor 1985, p. 254). As they smoke more and more cigarettes, they are therefore now at real risk of smoking-related diseases in a way they might not have been in the past.

Even before smoking-related diseases catch up with them, impoverished Third World smokers will have to confront problems (among them, health problems) associated with their poverty. Smoking exacerbates those, too. Cigarettes are expensive. It has been calculated that, in Bangladesh, the cost of the breadwinner in a poor household smoking only five cigarettes a day amounts in food-substitution terms to a monthly dietary deficit of 8,000 calories, which amounts to "nearly a quarter the monthly maintenance energy requirements . . . of a [young] child"; on certain sociologically plausible assumptions, the "result of income being used for smoking rather than for food" is that "each year the prospects of survival of some 18,000 children [in Bangladesh alone] would be halved" (Cohen 1981, p. 1092).

Furthermore, cigarettes are often consumed by smokers even when they can ill afford them. Given the addictive properties of their constituent chemicals, that is only to be expected. Still worse, as a result of the association between stress and smoking, smokers often end up consuming cigarettes most heavily precisely when they can least afford them: at times of unemployment or crop failure.[28]

Insofar as economically hard-pressed Third World smokers spend money on cigarettes instead of food for themselves and their families, smoking can truly be said to be a cause of malnutrition. In those countries where Third World smokers are consuming domestically produced cigarettes, smoking makes an indirect contribution in another way, too. Land devoted to cultivating tobacco is land not devoted to cultivating other more wholesome foodstuffs. In Bangladesh, again, "over 100,000 acres . . . of land that could produce food are planted with tobacco," resulting in an annual loss in rice production of some 43,000 tons. In recent years, Bangladesh has imported heavily to meet its cereal requirements, of course. But so far as problems of malnutrition are concerned, such imports "will not help much, for those who need the food most usually cannot afford to buy it" and they "hardly figure in existing ration distributions" either. "Maximum food self-sufficiency is indeed the only adequate protection for the small cultivator in Bangladesh" and elsewhere (Cohen 1981, pp. 1090–91). The shift from subsistence crops, like rice, to cash crops, like tobacco, helps frustrate that goal (see, more generally, Christensen 1978).

The longer terms effects of tobacco cultivation are even more serious. Intensive cultivation of tobacco leaches the soil of nutrients,

---

28. Chapman (1986, p. 119) quotes an observer of recent African famines as saying, "It is really tragic, but the worse the famine becomes, the more people smoke. It is like a war: people are worried and they want to smoke." Insofar as what I say in this paragraph and elsewhere in this section really turns on the differences between rich and poor, much the same will be true within nations as it is between them.

significantly impairing its productive capacity. Furthermore, the deforestation caused as trees are cut down to be used in curing tobacco leads to the familiar problems of topsoil erosion. It has been estimated that one in eight of all trees felled in the world are used for flue curing tobacco (Madeley 1981), and the effects in the Third World are particularly striking. Brazilian farmers alone need annually the wood of some 60 million trees—the equivalent of 1.5 million acres of forest—to cure their tobacco, according to one estimate (Taylor 1985, pp. 252–53; see, similarly, Wilkinson 1986, p. 127).

In most Third World countries, though, smokers will be consuming cigarettes imported from abroad, most often from the United States. Even in countries where tobacco is grown, there is often preference (born of aggressive promotion or a pure desire to emulate the West) for American "blond" tobacco that is milder than the "dark" varieties typically produced locally (Taylor 1985, chap. 15; Chapman 1986, pp. 123–24). Importing tobacco from abroad exacerbates the balance of payments deficit and drains a nation's hard currency reserves, upon which development plans so heavily rely (Chapman 1986, p. 119).

From the point of view of Third World governments, then, it would seem that smoking is something that ought to be discouraged. It rarely is. Whereas some 95 percent of developed nations have regulations pertaining to cigarette marketing and health warnings, only 24 percent of developing countries do so (Stebbins 1987, p. 528; see, further, Roemer 1986). Prohibitions on advertising on television are rare; so are prohibitions on sales to minors; so are mandatory health warnings on packets, which would anyway be irrelevant, given high rates of illiteracy and the practice of selling cigarettes by the stick rather than the packet (Stebbins 1987, p. 528). In consequence of this regulatory laxity, unhealthier cigarettes are sold in the Third World, and they are sold in unhealthier ways. Consider, for just one summary measure, the following comparisons of tar levels: "Tar concentrations for a range of popular cigarettes sold in the United Kingdom and in Australia in 1981 never exceeded 19 mg tar per cigarette. By contrast, the same cigarettes sold in Singapore give tar yields of 19 to 33 mg per cigarette. . . . In Pakistan, . . . two of the most popular brands, Capstan and Morven, each have a yield of 29 mg tar per cigarette" (Wilkinson 1986, p. 125).

Why Third World governments so conspicuously fail to regulate smoking is an open question. One answer might be in terms of the short-term economic benefits they get, in terms of employment in the tobacco industry or in terms of taxing tobacco consumed (Taylor 1985, p. 250). Another answer might be in the more venal terms of bribes paid by tobacco companies to foreign governments. Both R. J. Reynolds and Philip Morris—two of the largest cigarette manufacturers—have admitted to the U.S. Securities and Exchange Commission that "questionable" payments of $5 million and of $2.4 million, respectively, had been made to foreign governments on their behalf (Taylor 1985, pp. 263–64).

Be all that as it may, my primary focus here is upon the duties of the people and the governments of First World countries—principally the United States and Britain—with respect to smoking in the Third World. I shall simply take as settled the large argument over whether we have duties at all to foreigners; at the very least, we surely have duties not actually to harm them (Shue 1981; Goodin 1985, pp. 154–69). There are two particular problems, from that perspective, that should concern us with the tobacco trade. One has to do with harm done by our government itself; the other has to do with harm that our government allows tobacco companies under its control to do abroad.

Consider first the way in which our governments actively promote smoking in the Third World in various ways. One is under the U.S. government's Food for Peace program, which in effect compelled Third World consumers to buy $1 billion worth of U.S. tobacco between 1955 and 1980 in exchange for American economic assistance (Taylor 1985, p. 262; Stebbins 1987, p. 527).[29] Another is through their leading role in multilateral institutions—principally the United Nations Food and Agriculture Organisation (FAO) and the World Bank, which assist Third World governments in fostering an indigenous tobacco industry. These financial inducements are often at such a level that host nations find them irresistable. The $600 million in loans the World Bank gave out between 1974 and 1982 for tobacco-related rural development projects includes, for example, $30 million to Malawi, $4 million to Swaziland, $14 million to Tanzania, and so on (Taylor 1985, pp. 242–45).

These practices raise serious ethical problems, of an equally various sort. The immorality of giving out free samples of an addictive substance, with a view to cultivating future markets, is transparent—whether practiced at home by tobacco companies them-

---

29.   If this characterization seems less than generous, it is hard to see what else could be made of the administrative arrangements detailed by Tayor (1985, p. 262) as follows: "Developing countries could purchase American tobacco on federally guaranteed long term dollar loans (up to forty years) at low rates of interest (two to three percent). If their governments resold the tobacco locally and used the money to finance approved development projects, they could then be exempted of the debt obligation."

selves or abroad by governments on their behalves. Requiring the victims to pay for the privilege of being subjected to an addictive substance simply compounds the sin.

There is nothing quite so obviously immoral, perhaps, in the other practice. Giving out developmental assistance, on the strictly economic criterion of maximizing the rate of return on investments, seems perfectly reasonable. If tobacco cultivation qualifies for assistance under such criteria, well, so be it—or so economists would say. But there are certain sorts of profits that morally ought not to be made. Profiting from tobacco, in particular, might be regarded as tantamount to trading in lives, taking advantage of the helplessness of nicotine addicts. If tobacco profits are indeed immoral, ill-gotten gains, then it could easily be argued that those investments simply ought not be made, whatever their promised rate of return. In recent years, international financial institutions have come under increasing pressure to introduce a variety of ethical and social side-constraints into their calculations, alongside more standard considerations like the economic rate of return on investments (Ayres 1983). A principle of not poisoning people would presumably be among them. And as a—perhaps the—central actor in those international financial institutions, it is the peculiar responsibility of the United States to see to it that they adhere to these moral side-constraints in their dealings with Third World countries.

The first set of ethical issues concerns the acts of First World governments in themselves actively promoting smoking in the Third World. A second set of ethical issues surrounds the inactions or omissions of First World governments in permitting tobacco companies chartered there to export hazardous products (cigarettes) to Third World countries where they will be regulated much less stringently than they would have been in their home markets.[30]

The problems that arise in exporting American cigarettes to countries where they will be regulated less stringently is merely a special case of a much more general problem. That concerns the permissibility, in general, of exporting hazards—hazardous products, hazardous production processes and factories, hazardous wastes— which we would not be prepared to tolerate within our own country to some other (typically, much poorer) country that is prepared to accept them, for a price (Shue 1981; Castleman 1979; 1985; King

---

30. Typically, these offshore operations are carried out through foreign subsidiaries of the parent American tobacco companies. Insofar as the moral issue concerns the permissibility of exporting hazardous products from the United States, however, problems of corporate identity and parent-company control over operations of subsidiaries abroad need not arise. If the issue is whether it is permissible to export products that we know will be marketed immorally, the issue is the same whether the marketing will be done by ourselves or others.

1985; Ives 1985). We have no settled public policy on that more general issue. One of the last official acts of President Carter was to sign Executive Order 12264, sharply restricting the export of products or substances that are so hazardous that they are banned or significantly restricted at home. One of President Reagan's first acts in office revoked that order.[31]

The central moral issue involved here would seem to be one of ethical inconsistency. It is morally unacceptable to practice a double standard, applying one rule of conduct to yourself and another to others. It is, we might suppose, equally morally unacceptable to demand a higher standard of conduct from people when they deal with us than when they deal with others. This sense of an immoral double standard was effectively evoked by the plaintiff's complaint in recent Philippine litigation against two American tobacco companies and their local subsidiaries:

> Defendants [R.J.] Reynolds and Philip Morris voluntarily comply with the U.S. laws on labelling and advertising that educate and warn Americans and their children about, and protect them from, the adverse health effects of smoking. Yet . . . they callously and unconscionably refuse to extend the same minimum protection and treatment to . . . the children of the Philippines. . . .
>
> Reynolds and Philip Morris voluntarily complied with the [U.S.] federal laws, did not test their constitutionality and entered . . . into voluntary codes or agreements to regulate [cigarette] advertising. . . . In the face of the legal restrictions [there, they] shifted their advertising resources to Third World countries, including the Philippines. . . . To date, defendant cigarette companies refuse to adopt in the Philippines at the very least the same labelling and advertising restrictions to which they (and/or their licensors) are subject to in the United States.[32]

31. Carter's executive order of January 16, 1981, is printed under the heading, "On Federal Policy Regarding the Export of Banned or Significantly Restricted Substances," in the *Federal Register* 46 (1981): 4658–64; Reagan's repeal of February 17, 1981, "Federal Exports and Excessive Regulation," appears in the *Federal Register* 46 (1981): 12943. For background on this debate, see Shaikh and Reich (1981) and Ives (1985). Note that the Carter policy explicitly excluded tobacco—along with military weapons, nuclear fuels, alcohol, narcotic drugs, and hazardous production facilities (Shaikh and Reich 1981, p. 741).

32. Plaintiff's "Complaint with urgent petition for prohibitory and mandatory injunctions" in the case of Jardeleza v. R. J. Reynolds Tobacco Co., Civil Case no. Q-50436 in the Regional Trial Court, Quezon City Branch 106, Republic of the Philippines; reprinted in the *Tobacco Products Liability Reporter* 2, no. 7 (July/August 1987): 3.409–3.421, at p. 3.417.

Now, perhaps it is idle to address such complaints to tobacco companies themselves. As one Rothmans executive is quoted as remarking, "If there is no ban on TV advertising, then you [as a tobacco company] aren't going to be an idiot and impose restrictions on yourself" (quoted in Chapman 1986, p. 121). But we may well blame our government if, knowing that that is what will happen if it allows exports of tobacco products to the Third World, it does nothing to restrict them.

Defenders of allowing tobacco exports have two possible rejoinders available at this point. The less satisfactory one of them points to the fact that what is involved in the case of cigarette exports is a very much watered-down example of the standard case involved in exporting hazardous products. It is not as if the product were banned altogether for use in the United States and companies were trying to dump abroad products that they are prohibited from marketing at home. Cigarettes are perfectly lawful products, even in the United States.

Certainly the dumping of banned products abroad constitutes an even more egregious example of the same basic phenomenon. For that reason, perhaps, that is the example that has attracted most previous attention, among both philosophers and policymakers. But surely the same basic principles apply to both kinds of cases alike.

What matters morally, here, might best be phrased in terms of the "excess burden of risk" that is inflicted on foreign consumers from allowing exports of a product. What risks would Third World consumers be bearing as a result of the exported product, over and above the risks that U.S. policymakers are prepared to allow consumers in their own country to bear? For products banned at home but exported for use by foreign consumers, the whole of the risk borne by those foreign consumers would count as part of the "excess risk burden" in this way. For products that are allowed to be marketed, subject to certain restrictions, at home, the excess risk burden to foreign consumers is just a matter of how much greater risks they run from the less restrained way in which the product is marketed and consumed abroad than at home. If the product is a sufficiently dangerous one, however, and if it will be marketed and consumed in a sufficiently less restrained way abroad than at home, then that excess risk burden may be quite large. Indeed, depending upon the precise parameters associated with the variables in this pseudo-equation, the excess risk burden might actually be greater in the latter case than the former: it may well be that more people abroad die as a result of the less restrained way in which powerfully carcinogenic substances like tobacco are marketed and consumed there than die as a result of the sale abroad of mildly carcinogenic products that are banned at home. In any case, it is plain that enough more people die as a result of the less stringent control of tobacco abroad to make the export of this hazardous product a matter for real moral concern.

The more interesting rejoinder takes its lead from George Bernard Shaw's variation on the Golden Rule: "Do not do unto others as you would that they should do unto you. Their tastes may not be the same" (Shaw 1903/1965, p. 188). It would, on this argument, be wrong for us to impose our values on foreigners by refusing to export products that they want to buy from us, just because we do not want (or think our citizens should not want to risk) these products.[33] Still less, this argument would continue, should we refuse to export products that we ourselves actually enjoy consuming, just because foreign governments will allow their citizens to enjoy them in a more unrestrained way.

At root, this riposte points to the sad fact that the poor, by reason of their poverty, are forced to consume less goods (and less good goods) all the way across the board. They are forced, by their budgetary constraints, to buy fewer and lower quality consumer products. They are forced, by their budgetary constraints, to consume less leisure (the economist's way of saying they have to work harder and for longer hours). And they are forced, by their budgetary constraints, to consume less safety and hence to take more risks. Taking more chances is just part of what it is to be poor, in the Third World as surely as in the First.

None of this is to say that those outcomes are morally proper, of course. What it does suggest is that if we want to remedy those outcomes, the way to do so is by attacking their root causes—people's poverty—rather than by attacking the various surface manifestations of it just mentioned. Unless we do something about their poverty, poor people will be worse off than before as a result of consumer product safety legislation, for example: forcing people to buy safer (but more expensive) goods than they otherwise would have bought simply leaves them with less money for other purchases (Friedman and Friedman 1980, pp. 250–55; Wildavsky 1980).

33. "The Carter policy sought to resolve this ethical dilemma by instituting an orderly notification system," whereby U.S. corporations would notify the U.S. government of their intent to export substances banned or restricted for sale in the United States, and the U.S. government would notify governments of the recipient countries in turn; exports would then be permitted only with the recipient's permission. The advantage of that arrangement is that "the notification system works on the principle of informed consent." The disadvantage is that it "suffers from the difficulties of information transfer"—there is a real reason to fear that the importing countries might not fully appreciate the extent of the risks they would be running (Shaikh and Reich 1981, p. 741).

Despite the obvious truth of all that, I think a case can nonetheless be made for consumer product safety legislation domestically—and, by analogy, for banning exports of hazardous products to willing consumers abroad. The central point is simply that some manifestations of poverty are morally more unacceptable than others. It is bad that anyone is poor, and perhaps we should do something about it. But it is still worse that anyone, by reason of poverty, should suffer certain fates: starvation, homelessness, or debilitating illness or disease, for example. Hence, even if we do not engage in wholesale cash transfers to remedy poverty, *tout court,* we nonetheless arrange for the welfare state to allocate poor people nonfungible food stamps, public housing, and rights to a healthy environment (Tobin 1970). One reason we do so might have to do with the way in which all these conditions impinge upon a person's autonomy and capacity for future choice. In that way, all those sorts of policies might be morally on a par with prohibition upon selling oneself into slavery, however desperate one's debts and however a good price one might have fetched on the slave market (Mill 1859/1975, pp. 126–27).

A case for consumer product safety legislation domestically, and for banning the export of hazardous products abroad, might be cast in the selfsame terms. People may be poor. Their plight might be desperate. But precisely because they are so desperate, we are not prepared to let them engage in economically induced acts of self-mutilation, intentional or otherwise (Goodin 1982, chap. 8; 1985; 1988, chap. 6). Desperation bidding simply is too morally suspect.

By refusing to allow people, at home or abroad, to buy hazardous products that they want, we may be making them subjectively worse off. Insofar as those bans on more hazardous products force them to buy instead more expensive safer substitutes, we may be making them financially worse off, even. There is undoubtedly much to be said for more transfer payments, within nations and between them, both in general and specifically in order to compensate consumers for these extra expenses that we force upon them. But having said all that, the moral case for banning exports of hazardous products—cigarettes among them—remains strong.

4.9   OTHER POISONS

Perhaps the most standard objection to smoking regulations is in the form of a "slippery slope argument." Where will it all end? "The next victims of such rule making may be whistlers, gum chewers, bone crackers, dandruff scratchers, lint pickers and popcorn eaters," in the words of one opponent of a Washington state ban on smoking in enclosed public places (quoted in Demarest 1976, p. 43).

Of course, just how slippery the slope is depends upon just how close an analogy there is between smoking and those other activities. Historically, smoking has been discussed alongside other "hurtful indulgences" and "stimulants" of various forms. Herbert Spencer (1893, pt. 3, secs. 214–15) lumped tobacco together with alcohol and tea as "stimulants" that people ought not really require if they were leading the ideally good life. Today, discussions of healthy life-styles tend to focus upon overeating and the lack of exercise in the place of tea on Spencer's list (Wikler 1978/1983, p. 35). And archenemies of government paternalism tend to lump prohibitions on smoking in public together with prohibitions on possessing handguns, on sale or use of alcoholic beverages, and on riding a motorcycle without a crash helmet (Buchanan 1986, pp. 339–40). What seems to be a constant and central point of comparison, across all these lists, is between our attitude toward smoking and our attitude toward drinking.

The two forms of regulation have indeed tended to travel together, historically. Having begun her career in politics as a news-paperwoman crusading against saloonkeepers, Lucy Page Gaston went on to found the Anti-Cigarette League. By 1909, the movement had persuaded the legislatures of fifteen states to ban the sale of cigarettes. Come World War I, though, the antismoking campaign was doomed: General Pershing cabled Washington insisting that "tobacco is as indispensable as the daily ration" for the fighting troops; and those speaking out against tobacco during the war were threatened with prosecution under the Espionage Act of 1917, so unpatriotic was their stand seen to be. Capitalizing on such sentiments, opponents of cigarette sales bans managed to get them repealed in all states by 1927, shortly before repeal of the antidrinking ordinances that had spawned the antismoking ones (Troyer and Markle 1983, pp. 34–41; U.S. DHHS 1986, p. 267).

Politically, there is a perfectly good explanation of how such linkages between different political issues come about. Studying the way in which the U.S. Senate's "safety" agenda evolved over the 1960s and 1970s, Walker (1977) tells the tale of a coalition organized around one good cause refusing simply to disband once it had won that war; instead, it went in search of other analogous battles to fight. Thus, the safety lobby was initially formed to press for mine safety regulations, based on well-established scientific principles. But it went on to lobby first for auto safety and then for occupational health and safety legislation, on which the science was substantially less secure, as one battle after another was won by the safety lobby. Politics, some say, is always a matter of problems looking for solutions, solutions looking for problems, and people looking for something to do next (Olsen 1972). Perhaps it is inevitable, therefore, that a prohibitionist lobby, established to stamp out one particularly odious product, will naturally seek some other products to try and prohibit once victory on the first front is within sight. At the beginning of the century, the path led from banning drinking to banning smoking, as "the success of the drys went to their heads" (Sinclair 1962, p. 201). Now the path looks like it is leading the other way.

There is, however, a certain philosophical point as well as a certain political inevitability in looking at the case for curtailing smoking alongside the case for curtailing other activities like drinking. One good way of testing to see whether we have found the right general principles for our smoking control policies is to see if we would be prepared to see the same broad policies applied, in similar circumstances, to the control of other activities. Or—what is merely another way of putting the same point—if we want to resist applying the same policies to other apparently analogous cases, we must either show that they are not really analogous at all or else we will be forced to abandon those principles for purposes of our smoking control policies as well.

Even having narrowed my focus to one particular comparison— the tobacco-alcohol analogy—I will be unable to do the other half of that pair full justice. There is as large a literature on the effects of alcohol and policies for controlling them as there is on tobacco. To discuss that literature and its philosophical implications fully would be to write a whole other book.

What I shall do here instead is something much more modest. I shall simply look at alcohol in light of the arguments I have given for controlling tobacco, to see to what extent the same arguments really would commit me to supporting controls on alcohol as well. My conclusions, to foreshadow, will be that the two products are importantly different on all these points of comparison, so the arguments I have given for controlling tobacco really do not commit me to supporting analogous controls on alcohol after all.

That, of course, is not to say that controls on drinking are not justified. There may well be some other principles altogether, irrelevant in the case of smoking but central to the case of drinking, that would justify the most stringent controls on alcohol. If so, my procedure here simply will not uncover them. Still, this limited attempt merely at breaking the analogy between tobacco and alcohol is the most ambitious task to which a book that is principally about the ethics of smoking can reasonably aspire.

The case against tobacco, laid out in Chapters 2 and 3 above, has been couched first in terms of harm to self from smoking and then in terms of harm to others from smoking. The question now before us is simply whether similar indictments can be made to stick in similar ways against alcohol.

Under the heading of "harm to self," the first point of disanalogy to be noted is this. Tobacco is harmful whenever it is smoked. As with all known carcinogens, there is no "safe" dose. The dose-response curve relating cigarettes smoked to lung cancer risk is monotonically increasing throughout its range. Alcohol, in contrast, seems medically "safe" in moderate doses and actually beneficial in small doses. How, exactly, it produces those results is still somewhat unclear: at present, the best guess is by reducing risk of cardiovascular disease, somehow. What is perfectly clear, however, is that the curve relating alcohol consumption to mortality takes on a U-shape: both nondrinkers and heavy drinkers have an age-adjusted mortality risk over half again higher than do moderate drinkers (Marmot et al. 1981, p. 581); and that relationship stands up perfectly well when all confounding factors (e.g., smoking) and selection biases (e.g., abstainers may have given up drinking because they were already sick) are taken into account.

Where exactly to set the limits to "safe" drinking has not yet been resolved. Anxious to "give clear information as to what constitutes safe or dangerous levels of drinking," the British Royal College of Psychiatrists (1979, p. 140) recommends "an intake of four pints of beer a day, four doubles of spirits, or one standard-sized bottle of wine constitutes reasonable guidelines for the upper limit of drinking." (Of course, as the Royal College goes on to say, "it is unwise to make a habit of drinking even at these levels, and anyone driving a vehicle should not drink at all before driving.") The U-shaped curve mentioned above begins turning up again at about half those levels of drinking—at about half those levels, drinking stops helping and starts harming health. But drinking does not seem to undo all the good it has done your health until those really rather high levels of consumption have been reached.

Debates over how exactly alcohol produces its beneficial effects on health, and where exactly to set the limits to safe drinking, should not obscure what is the central point for the present purposes. This is well captured by Congressman Mike Synar's regard that "tobacco is a unique product. It's the only product that . . . when used as intended still is harmful to your health. A doctor may say, 'Have a drink before you go to bed,' but I've never heard of one saying, 'Have a cigarette before you go to bed' " (quoted in Rovner 1986, p. 3052). To recall a statistic presented in section 2.1 above, cigarettes kill a quarter of their users. No other legal product can claim such a record.

Furthermore, and in a way following from that, is the sheer fact that very many fewer people die from alcohol than from tobacco. The number of deaths attributed to smoking is five times that attributable to alcohol in the United States (Ravenholt 1984, pp. 712–13). According to official estimates prepared by the U.S. Office of Management and Budget and the U.S. Council of Economic Advisers (1987, p. 184), the annual number of fatalities per million Americans is 2,950 from smoking but only 541 from drinking.

Equally significant, in light of what will be said later in this section, less than a third of alcohol-related deaths arise from diseases, per se, directly or indirectly attributable to the person's drinking. A clear majority arise from drink-related accidents rather than diseases (Ravenholt 1984, pp. 712–13; U.S. CEA, p. 184), and a very significant portion of those drink-related accidents result from the conjunction of drinking plus certain other forms of behavior on the part of the drinker, like drinking and driving. Indeed, fully a quarter of drinking-related deaths arise from motor vehicle accidents alone (Ravenholt 1984, pp. 712–13). In such cases, if we want to reduce the fatality toll we have the option of restraining either the drinking or the other behavior that, together with the drinking, causes death.

In short, the first thing that must be said about the harm to self arising from drinking is that there is very much less of it than the harm to self that arises from smoking—calculated in terms of deaths per annum, anyway. That does not take into account nonfatal harms from impaired functioning (the costs of loss of employment, family breakdown, etc.) that are more common with alcohol than tobacco, however. And in any case, even in terms of fatalities, although the numbers involved are fewer than with smoking they still are impressively large, with estimated fatalities in the United States from alcohol abuse edging toward 100,000 per year (Ravenholt 1984, p. 713). Fingarette (1988a, p. 11) is thus right to say that "chronic heavy drinking is rivalled only by habitual smoking as a major contributor to the nation's hospital and morgue populations." As such, it is undoubtedly a fit subject for moral concern—even if not quite so acute concern as smoking, perhaps.

Central to my discussion of the ethics of regulating tobacco to prevent harm to self, in Chapter 2 above, was the finding that smoking was addictive. If people start smoking before they are of the age of consent, and are addicted by the time they reach that age, then they have never had the opportunity to give their informed consent in any morally meaningful way to the risks of smoking. The risks cannot then be said to be voluntarily run, and legislation interfering with that risky behavior can be much more easily justified in consequence.

Much the same might be said of drinking. People start drinking before they are of the age of consent. By the World Health Organization standards, alcohol is addictive for at least some of its users

(WHO 1977; 1978; Royal College of Psychiatrists 1979, chap. 4). In the case of alcohol, that addiction evidence is more suspect, perhaps. For what it is worth, the great majority of alcohol-dependent smokers seeking treatment for alcohol abuse at a Toronto clinic reported that their strongest urges for cigarettes were at least as strong as their strongest urges for alcohol and that it would be harder for them to stop smoking than drinking (Kozlowski et al. 1989). We may be wary of subjective perceptions as an imperfect indicator of addictiveness, of course, but the behavioral evidence seems to suggest that those perceptions are correct in this case. Findings suggest that "one half of alcoholics will be abstinent . . . in any given month" (Marc Schuckit, quoted in Fingarette 1988a, p. 10); and that hardly looks like a matter of getting a regular "hit" of the substance to keep up the blood level, as is the case with heroin or even nicotine addiction. Still, the studies summarized and criticized by Fingarette (1970, 1988a, 1988b) are sufficiently convincing—despite his various criticisms—to suggest that problem drinking is not a purely behavioral problem.

Crucially, however, there is nothing in those studies to suggest that alcohol is addictive for everyone who starts using it, in a way that heroin and nicotine apparently are for the vast majority of people, anyway, who start using them. What those studies of the "alcohol dependence syndrome" suggest is, instead, that "a significant minority of the population has a distinctive biological vulnerability" to alcohol (Fingarette 1988a, p. 5).[34] In the words of the Royal College of Psychiatrists (1979, p. 1), "alcohol is a substance which is used widely and well by the majority of people who drink, and who derive nothing but pleasure and benefit from its use." In the words of the British government, "for the majority of drinkers of alcohol is harmless. It is the minority—the misusers—who can cause harm to themselves, and to others" (U.K. Department of Health and Social Security [DHSS] 1981).

The policy implications of the difference between a substance that is harmful for all users and one that is harmful only for some of its users are potentially enormous. If only some people are at risk,

---

34. It is therefore true but misleading to say that the relapse rates for drinkers trying to give up are about the same as for smokers and for heroin addicts (U.S. DHHS 1988, p. 314). The crucial question is how many, and which, drinkers are the ones trying to give up. In the case of smoking, the evidence is that most try to give up at some point or another, and then suffer a relapse. In the case of drinking, there is not the same evidence that all drinkers try at some point or another to give up. Insofar as it is only "problem drinkers" who try to give up in the first place, evidence of high relapse rates among those who do try to give up merely shows that those "problem drinkers" are addicted; it does not show that the vast majority who never felt the need to try to give up could not do so if they tried, or hence that they are addicted.

then the best policy would be one of screening for the vulnerability and targeting antidrinking policies at those most at risk, where possible. Insofar as screening or targeting is impossible, we may—depending upon exactly how many people are at risk, and on exactly how much of a risk they run—decide to run an antidrinking campaign aimed at the whole population. But really stringent measures will be necessarily less justifiable the fewer people in the population who are genuinely at risk.[35]

In any case, if we are concerned about the addictiveness of alcohol principally in connection with problems of informed consent, concern must principally be with people getting addicted before they reach the age of consent. And if that is our concern, then there are various policy measures we can pursue to prevent underage drinking. One is to impose—and genuinely enforce—a minimum legal drinking age of twenty-one.[36] By one estimate, that would reduce the number of heavy drinkers among American youths by more than 25 percent (Coate and Grossman 1988, p. 168).

When discussing the ethics of regulating tobacco to prevent harm to self in Chapter 2, I also considered utilitarian as well as informed-consent aspects of the problem. But for purposes of this brief comparison to the case of alcohol abuse, that discussion can be merged with the one of harm to others. The central point to be made

35. It may be true that there are advantages in focusing on "more malleable medium risk groups" rather than on very "high risk groups" who tend "to be intractable or treatment-resistent." But by Kreitman's (1986, pp. 361, 353) own calculations, it would take an across-the-board reduction of about 30 percent of current alcohol intake per capita to achieve the same health effects, in Britain, as if everyone were to drink within the "safe limits" set out above. Obviously, it is unrealistic to expect everyone to keep within the safe limits. By the same token, it is unrealistic—surely substantially more unrealistic—to expect everyone to cut consumption by almost a third.

36. That is being attempted, circuitously, via incentives built into the U.S. federal highway construction fund formula (Coate and Grossman 1988, pp. 145–46). Another way would be to impose swingeing new taxes on alcohol, particularly the beer that is the drink of choice among youths. Coate and Grossman (1988, pp. 1699–71) estimate that an eightfold increase in the federal excise tax on beer—which could be rationalized in terms of the tax's keeping pace with inflation, and of bringing the beer tax into line with that on spirits—might reduce the number of heavy drinkers among youths between 20 and 40 percent. These estimates have the support of President Reagan's Council of Economic Advisers (U.S. CEA 1987, pp. 187–88), which commends this strategy warmly. But Coate and Grossman (1988, p. 171) admit, "excise tax hikes impose welfare costs on all segments of the population, while a drinking age policy is targeted at the group in the population" that accounts for the problem—both the problem of addiction impairing informed consent, which is my focus here, and the problem that the young "account for a disproportionate share of motor accidents and deaths," which is Coate and Grossman's focus and mine below.

in both connections is this: whereas the harms under these headings from smoking arose as the inevitable consequences of smoking itself, the harms that indisputably do arise under these headings from drinking arise incidentally, from the conjunction of drinking with some other behavior (e.g., driving).[37] Thus, if we are to prevent harms under these headings from smoking, we must curtail smoking itself, either altogether or at least in confined public places. To prevent harms under these headings from drinking, it would be enough to prevent those other behaviors which, when conjoined with drinking, cause the harms.

Which strategy we should favor depends—based on the precepts set out in section 4.2 above—simply upon which factor is most under our control. No one would claim that laws against drunk driving work perfectly, as they stand. "None of the programs . . . to date has been able to sustain an increase in the probabilities of apprehending and punishing drunk drivers" (U.S. CEA 1987, p. 187), most importantly. Whether the flaw is in the whole approach, or merely in the implementation, remains unclear. Neither, however, is it easy to stop people from drinking. Like laws against drunk driving, laws against underage drinking will catch only part of all offenders; insofar as they raid the parental liquor cupboard, teenaged drinkers might similarly be undeterred by higher excise taxes. So all approaches are imperfect, and it remains to be seen which among them is least imperfect. It is entirely possible, though, that it will prove easier to stop people from driving when drunk than it is to stop them from drinking altogether. If so, then it is the driving rather than the drinking side of the drunk-driving conjunction that should be of preeminent concern to policymakers

Were this a book about drinking rather than smoking, all those points should be elaborated at much greater length, and many others added. For present purposes, however, perhaps those brief comments

37. Here I concentrate on indisputable physical harm. Notice, however, that insofar as the problem is one of others being bothered by an offensive nuisance, we already have in the case of drinking precisely the sorts of statutes I would like to see enacted for the case of smoking. In most American cities and states, it is an offense to drink in public, outside certain designated (i.e., licensed) premises; walking down the street with an open container of alcohol is characteristically illegal, in a way that walking down the corridor of a public building with a lit cigarette is not. Or, again, an offensive display of drunken excess in public invites arrest for being "drunk and disorderly" and spending the night in the drunk tank at the local jail. There is no equivalent in the case of smoking. Those emitting offensive odors from particularly smelly cigars are at no risk of being arrested (unless they are doing so in a legally designated no-smoking area). On the contrary, it will ordinarily be the offended nonsmoker who is locked up for starting a public affray when he throws water over the offending cigar in an attempt to douse it.

will be enough to demonstrate the disanalogies between drinking and smoking. At the very least, they allow me to say that the principles I have used to justify strict controls on smoking do not necessarily commit me to similarly strict controls on drinking.

4.10   BUSINESS ETHICS AND THE TOBACCO TRADE

Tobacco companies, like all public corporations, are fond of presenting themselves as "good corporate citizens." They give to charities. ("Buck" Duke, founder of the tobacco company American Brands, generously endowed Duke University.) They sponsor medical research. Generally, they live within the law and make their community a little better place. Or so they would have us believe.

Almost in passing, over the course of the preceding pages, I have mentioned evidence of various sorts that would suggest that this image of good corporate citizenship may be largely illusory. If true, this evidence would seem to suggest:

1. Tobacco companies have, apparently knowingly, marketed products that kill a quarter of their users even when used as intended; having done so knowingly, this harm might plausibly be said to have been inflicted intentionally rather than merely recklessly or in negligent disregard of the "duty of care" that companies are under, legally and morally, to provide customers with products that are safe.
2. There has been a conspiracy, within tobacco companies and between tobacco companies, to suppress or discredit these facts about their products, and in that way to defraud their customers by selling them products under false pretenses.
3. Tobacco companies have, apparently knowingly, engaged in deceptive advertising, implicitly or explicitly making untrue health claims for their products and appealing illicitly for youngsters to start smoking.
4. Tobacco companies have sponsored research that is biased in its conclusions, apparently in a deliberate effort to reassure worried smokers that "the jury is still out" on issues that by any reasonable scientific standards have long been settled.[38]
5. Tobacco companies or their subsidiaries have apparently bribed public officials abroad to facilitate the marketing of their products in those countries.

38. See Troyer and Markle 1983, pp. 95 ff. for details. They also sponsor social scientists and philosophers—who sometimes declare their interest (Tollison and Wagner 1988, p. x) and sometimes do not (Tollison 1986; see White 1988, pp. 219–20)—presumably in a similar attempt to muddy the moral waters.

All of those allegations have been made against tobacco companies. All would seem to be supported by some good evidence. Whether, ultimately, such allegations can be sustained will depend upon the fruits of factual enquiries that lie well outside the scope of this book. I do not want to get into those factual matters here.[39] Instead, I want merely to ask what would follow, should those allegations turn out to be true.

Certainly corporations that behaved in ways that tobacco companies are said to have behaved would be substantially at variance from ordinary canons of business ethics (Beauchamp and Bowie 1979). What, however, follows from the finding that a firm or an industry is "unethical"? Some might say that it was naive ever to expect otherwise. Business is business. Nice guys finish last.

Depending upon the depths of the immorality involved, much might follow from a judgment of unethical practice. Corporations might, most dramatically, be liable to criminal prosecution—as Ford Motor Company found with regard to the Pinto—if the facts of the case can sustain a charge of manslaughter, reckless homicide, or some such (Epstein 1980). Conspiracy to defraud is, similarly, a criminal offense. And "intentional torts," though arising from a civil action, carry exemplary, punitive damages that might vastly outstrip the purely compensatory damages for harm actually done to plaintiffs. The corporation is—and has, since at least the mid-nineteenth century, been—indisputably a person for purposes of criminal prosecution, as for so much else (Anonymous 1979). And that is morally as it should be (French 1984, chaps. 13, 14).

---

39. Not least because I do not want to be sued. Despite the tobacco industry's strong defense of free speech when it comes to banning cigarette advertising, it has no hesitation in using the legal system to silence its critics wherever possible. The largest court-ordered libel award ever upheld on appeal—for some $3 million in presumed and actual punitive damages—was against the Columbia Broadcasting System and a commentator on its Chicago affiliate, Walter Jacobson, for a 1981 broadcast drawing on an FTC study of the ways in which tobacco companies try to attract new smokers (Taylor 1988). The U.S. Court of Appeals prefaces its decision by saying that it is "difficult to imagine how the tobacco people can be libeled." But it concludes that a tobacco company was libeled when Jacobson attributed to them a marketing strategy of relating the cigarette to "pot, wine, beer, and sex." The company's argument, which the court upheld, was that that constitutes libel because the document being quoted there was merely a recommendation from a marketing-and-research firm to the company's advertising agency; and there was no evidence that the tobacco company ever actually implemented that strategy, in precisely the form that recommendation suggested (Bauer 1987, pp. 1122–25). The record contains much to cast the reporter in this case in a very bad light indeed. But it should also be noted that "Jacobson's case was fatally weakened by the judge in the case, who refused to admit the testimony of the author of the report, a Federal Trade Commission employee, who was not allowed to say to the jury what he said to reporters outside the courtroom—that he thought Jacobson's commentary fairly reflected the FTC's report about cigarette advertising" (White 1988, p. 218).

Even if we stop short of criminal prosecution of an offending corporation, a long chain of ethical abuses might lead us to conclude that a firm or a whole industry was unworthy of our trust. The loss of reputation is much feared among corporations, and in general publicity is one of the most powerful sanctions to be used against corporate offenders (Fisse and Braithwaite 1983).

The effects of this sanction have traditionally been felt through the market, as individuals refrain from doing business with untrustworthy corporations. As President Reagan's Council of Economic Advisers (U.S. CEA 1987, p. 181) says, "safety is a desirable product characteristic," and "companies that earn reputations for making unsafe products face retribution in the marketplace, just as if they charged excessive prices or offered shoddy goods." A reputation for being unworthy of trust will have similar consequences. Insofar as consumers are incapable of monitoring product quality perfectly for themselves—and few of us have the laboratories in the back shed that that would require—we must trust corporations to produce according to acceptable standards. If we cannot trust them to do so, we seek some other producer whom we can trust, or we shun the product altogether (Arrow 1973).

The public has already lost faith in the tobacco industry as a whole. A panel of the U.S. Court of Appeals that included Richard Posner—hardly an opponent of business in general—commented recently that "the attitude of most knowledgeable and disinterested persons toward the tobacco industry is certainly negative" and "it has been negative for the past decade" at least (Bauer 1987, p. 1122). The addiction evidence cited in section 2.2.2 may help to explain why this has not had quite such catastrophic consequences for sales of the industry's product as Arrow predicts it should for rational consumers.

If a firm or a whole industry has shown itself to be systematically unworthy of public trust, there might be a sanction to be collectively imposed, as well. Governments might consider lifting the license or revoking the charter of a corporation or a set of corporations, in really dire circumstances. Corporations, after all, operate under a public charter and often under license from the state; if the terms and conditions implicitly and explicitly contained within them have been breached, revocation is always possible (French 1984, pp. 188–90).[40]

---

40. The courts, of course, are reluctant to pursue this option on their own, so the impetus here might have to come from the legislative rather than judicial branch. But the Model Penal Code does contain the following provision: "The (prosecuting attorney) is authorized to institute civil proceedings in the appropriate court of general jurisdiction to forfeit the charter of a corporation organized under the laws of this state

At the very least, a persistent pattern of unethical conduct would make us systematically suspicious of any claims made by or on behalf of a firm or industry. In general, arguments from authority cut no ice in philosophy: the fact that Aristotle thought X was true is, in and of itself, no reason for our believing that X is true. And, conversely, the fact that a certain argument is being advanced by someone known not to be a reliable reporter does not, in and of itself, provide any reason for believing that that argument is necessarily false. But when agents who are known to be unscrupulous have a vested interest in the matter, we reasonably suspect that they will bias accounts in their favor (Galbraith 1959). For this reason, we may well be suspicious of medical evidence casting doubt on the harms of smoking coming from research sponsored by the tobacco industry. Ordinary social intercourse requires us to operate a principle of charity, presuming the veracity of others' statements unless we have reason to doubt them. In the case of agents with a known pattern of immoral conduct, that presumption must be reversed, at least in cases where we know their interests would be well served by falsehoods.

Insofar as it is important to us, in any of these ways, to single out certain firms or industries for special treatment, it follows that it is important not to let them hide their identities through diversification or corporate mergers. Tobacco companies are busily diversifying, with American Brands making Sunshine Hydrox cookies, Philip Morris brewing Miller beer, and R. J. Reynolds producing both Chun King and Del Monte foods (Moskowitz, Katz, and Levering 1980, pp. 765–83). If the evidence of their past practices suggests that they are pariah corporations deserving of some special social stigma, perhaps we ought not let them merge their identities with those of other more respectable enterprises in this fashion, whatever the corporate logic underlying the merger.

---

or to revoke the certificate authorizing a foreign corporation to conduct business in this state. The court may order the charter forfeited or the certificate revoked upon finding (i) that the board of directors or a high managerial agent acting on behalf of the corporation has, in conducting the corporation's affairs, purposely engaged in a persistent course of criminal conduct and (ii) that for the prevention of future criminal conduct of the same character, the public interest required the charter of the corporation to be forfeited and the corporation to be dissolved or the certificate to be revoked" (ALI 1974, sec. 6.04, clause 2a).

5   Conclusion

Forty-two states have now enacted restrictions—in at least nine cases extensive ones—on smoking in public places. Smoking is now banned or restricted in over a third of private-sector business establishments (U.S. DHHS 1986, pp. 267, 285; 1989, pp. 571–80). New regulations require that in U.S. government buildings "smoking is to be held to an absolute minimum in areas where there are nonsmokers" (U.S. General Services Administration [GSA] 1986). Smoking is banned on U.S. domestic flights of less than two hours' duration (PL 100–202, enacted 1987). Clearly, those responsible for governing our society have increasingly come to conclude that clean indoor air is a quality-of-life issue that is a fitting concern for socially enforced sanctions.[1]

To date, the argument has been won principally on the basis of harm-to-other style claims. President Reagan's Council of Economic Advisers (U.S. CEA 1987, p. 181) is strongly predisposed to say, "If responsible adults voluntarily undertake risky activities . . . , their choices must be respected in a society that values individual liberty and autonomy." Still, even they must concede that "this general principle of respecting personal choice is compatible . . . with governmental action to reduce risk . . . when the actions of some increase the risks to others." Evidence on the harmfulness of passive smoking has convinced policymakers that smoking is one such action, and they have increasingly restricted it in enclosed public places in consequence.

In future, the argument will inevitably shift more to harm-to-self style propositions. If the addiction evidence discussed in Chapter 2 is indeed persuasive, then we can no longer treat smoking as a case of

---

1. The focus here is on one particular pollutant—tobacco smoke. See, more generally, Doggett and Friedman (1973), U.S. General Accounting Office (1980), Repace (1982), and Kerr (1988).

"responsible adults voluntarily undertaking risky activities," in the Council of Economic Advisers' formula. People begin smoking before they are responsible adults; by the time they are responsible adults, their nicotine addiction will have rendered their continued smoking largely involuntary. Policies justified as aids in preventing harms to oneself are bound to be opposed as paternalistic. But helping addicts who want to break the habit is not offensively paternalistic; nor is helping people avoid acquiring addictions they would later want to renounce. Advertising bans, swingeing taxes, and perhaps even prohibiting over-the-counter sales of cigarettes can all be justified on grounds of that inoffensively weak-paternalistic sort.

In short, on the best scientific evidence available, smoking has long ago ceased to be a private-regarding vice best treated as such. It is high time that philosophers stopped talking as if it were.

Of course, what practical consequences might follow from philosophers talking one way rather than another is an open question. The slide between "is" and "ought" is blocked in both directions. Just as we cannot infer that something ought to be done merely because it has long been done, so too we cannot infer that something is or will soon be the case merely because it should be.

The political punch of moral philosophy is distinctly limited, especially when it is up against the entrenched economic interests and the consequently well-funded lobby of the tobacco industry. The tales of its shenanigans are legion. Anything like a complete account would fill many a book.[2]

In being realistic about the political power of moral philosophy, however, we ought not be unduly sanguine. Its power is limited, but nonetheless real and perhaps crucial. More than moralizing will be required to carry into practice the reforms here recommended. Still, moral philosophy is an indispensible first step in that larger political campaign. We need to be persuaded that something ought be done before there is any hope whatsoever that it will.

---

2. Indeed, many excellent books already have been written on precisely these themes: Neuberger 1963; Fritschler 1969; Taylor 1985; Wilkinson 1986; White 1988. Those interested in political war stories should look there.

References

This list provides details of all the studies cited in the text. Scholars and students wishing to pursue these issues further should turn first to the asterisked, and especially the double-asterisked, items.

Ackerman, Bruce A. 1977. *Private Property and the Constitution.* New Haven, Conn.: Yale University Press.

Aitken, P. P.; Leather, D. S.; and O'Hagan, F. J. 1985. Children's Perceptions of Advertisements for Cigarettes. *Social Science and Medicine* 21:785–97.

Aitkin, P. P.; Leather, D. S.; O'Hagan, F. J.; and Squair, S. I. 1987. Children's Awareness of Cigarette Advertisements and Brand Imagery. *British Journal of Addiction* 82:615–22.

Alexander, H. M.; Calcott, R.; and Dobson, A. J. 1983. Cigarette Smoking and Drug Use in Schoolchildren. IV. Factors Associated with Changes in Smoking Behaviors. *International Journal of Epidemiology* 12:59–65.

American Law Institute (ALI). 1974. Model Penal Code. In *Uniform Laws Annotated*, vol. 10, pp. 433–746. St. Paul, Minn.: West.

*American Medical Association (AMA). Office of the General Counsel. 1986. Tobacco Product Liability. *Journal of the American Medical Association* 255:1034–37.

American Psychiatric Association (APA). 1987. *Diagnostic and Statistical Manual of Mental Disorders.* 3d ed. Washington, D.C.: APA.

Anonymous. 1979. Developments in the Law: Corporate Crime—Regulating Corporate Behavior Through Criminal Sanctions. *Harvard Law Review* 92:1227–1375.

Anonymous. 1981. Note: Quasi-suspect Classes and Proof of Discriminatory Intent: A New Model. *Yale Law Journal* 90:912–31.

Anonymous. 1984. Note: Handguns and Product Liability. *Harvard Law Review* 97:1912–28.

*Anonymous. 1986. Note: Plaintiff's Conduct as a Defense to Claims against Cigarette Manufacturers. *Harvard Law Review* 99:809–27.

Anonymous. 1988. Busman's Damages Could Shock Employers into Smoking Ban. *Sydney Morning Herald*, July 22, p. 1.

Armitage, P. 1978. Discussion of Burch 1978. *Journal of the Royal Statistical Society*, ser. A, 141:458–60.

Arrow, Kenneth J. 1973. Social Responsibility and Economic Efficiency. *Public Policy* 21:303–17.

140   *References*

Atkins, Liz, and Jarrett, David. 1979. The Significance of "Significance" Tests. In *Demystifying Social Statistics*, ed. Ian Miles and Jeff Evans, pp. 87–109. London: Pluto Press.

*Atkinson, A. B. 1974. Smoking and the Economics of Government Intervention. In *The Economics of Health and Medical Care*, ed. Mark Perlman, pp. 428–41. London: Macmillan.

Atkinson, A. B.; Gomulka, Joanna; and Stern, Nicholas. 1984. Household Expenditure on Tobacco, 1970–1980: Evidence from the Family Expenditure Survey. Working Paper no. 57, Economic & Social Research Council Programme on Taxation, Incentives and the Distribution of Wealth. London: London School of Economics.

Atkinson, A. B., and Meade, T. W. 1974. Methods and Preliminary Findings in Assessing the Economic and Health Services Consequences of Smoking, with Particular Reference to Lung Cancer. *Journal of the Royal Statistical Society,* ser. A, 137:297–312.

Atkinson, A. B., and Skegg, J. L. 1973. Antismoking Publicity and the Demand for Tobacco in the UK. *Manchester School of Economic and Social Studies* 41:265–82.

Atkinson, A. B., and Townsend, J. L. 1977. Economic Aspects of Reduced Smoking. *Lancet* 8036:492–94.

Ayres, Robert L. 1983. *Banking on the Poor: The World Bank and World Poverty.* Cambridge, Mass.: MIT Press.

Baggott, Rob. 1986. By Voluntary Agreement: The Politics of Instrument Selection. *Public Administration* (London) 64:51–67.

Barrett, James E. 1987. Opinion of the U.S. Court of Appeals. *Grusendorf v. City of Oklahoma City.* 816 F.2d 539 (10th Cir. 1987).

Barry, Brian. 1965. *Political Argument.* London: Routledge & Kegan Paul.

Barry, Brian. 1979. Is Democracy Special? In *Philosophy, Politics and Society,* 5th ser., ed. Peter Laslett and James S. Fishkin, pp. 155–96. Oxford: Blackwell.

Battin, Margaret P. 1987. Age Rationing and the Just Distribution of Health Care: Is There a Duty to Die? *Ethics* 97:317–40.

Bauer, William J. 1987. Opinion of the U.S. Court of Appeals. *Brown & Williamson Tobacco Corp. v. Jacobson.* 827 F.2d 1119 (7th Cir. 1987).

Beauchamp, Tom L., and Bowie, Norman E., eds. 1979. *Ethical Theory and Business.* Englewood Cliffs, N.J.: Prentice-Hall.

Benfari, Robert C.; Ockene, Judith K.; and McIntyre, Kevin M. 1982. Control of Cigarette-Smoking from a Psychological Perspective. *Annual Review of Public Health* 3:101–28.

Benham, Lee. 1981. Comments on Lewit, Coate and Grossman (1981). *Journal of Law and Economics* 24:571–73.

Berle, A. A., Jr. 1952. Constitutional Limitations on Corporate Activity—Protection of Personal Rights from Invasion through Economic Power. *University of Pennsylvania Law Review* 100:933–55.

Blackstone, William. 1783. *Commentaries on the Laws of England.* London: W. Strahan.

Blasi, Vincent, and Monaghan, Henry Paul. 1986. The First Amendment and Cigarette Advertising. *Journal of the American Medical Association* 256:502–9

Bleda, P. R., and Sandman, P. H. 1977. In Smoke's Way: Socioemotional Reactions to Another's Smoking. *Journal of Applied Psychology* 62:452–58.

Boddewyn, J. J. 1986. Tobacco Advertising in a Free Society. In Tollison, ed., 1986, pp. 309–32.

Bohlen, F. H. 1908. The Moral Duty to Aid Others as a Basis of Tort Liability. *University of Pennsylvania Law Review* 56:217–44, 316–38.

Borgida, E., and Nisbett, R. E. 1977. The Differential Impact of Abstract vs. Concrete Information on Decisions. *Journal of Applied Social Psychology* 7:258–71.

Botkin, Jeffrey R. 1988. The Fire-safe Cigarette. *Journal of the American Medical Association* 260:226–29.

Bradford Hill, Austin. 1965. The Environment and Disease: Association or Causation? *Proceedings of the Royal Society of Medicine* 58, no. 5:7–12.

Brandt, R. B. 1985. A Motivational Theory of Excuses in the Criminal Law. In *Nomos XXVII: Criminal Justice*, ed. J. R. Pennock and J. W. Chapman, pp. 165–98. New York: New York University Press.

Bremner, Charles. 1988. US Tobacco Giants "Plotted to Mislead Smokers." *Times* (London), April 23, p. 7.

Breslow, Lester. 1982. Control of Cigarette Smoking from a Public Policy Perspective. *Annual Review of Public Health* 3:129–52.

Breyer, Stephen. 1982. *Regulation and Its Reform*. Cambridge, Mass.: Harvard University Press.

British Medical Association (BMA). Public Affairs Division. 1986. *Smoking Out the Barons: The Campaign against the Tobacco Industry.* Chichester: Wiley, for the BMA.

Brown, John R. 1987. Opinion of the U.S. Court of Appeals. *Palmer v. Liggett Group, Inc.* 825 F.2d 620 (1st Cir. 1987).

Brownlee, K. A. 1965. A Review of "Smoking and Health" (U.S. DHEW 1964). *Journal of the American Statistical Association* 60:722–39.

*Buchanan, James M. 1970. In Defense of *Caveat Emptor*. *University of Chicago Law Review* 38:64–73.

Buchanan, James M. 1986. Politics and Meddlesome Preferences. In Tollison, ed., 1986, pp. 335–42.

*Burch, P. R. J. 1978. Smoking and Lung Cancer: The Problem of Inferring Cause. *Journal of the Royal Statistical Society*, ser. A, 141:437–58.

Burch, P. R. J. 1986. Health Risks of Passive Smoking: Problems of Interpretation. *Environment International* 12:23–28.

Cain, Glen G., and Watts, Harold W. 1970. Problems in Making Policy Inferences from the Coleman Report. *American Sociological Review* 35:228–42.

Calabresi, Guido. 1970. *The Costs of Accidents*. New Haven, Conn.: Yale University Press.

Calfee, John E. 1986. The Ghost of Cigarette Advertising Past. *Regulation* 10, no. 6:35–45.

Califano, Joseph A., Jr. 1981. *Governing America*. New York: Simon & Schuster.

Castleman, Barry I. 1979. The Export of Hazardous Factories to Developing Countries. *International Journal of Health Services* 9:569–606.

Castleman, Barry I. 1985. The Double Standard in Industrial Hazards. In Ives, ed., 1985, pp. 60–89.

Cederlof, R.; Friberg, L.; and Lundman, T. 1977. The Interactions of Smoking, Environment and Heredity and Their Implications for Disease Etiology. *Acta Medica Scandinavica*, vol. 612 (suppl. 1).

Chapman, Simon. 1985. *Cigarette Advertising and Smoking: A Review of the Evidence*. London: British Medical Association. Reprinted in BMA 1986, pp. 79–98.

Chapman, Simon. 1986. *Great Expectorations: Advertising and the Tobacco Industry.* London: Comedia.

Chapman, Simon, and Fitzgerald, Bill. 1982. Brand Preferences and Advertisement Recall in Adolescent Smokers: Some Implications for Health Promotion. *American Journal of Public Health* 72:491–94.

Chase Econometrics. 1985. *The Economic Impact of the Tobacco Industry on the United States Economy.* Bala Cynwyd, Penn.: Chase Econometrics, for the Tobacco Institute.

Christensen, Cheryl. 1978. World Hunger: A Structural Approach. *International Organization* 32:745–74.

Coase, R. H. 1960. The Problem of Social Cost. *Journal of Law and Economics* 3:1–44.

Coate, Douglas, and Grossman, Michael. 1988. Effects of Alcoholic Beverage Prices and Legal Drinking Ages on Youth Alcohol Use. *Journal of Law and Economics* 31:145–71.

Cohen, Marc I. 1987. *Cigarette Product Liability Litigation.* New York: Bernstein/James Capel.

Cohen, Nicholas. 1981. Smoking, Health, and Survival Prospects in Bangladesh. *Lancet* 8229:1090–93.

Coleman, Geoff. 1985. The Great Ad Wars. *Australian Society* 4, no. 10:11–14.

Cox, Archibald. 1980. Forward: Freedom of Expression in the Burger Court. *Harvard Law Review* 94:1–73.

Cox, Howard, and Smith, Ron. 1984. Political Approaches to Smoking Control: A Comparative Analysis. *Applied Economics* 16:569–82.

Crain, W. M.; Deaton, T.; Holcombe, R.; and Tollison, R. 1977. Rational Choice and the Taxation of Sin. *Journal of Public Economics* 8:239–45.

Cushner, I. M. 1981. Maternal Behavior and Perinatal Risks: Alcohol, Smoking and Drugs. *Annual Review of Public Health* 2:201–18.

Daniels, Norman. 1985. *Just Health Care.* Cambridge: Cambridge University Press.

Davis, Ronald M. 1987. Current Trends in Cigarette Advertising and Marketing. *New England Journal of Medicine* 316:725–32.

Day, Charles W. 1836. *Hints on Etiquette and the Usages of Society, with a Glance at Bad Habits.* 3d ed. London: Turnstile Press, 1947.

*Daynard, Richard A. 1988. Tobacco Liability Litigation as a Cancer Control Strategy. *Journal of the National Cancer Institute* 80, no. 1:9–13.

*Daynard, Richard A.; Popper, Edward T.; and Gruzalski, Bart K. 1986. *Selling Death: Individual and Organizational Responsibility and the Tobacco Industry.* A faculty colloquium, Northeastern University. Boston, Mass.: Northeastern University, Office of the Provost, video.

Demarest, Michael. 1976. Smoking: Fighting Fire with Ire. *Time* 107, no. 2 (January 12):42–43.

Den Uyl, Douglas J., and Machan, Tibor R. 1988. Should Cigarette Advertising Be Banned? *Public Affairs Quarterly* 2:19–30.

Doggett, K. M., and Friedman, D. J. 1973. Note: Legislation for Clean Air: An Indoor Front. *Yale Law Journal* 82:1042–54.

Doll, Richard; and Peto, Richard. 1981. The Causes of Cancer: Quantitative Estimates of Avoidable Risks of Cancer in the United States Today. *Journal of the National Cancer Institute* 66:1193–1308. Reprinted as *The Causes of Cancer.* Oxford: Oxford University Press, 1981.

*Dworkin, Gerald. 1972. Paternalism. *Monist* 56, no. 1:64–84. Reprinted in Sartorius, ed., 1983, pp. 19–34.

Edell, Marc Z., and Gisser, Stewart M. 1985. *Cipollone v. Liggett Group, Inc.:* The Application of Theories of Liability in Current Cigarette Litigation. *New York State Journal of Medicine* 85, no. 7:318–21.

Eichenwald, Kurt. 1988. Setback to Tobacco Industry Is Termed Slim by Analysts. *New York Times,* June 14, p. B4.

Epstein, Richard A. 1980. Is Pinto Criminal? *Regulation* 4, no. 2:15–21.

Etzioni, Amitai. 1978. Individual Will and Social Conditions: Toward an Effective Health Maintenance Policy. *Annals of the American Academy of Political and Social Science* 437:62–73.

Eysenck, H. J. 1980. *The Causes and Effects of Smoking.* London: Maurice Temple Smith.

*Eysenck, H. J. 1986. Smoking and Health. In Tollison, ed., 1986, pp. 17–88.

Feinberg, Joel. 1970. *Doing and Deserving.* Princeton, N.J.: Princeton University Press.

Feinberg, Joel. 1971. Legal Paternalism. *Canadian Journal of Philosophy* 1:106–24. Reprinted in Sartorius, ed., 1983, pp. 3–18.

Feinberg, Joel. 1984. *Harm to Others.* New York: Oxford University Press.

Feinberg, Joel. 1985. *Offense to Others.* New York: Oxford University Press.

Feinberg, Joel. 1986. *Harm to Self.* New York: Oxford University Press.

**Fielding, Jonathan E. 1985. Smoking: Health Effects and Control. *New England Journal of Medicine* 313:491–98, 555–61.

Fingarette, Herbert. 1970. The Perils of *Powell:* In Search of a Factual Foundation for the "Disease" Concept of Alcoholism. *Harvard Law Review* 83:793–812.

Fingarette, Herbert. 1975. Addiction and Criminal Responsibility. *Yale Law Journal* 84:413–44.

Fingarette, Herbert. 1988a. Alcoholism: The Mythical Disease. *Public Interest* 91:3–22.

Fingarette, Herbert. 1988b. *Heavy Drinking: The Myth of Alcoholism as a Disease.* Berkeley and Los Angeles: University of California Press.

Fischer, P. M.; Richards, J. W.; Berman, E. J.; and Krugman, D. M. 1989. Recall and Eye Tracking Study of Adolescents Viewing Tobacco Advertisements. *Journal of the American Medical Association* 261:84–89.

Fisher, Ronald A. 1957. Letter to the Editor: Dangers of Cigarette Smoking. *British Journal of Medicine* 2:297–98. Reprinted in Fisher 1959 and Fisher 1974, vol. 5, pp. 378–9.

Fisher, Ronald A. 1958. Cigarettes, Cancer and Statistics. *Centennial Review* 2:151–66. Reprinted in Fisher 1959 and Fisher 1974, 5:407–22.

Fisher, Ronald A. 1959. *Smoking: The Cancer Controversy: Some Attempts to Assess the Evidence.* Edinburgh: Oliver & Boyd. Reprinted in Fisher 1974, 5:377–80, 385–432.

Fisher, Ronald A. 1974. *Collected Papers,* ed. J. H. Bennett. Adelaide: University of Adelaide.

Fisse, Brent, and Braithwaite, John. 1983. *The Impact of Publicity on Corporate Offenders.* Albany: State University of New York Press.

Fitzgerald, P. J. 1961. Voluntary and Involuntary Acts. In *Oxford Essays in Jurisprudence,* 1st ser., ed. A. G. Guest, pp. 1–28. Oxford: Clarendon.

Fletcher, George P. 1978. *Rethinking Criminal Law.* Boston: Little, Brown.

Fletcher, John C. 1981. The Fetus as Patient: Ethical Issues. *Journal of the American Medical Association* 246:772–73.

Fortas, Abe. 1968. Dissenting Opinion. *Powell v. Texas.* 392 US 514, 554–70.

Fox, S. J. 1963. Physical Disorder, Consciousness and Criminal Liability. *Columbia Law Review* 63:645–68.

Frankfurt, Harry G. 1971. Freedom of the Will and the Concept of a Person. *Journal of Philosophy* 68:5–20.

Freedman, Alix M. 1988. Smokers' Rights Campaign Suffers from Lack of Dedicated Recruits. *Wall Street Journal,* April 11.

Freedman, Alix M. 1989. Past Is Ominous for Substitute Smokes. *Wall Street Journal,* June 15.

French, Peter A. 1984. *Collective and Corporate Responsibility.* New York: Columbia University Press.

Friedman, Milton, and Friedman, Rose. 1980. *Free to Choose.* Harmondsworth, Mddx.: Penguin.

Fritschler, A. Lee. 1969. *Smoking and Politics: Policymaking and the Federal Bureaucracy.* New York: Appleton-Century-Crofts.

Froggatt, P., chairman. 1988. *Smoking and Health.* Fourth Report of the Independent Scientific Committee, UK Department of Health and Social Security. London: Her Majesty's Stationery Office.

Fuchs, Victor R. 1982. Time Preference and Health: An Exploratory Study. In *Economic Aspects of Health,* ed. Victor R. Fuchs, pp. 93–120. Chicago: University of Chicago Press.

Fujii, E. T. 1980. The Demand for Cigarettes: Further Empirical Evidence and Its Implications for Public Policy. *Applied Economics* 12:479–89.

Galbraith, John Kenneth, 1959. Letter to the Editor: Findings on Smoking. *New York Times,* August 19, p. 28.

Garland, C.; Barret-Connor, E.; Suarez, L.; Criqui, M. H.; and Wingard, D. L. 1985. Effects of Passive Smoking on Ischemic Heart Disease Mortality in Nonsmokers. *American Journal of Epidemiology* 121:645–50.

Garner, Donald W. 1977. Cigarettes and Welfare Reform. *Emory Law Journal* 26:269–335.

Garner, Donald W. 1980. Cigarette Dependency and Civil Liability: A Modest Proposal. *Southern California Law Review* 53:1371–1465.

Gewirth, Alan. 1980. Health Rights and the Prevention of Cancer. *American Philosophical Quarterly* 17:117–25.

Gibson, Mary. 1985. Consent and Autonomy. In *To Breathe Freely,* ed. Mary Gibson, pp. 141–68. Totowa, N.J.: Rowman & Allanheld.

Godfrey, Christine, and Maynard, Alan. 1988. Economic Aspects of Tobacco Use and Taxation Policy. *British Medical Journal* 297:339–43.

Goodin, Robert E. 1980. No Moral Nukes. *Ethics* 90:417–49.

Goodin, Robert E. 1982. *Political Theory and Public Policy.* Chicago: University of Chicago Press.

Goodin, Robert E. 1985. *Protecting the Vulnerable.* Chicago: University of Chicago Press.

Goodin, Robert E. 1986. The Principle of Voluntary Agreement. *Public Administration* (London) 64:435–44.

Goodin, Robert E. 1988. *Reasons for Welfare.* Princeton, N.J.: Princeton University Press.

Goodin, Robert E. 1989. Theories of Compensation. *Oxford Journal of Legal Studies,* 9:56–75.

Gori, G. B.; Richter, B. J.; and Yu, W. K. 1984. Economics and Extended Longevity: A Case Study. *Preventive Medicine* 13:396–410.

Gorovitz, Samuel. 1982. *Doctors' Dilemmas.* New York: Oxford University Press.

Grabosky, Peter, and Braithwaite, John. 1986. *Of Manners Gentle: Enforcement Strategies of Australian Business Regulatory Agencies.* Melbourne: Oxford University Press.

Gray, H. P., and Walter, I. 1986. The Economic Contribution of the Tobacco Industry to the Aggregate Economy. In Tollison, ed., 1986, pp. 271–84.

Gray, Nigel. 1989. Taking Money from the Devil in Victoria. *British Medical Journal* 298:141.

Gray, P. B. 1988. Smoking Foes Cite New Evidence Emerging in Tobacco Liability Suit. *Wall Street Journal,* April 4.

Grotius, Hugo. 1625. *The Law of War and Peace,* trans. F. W. Kelsey, ed. J. B. Scott. New York: Oceana, 1964.

Hale, Matthew. 1694. *The History of the Pleas of the Crown.* Rev. ed. London: Sollom Emlyn, 1736.

Hall, Jerome. 1944. Intoxication and Criminal Liability. *Harvard Law Review* 57:1045–84.

Hamilton, James L. 1972. The Demand for Cigarettes: Advertising, the Health Scare, and the Cigarette Advertising Ban. *Review of Economics and Statistics* 54:401–11.

Hanushek, Eric A., and Kain, John F. 1972. On the Value of *Equality of Educational Opportunity* as a Guide to Public Policy. In *On Equality of Educational Opportunity,* ed. Frederick Mosteller and D. P. Moynihan, pp. 116–45. New York: Random House.

Harrison, Larry. 1986. Tobacco Battered and the Pipes Shattered: A Note on the Fate of the First British Campaign against Tobacco Smoking. *British Journal of Addiction* 81:553–58.

Hart, H. L. A., and Honoré, Tony. 1985. *Causation in the Law,* 2d ed. Oxford: Clarendon.

Helyar, John. 1987. RJR Is Expected to Unveil "Smokeless" Cigarette Today. *Wall Street Journal,* September 14.

Helyar, John. 1988. RJR Plans to Market Smokeless Cigarette as Breakthrough with Hefty Price Tag. *Wall Street Journal,* August 30.

Hencke, D. 1989. Tobacco Ad Curb Planned. *Guardian* (London), April 21.

Himmelfarb, Gertrude. 1988. Manners into Morals: What the Victorians Knew. *American Scholar* 57, no. 2:332–33.

Hobbes, Thomas. 1651. *Leviathan.* London: Andrew Crooke.

Hume, David. 1760. Of the Original Contract. In *Essays, Literary, Moral and Political.* London: A. Millar.

Infante, G. Cabrera. 1985. *Holy Smoke.* London: Faber & Faber.

Ives, Jane H., ed. 1985. *The Export of Hazards.* London: Routledge & Kegan Paul.

Jackson, Thomas H., and Jeffries, John Calvin, Jr. 1979. Commercial Speech: Economic Due Process and the First Amendment. *Virginia Law Review* 65:1–41.

Jacobson, Philip. 1989. Allez les Fumeurs! *Times* (London), April 6, p. 12.

Janson, Donald. 1988. Cigarette Maker Assessed Damages in Smoker's Death. *New York Times,* June 14, pp. A1, B4.

Jenkins, Maggie; McEwan, James; Moreton, Wendy J.; East, Robert; Seymour, Linda; and Goodin, Margo. 1987. *Smoking Policies at Work.* London: Health Education Authority.

Jones, Peter. 1980. Blasphemy, Offensiveness and the Law. *British Journal of Political Science* 10:129–48.

Kahneman, D.; Slovic, P.; and Tversky, A., eds. 1982. *Judgment under Uncertainty.* Cambridge: Cambridge University Press.

Kelman, Mark. 1979. Choice and Utility. *Wisconsin Law Review* 1979:769–97.

Kerr, Robert A. 1988. Indoor Radon: The Deadliest Pollutant. *Science* 240:606–8.

King, Susan B. 1985. Hazardous Exports: A Consumer Perspective. In Ives, ed., 1985, pp. 1–17.

Kirchheimer, Otto. 1942. Criminal Omissions. *Harvard Law Review* 55:615–42.

Kmiec, Douglas. 1986. Should Tobacco Advertising Be Banned? The Wrong Solution. *American Bar Association Journal* 72, no. 12:39.

Knowles, John H. 1977. The Responsibility of the Individual. *Daedalus* 106, no. 1:57–80.

Kozlowski, Lynn T.; Appel, C.-P.; Frecker, Richard C.; and Khouw, Virginia. 1982. Nicotine, a Prescription Drug Available without Prescription. *Lancet* 8267:334.

Kozlowski, L. T.; Wilkinson, A.; Skinner, W.; Kent, C.; Franklin, T.; and Pope M. , 1989. Comparing Tobacco Cigarette Dependence with Other Drug Dependencies. *Journal of the American Medical Association* 261:898–901.

Kreitman, Norman. 1986. Alcohol Consumption and the Preventive Paradox. *British Journal of Addiction* 81:353–63.

Kristein, M. M. 1983. How Much Can Business Expect to Profit from Smoking Cessation? *Preventive Medicine* 12:358–81.

Lazurus, Peter, chairman. 1988. *First Report of the Committee for Monitoring Agreements on Tobacco Advertising and Sponsorship.* London: Her Majesty's Stationery Office.

Lazarus, Peter, chairman. 1989. *Second Report of the Committee for Monitoring Agreements on Tobacco Advertising and Sponsorship.* London: Her Majesty's Stationery Office.

Ledwith, Frank. 1984. Does Tobacco Sports Sponsorship on Television Act as Advertising to Children? *Health Education Journal* 43:85–88. Reprinted in BMA 1986, pp. 173–85.

Leu, Robert E. 1984. Anti-smoking Publicity, Taxation and the Demand for Cigarettes. *Journal of Health Economics* 3:101–16.

Leu, Robert E., and Schaub, Thomas. 1983. Does Smoking Increase Medical Care Expenditures? *Social Science and Medicine* 17:1907–14.

*Leventhal, Howard, and Cleary, Paul D. 1980. The Smoking Problem: A Review of the Research and Theory in Behavioral Risk Modification. *Psychological Bulletin* 88:370–405.

**Leventhal, Howard; Glynn, Kathleen; and Fleming, Raymond. 1987. Is the Smoking Decision an "Informed Choice"? *Journal of the American Medical Association* 257:3373–76.

*Lewit, E. M.; Coate, D.; and Grossman, M. 1981. The Effects of Government Regulation on Teenage Smoking. *Journal of Law and Economics* 24:545–69.

Lichtenstein, S.; Slovic, P.; Fischhoff, B.; Layman, M.; and Combs, B. 1978. Judged Frequency of Lethal Events. *Journal of Experimental Psychology (Human Learning and Memory)* 4:551–78.

Littlechild, S. C. 1986. Smoking and Market Failure. In Tollison, ed., 1986, pp. 271–84.

*Littlechild, S. C., and Wiseman, J. 1984. Principles of Public Policy Relevant to Smoking. *Policy Studies* 4, no. 3:54–67.

Locke, John. 1690. *Second Treatise of Government,* ed. Peter Laslett. Cambridge: Cambridge University Press, 1960.

Luce, B. R., and Schweitzer, S. O. 1978. Smoking and Alcohol Abuse: A Comparison of Their Economic Consequences. *New England Journal of Medicine* 298:569–71.

Lundberg, George D., and Knoll, Elizabeth. 1986. Editorial: Tobacco for Consenting Adults in Private Only. *Journal of the American Medical Association* 255:1051–53.

McGuinness, Tony, and Cowling, Keith. 1975. Advertising and the Aggregate Demand for Cigarettes. *European Economic Review* 6:311–28.

Machan, Tibor R. 1986. Smoking and Politics. *Economic Affairs* 7, no. 1:50–51.

Mackie, J. L. 1955. Responsibility and Language. *Australasian Journal of Philosophy* 33:143–59.

Madeley, John. 1981. The Environmental Impact of Tobacco Production in Developing Countries. *New York State Journal of Medicine* 83, no. 3:1310–11.

Manchester, P. B. 1976. Interstate Cigarette Smuggling. *Public Finance Quarterly* 4:225–37.

Marmot, M. G.; Rose, Geoffrey; Shipley, M. J.; Thomas, B. J. 1981. Alcoholism and Mortality: A U-Shaped Curve. *Lancet* 8220:580–82.

Marsh, Alan. 1985. Smoking and Illness: What Smokers Really Believe. *Health Trends* 17:7–12.

Marshall, Thurgood. 1968. Opinion of the U.S. Supreme Court. *Powell v. Texas,* 392 U.S. 514, 516–37.

Martin, Judith. 1983. *Miss Manners' Guide to Excruciatingly Correct Behavior.* New York: Warner Books.

Martin, Terry R., and Bracken, Michael B. 1986. Association of Low Birth Weight with Passive Smoke Exposure in Pregnancy. *American Journal of Epidemiology* 124:633–42.

Mathieu, Deborah. 1985. Respecting Liberty and Preventing Harm: Limits of State Intervention in Prenatal Choice. *Harvard Journal of Law and Public Policy* 8:19–55.

Matthews, Robert. 1988. Tobacco Company "Refused to Sell Safe Cigarettes." *Times* (London), July 4, p. 1.

Mattson, M. E.; Boyd, G.; Byar, D.; Brown, C.; Callahan, J. S.; Corle, D.; Cullen, J. W.; Greenbatt, J.; Haley, N. J.; Hammond, S. K.; Lewtas, J.; and Reeves, W. 1989. Passive Smoking on Commercial Airline Flights. *Journal of the American Medical Association* 261:867–72.

Maynard, Alan, and Kennan, Patricia. 1981. *The Economics of Addiction: A Survey of the Literature and a Proposed Research Strategy.* Report to the Social Science Research Council Panel on Addiction Research. York: University of York, Institute of Social and Economic Research.

Meenan, Robert F. 1976. Improving the Public's Health—Some Further Reflections. *New England Journal of Medicine* 294:45–47.

Mill, John Stuart. 1859. *On Liberty.* In *Three Essays,* ed. Richard Wollheim, pp. 1–141. Oxford: Oxford University Press, 1975.

Miller, Matthew L. 1985. Note: The First Amendment and Legislative Bans of Liquor and Cigarette Advertisements. *Columbia Law Review* 85:632–55.

Mintz, Morton. 1987. A Pack of Whys: A Tobacco Company Faces a Trial in the Death of a Smoker. *Washington Post National Weekly Edition,* February 9, pp. 21–22.

Mintz, Morton. 1988a. Cigarette Trial Breaks New Ground. *Washington Post,* March 27, pp. H1, H8. Reprinted in *Washington Post National Weekly Edition,* April 11, pp. 20–21.

Mintz, Morton. 1988b. Foes of Smoking Call for Congressional Probe: Tobacco Industry Lawyer Decries "Media Circus." *Washington Post,* March 27, p. A6.

Mishan, E. J. 1967. Pareto Optimality and the Law. *Oxford Economic Papers* 19:255–87.

Morris, Betty, and Waldman, Peter. 1989. The Death of Premier. *Wall Street Journal*, March 10, pp. B1, B4.

Morrison, Denton E., and Henkel, Ramon E., eds. 1970. *The Significance Test Controversy.* London: Butterworths.

Mosey, Christopher. 1985. Posthumous Victory for Passive Smoker. *Times* (London), December 2, p. 8.

Moskowitz, Milton; Katz, Michael; and Levering, Robert. 1980. *Everybody's Business.* San Francisco: Harper & Row.

Neuberger, Maurine B. 1963. *Smoke Screen: Tobacco and Public Welfare.* Englewood Cliffs, N.J.: Prentice-Hall.

Nozick, Robert. 1972. Coercion. In *Philosophy, Politics, and Society,* 4th ser., ed. P. Laslett, W. G. Runciman, and Q. Skinner, pp. 101–35. Oxford: Blackwell.

Oken, Donald. 1985. Tobacco Addiction and Compassion. *Journal of the American Medical Association* 253:2958.

Olsen, Johan P. 1972. Public Policy-Making and Theories of Organisational Choice. *Scandinavian Political Studies* 7:45–62.

Owen, David. 1987. Octane and Knock. *Atlantic Monthly* 260, no. 2:53–60.

Page, Talbot. 1978. A Generic View of Toxic Chemicals and Similar Risks. *Ecology Law Quarterly* 7:207–44.

Parfit, Derek. 1984. *Reasons and Persons.* Oxford: Clarendon.

Pears, David. 1984. *Motivated Irrationality.* Oxford: Clarendon.

Pease, Charles. 1911. Letter to the Editor. *New York Times,* November 10, p. 10.

Peltzman, Sam. 1987. The Health Effects of Mandatory Prescriptions. *Journal of Law and Economics* 30:207–38.

Peto, Richard. 1980. Possible Ways of Explaining to Ordinary People the Quantitative Dangers of Smoking. *Health Education Journal* 39:45–46.

Philips, Melanie. 1980. Why Smoking, Not Health, Wins the Day. *Guardian* (London), May 6, p. 2.

*Pollin, William. 1984. The Role of the Addictive Process as a Key Step in Causation of All Tobacco-related Diseases. *Journal of the American Medical Association* 252:2874.

Preston, M. H. 1971. Economics of Cigarette Smoking. In *Proceedings of the Second World Conference on Smoking and Health,* ed. Robert G. Richardson, pp. 100–110. London: Pittman Medical.

Prevezer, S. 1958. Automatism and Involuntary Conduct. *Criminal Law Review* 1958:361–67, 440–52.

Pufendorf, Samuel. 1672. *Of the Law of Nature and Nations,* trans. B. Kennett. 3d ed. London: Sare, 1717.

Rae, Douglas. 1975. The Limits of Consensual Decision. *American Political Science Review* 69:1270–94.

Ravenholt, R. T. 1984. Addiction Mortality in the United States, 1980: Tobacco, Alcohol, and Other Substances. *Population and Development Review* 10:697–724.

Rehnquist, William. 1986. Opinion of the U.S. Supreme Court. *Posadas de Puerto Rico Assoc. v. Tourism Co. of Puerto Rico,* 92 LEd2d 266, 274–85.

Repace, James L. 1982. Indoor Air Pollution. *Environment International* 8:21–36.

**Repace, James L. 1985. Risks of Passive Smoking. In *To Breathe Freely,* ed. Mary Gibson, pp. 3–30. Totowa, N.J.: Rowman & Allanheld.

Repace, James L., and Lowrey, A. H. 1980. Indoor Air Pollution, Tobacco Smoke and Public Health. *Science* 208:464–72.

Repace, James L., and Lowrey, A. H. 1985. A Quantitative Assessment of Nonsmokers' Lung Cancer Risk from Passive Smoking. *Environment International* 11:3–22.

Repace, James L., and Lowrey, A. H. 1986. A Rebuttal to Criticism of Repace and Lowrey (1985). *Environment International* 12:33–38.

Rice, Dorothy P.; Hodgson, Thomas A.; Sinsheimer, Peter H.; Browner, Warren; and Kopstein, Andrea N. 1986. The Economic Costs of the Health Effects of Smoking, 1984. *Milbank Quarterly* 64:489–547.

R. J. Reynolds Tobacco Co. 1986. The Health Effects of Smoking. A Submission in the Case of *Browner v. R.J. Reynolds* (California Superior Court, County of Contra Costa). Reprinted in *Tobacco Products Litigation Reporter* 1, no. 4:5.45–56.

Roberts, John L. 1986. *Code Busting by Tobacco Companies*. A Report for the Health Education Council from the North Western Regional Health Authority. Manchester: Project Smoke Free.

Robins, L. 1973. *A Follow-up of Vietnam Drug Users*. Interim Final Report, Special Actions Office for Drug Abuse Prevention. Washington, D.C.: Executive Office of the President.

Robinson, James C. 1986. Philosophical Origins of the Economic Valuation of Life. *Milbank Quarterly* 64:133–55.

Roemer, Ruth. 1986. *Recent Developments in Legislation to Combat the World Smoking Epidemic*. Division of Non-communicable Diseases, Smoking and Health Program. WHO/SMO/HLE/86.1. Geneva: World Health Organization.

Rose-Ackerman, Susan. 1985. Inalienability and the Theory of Property Rights. *Columbia Law Review* 85:931–69.

Rosenberg, David. 1984. The Causal Connection in Mass Exposure Cases: A "Public Law" Vision of the Tort System. *Harvard Law Review* 97:849–929.

Rothenberg, Randall. 1988. Verdict Expected to Focus Attention on Early Tobacco Ads. *New York Times*, June 15, p. B7.

Rothstein, M. 1983. Employee Selection Based on Susceptibility to Occupational Illness. *Michigan Law Review* 81:1379–1496.

Rovner, Julie. 1986. Anti-smoking Forces Stoke Legislative Fires. *Congressional Quarterly Weekly Report* 44:3049–54.

Royal College of Physicians. 1962. *Smoking and Health*. London: Pittman Medical.

Royal College of Physicians. 1971. *Smoking and Health Now*. London: Pittman Medical.

Royal College of Physicians. 1983. *Health or Smoking?* London: Pittman Medical.

Royal College of Psychiatrists. 1979. *Alcohol and Alcoholism*. The Report of a Special Committee of the Royal College of Psychiatrists. London: Tavistock.

Russell, M. A. H. 1974. Realistic Goals for Smoking and Health. *Lancet* 7851:254–58.

Sarokin, H. Lee. 1988. Opinion on Defendant's Motion for Directed Verdict. Cipollone v. Liggett Group, Inc. 683 F. Supp. 1487–1500 (D.N.J. 1988).

*Sartorius, Rolf, ed. 1983. *Paternalism*. Minneapolis: University of Minnesota Press.

Savarese, J. M., and Shughart, W. F. II. 1986. The Incidence of Taxes on Tobacco. In Tollison, ed., 1986, pp. 285–308.

Schelling, Thomas C. 1968. The Life You Save May Be Your Own. In *Problems in Public Expenditure Analysis*, ed. Samuel B. Chase. Washington, D.C.: Brookings Institution. Reprinted in Schelling 1984a, pp. 113–46.

Schelling, Thomas C. 1980. The Intimate Contest for Self-Command. *Public Interest* 60:94–118. Reprinted in Schelling 1984a, pp. 57–82.

*Schelling, Thomas C. 1983. Ethics, Law and the Exercise of Self-command. *Tanner Lectures on Human Values* 4:44–79. Reprinted in Schelling 1984a, pp. 83–113.

Schelling, Thomas C. 1984a. *Choice and Consequence.* Cambridge, Mass.: Harvard University Press.

Schelling, Thomas C. 1984b. Self-Command in Practice, in Policy, and in a Theory of Rational Choice. *American Economic Review (Papers and Proceedings)* 74:1–11.

Schelling, Thomas C. 1985. Enforcing Rules on Oneself. *Journal of Law, Economics and Organization* 1:357–74.

*Schelling, Thomas C. 1986a. Economics and Cigarettes. *Preventive Medicine* 15:549–60.

*Schelling, Thomas C. 1986b. Whose Business Is Good Behavior? In *American Society: Public and Private Responsibilities,* ed. Winthrop Knowlton and Richard Zeckhauser, pp. 153–80. Cambridge, Mass.: Ballinger.

Schlesinger, A. M. 1946. *Learning How to Behave.* New York: Macmillan.

Schneider, L.; Klein, B.; and Murphy, K. M. 1981. Governmental Regulation of Cigarette Health Information. *Journal of Law and Economics* 24:575–612.

Schoeman, Ferdinand. 1987. Statistical vs. Direct Evidence. *Noûs* 21:179–98.

Schuck, Peter H. 1988. The New Ideology of Tort Law. *Public Interest* 92:93–109.

Schwartz, Alan. 1989. Views of Addiction and the Duty to Warn. *Virginia Law Review* 75:509–60.

Sen, Amartya. 1973. Behaviour and the Concept of Preference. *Economica* 40:241–59.

Sen, Amartya. 1977. Rational Fools: A Critique of the Behavioral Foundations of Economic Theory. *Philosophy and Public Affairs* 6:317–44.

Shaikh, Rashid, and Reich, Michael R. 1981. Haphazard Policy on Hazardous Exports. *Lancet* 8249:740–42.

Shaw, George Bernard. 1903. Maxims for Revolutionists, from *Man and Superman.* In *The Complete Prefaces of Bernard Shaw,* pp. 188–95. London: Paul Hamlyn, 1965.

Shelton, A. 1984. Tobacco Tomorrow: Cigarette Sales and Markets. *Tobacco Reporter* 111, no. 4:54, 56–57.

Sherman, Jill. 1988. Doctors Demand a Law to Forbid All Smoking at Work. *Times* (London), March 24, p. 3.

Shipp, E. R. 1988. After the Smoke Has Cleared, Both Sides Declare Victory. *New York Times,* June 15, p. B7.

Shue, Henry. 1981. Exporting Hazards. *Ethics* 91:579–606.

Shughart, W. F. II, and Tollison, R. D. 1986. Smokers vs. Nonsmokers. In Tollison, ed., 1986, pp. 217–24.

Sidgwick, Henry. 1907. *The Methods of Ethics.* 7th ed. London: Macmillan.

Sinclair, Andrew. 1962. *Prohibition: The Era of Excess.* London: Faber & Faber.

Slade, J.; Kopelowicz, A.; Hahn, A.; Gill, J.; Kabis, S.; and Vasen, A. 1986–87. An Analysis of R. J. Reynolds' Position Paper on the Health Effects of Smoking. *Tobacco Products Litigation Reporter* 1, no. 8:5.97–105; 1, no. 10:5.115–21; 2, no. 2:5.11–21.

Slovic, P.; Fischhoff, B.; and Lichtenstein, S. 1982. Fact vs. Fears: Understanding Perceived Risks. In Kahneman, Slovic, and Tversky, eds., 1982, pp. 463–89.

Smith, R. C. 1978. The Magazines' Smoking Habit. *Columbia Journalism Review* 15, no. 5:29–31.

Sosa, Ernest, ed. 1975. *Causation and Conditionals.* Oxford: Oxford University Press.

Spencer, Herbert. 1893. *The Principles of Ethics.* London: Williams & Norgate.

Spielberger, C. D. 1986. Psychological Determinants of Smoking Behavior. In Tollison, ed., 1986, pp. 89–134.

Starr, Chauncey. 1969. Social Benefits vs. Technological Risks. *Science* 165:1232–38.

Stebbins, Kenyon R. 1987. Tobacco or Health in the Third World. *International Journal of Health Services* 17:521–36.

Stewart, Potter. 1962. Opinion of the U.S. Supreme Court. *Robinson v. California,* 370 U.S. 660.

Steyer, Robert. 1988. "Smokeless" Cigarette to be Tested. *St. Louis Post-Dispatch,* August 31, pp. 1, 14.

Stigler, George J., and Becker, Gary S. 1977. De Gustibus Non Est Disputandum. *American Economic Review* 67:76–90.

Stoddart, Greg L.; Labelle, Roberta J.; Barer, Morris L.; and Evals, Robert G. 1986. Tobacco Sales and Health Care Costs: Do Canadian Smokers Pay Their Way? *Journal of Health Economics* 5:63–80.

Sunstein, Cass R. 1986. Legal Interference with Private Preferences. *University of Chicago Law Review* 53:1129–74.

Sunstein, Cass R. 1988. Disrupting Voluntary Transactions. In *Nomos XXXI: Markets and Justice,* ed. J. W. Chapman and J. R. Pennock, pp. 279–302. New York: New York University Press.

Taylor, Peter. 1985. *The Smoke Ring.* London: Sphere Books.

Taylor, Stuart, Jr. 1988. CBS Is Ordered to Pay $3 Million Libel Award. *New York Times,* April 5, p. A17.

Temin, Peter. 1979. The Origin of Compulsory Drug Prescriptions. *Journal of Law and Economics* 22:91–106.

Thomson, Judith Jarvis. 1971. A Defense of Abortion. *Philosophy and Public Affairs* 1:47–66. Reprinted in Thomson 1986, chap. 1.

Thomson, Judith Jarvis. 1986. *Rights, Restitution and Risk.* Cambridge, Mass.: Harvard University Press.

Tobacco Advisory Council (TAC). 1987. *Smoking at Work.* London: TAC.

Tobin, James, 1970. On Limiting the Domain of Inequality. *Journal of Law and Economics* 13:363–78.

*Tollison, Robert D., ed. 1986. *Smoking and Society.* Lexington, Mass.: Lexington Books, D. C. Heath.

*Tollison, Robert D., and Wagner, Richard E. 1988. *Smoking and the State: Social Costs, Rent Seeking, and Public Policy.* Lexington, Mass.: Lexington Books, D. C. Heath.

Townsend, Joy L. 1987. Cigarette Tax, Economic Welfare and Social Class Patterns of Smoking. *Applied Economics* 19:355–65.

Tribe, Laurence H. 1971. Trial by Mathematics. *Harvard Law Review* 84:1329–93.

Tribe, Laurence H. 1986. Federalism with Smoke and Mirrors. *The Nation* 242:788–90.

Troyer, Ronald J., and Markle, Gerald E. 1983. *Cigarettes: The Battle Over Smoking.* New Brunswick, N.J.: Rutgers University Press.

Tufte, Edward R. 1974. *Data Analysis for Politics and Policy.* Englewood Cliffs, N.J.: Prentice-Hall.

Tushnet, Mark. 1982. Corporations and Free Speech. In *The Politics of Law,* ed. David Kairys, pp. 253–61. New York: Pantheon.

United Kingdom. Central Statistical Office. 1987. The Effects of Taxes and Benefits on Household Income in 1985. *Economic Trends* 405:101–17.

United Kingdom. Department of Health and Social Security. 1981. *Drinking Sensibly.* London: Her Majesty's Stationery Office.

United Kingdom. Her Majesty's Treasury. 1980. The Change in Revenue from an Indirect Tax Change. *Economic Trends* 317:97–107.

U.S. Advisory Commission on Intergovernmental Relations (U.S. ACIR). 1977. *Cigarette Bootlegging: A State and Federal Responsibility.* Washington, D.C.: ACIR.

U.S. Congress. Office of Technology Assessment (U.S. OTA). 1985. *Smoking-related Deaths and Financial Costs.* OTA Staff Memorandum, Health Program, OTA, U.S. Congress. Washington, D.C.: OTA.

U.S. Council of Economic Advisers (U.S. CEA). 1987. Annual Report of the Council of Economic Advisers, 1987. In *Economic Report of the President,* pp. 9–368. Washington, D.C.: Government Printing Office.

U.S. Department of Health, Education and Welfare (U.S. DHEW). 1964. *Smoking and Health.* Report of the Advisory Committee to the Surgeon General of the Public Health Service. Washington, D.C.: Government Printing Office.

U.S. DHEW. Surgeon General. 1976. *The Health Consequences of Smoking: A Reference Edition.* Washington, D.C.: Government Printing Office.

U.S. Department of Health and Human Services (U.S. DHHS). Various years. *Bibliography on Smoking and Health.* Washington, D.C.: Government Printing Office.

U.S. DHHS. Various years. *Smoking and Health Bulletin.* Washington, D.C.: Government Printing Office.

U.S. DHHS. Surgeon General. 1979. *Smoking and Health.* Washington, D.C.: Government Printing Office.

U.S. DHHS. Surgeon General. 1980. *The Health Consequences of Smoking for Women.* Washington, D.C.: Government Printing Office.

U.S. DHHS. Surgeon General. 1981. *The Health Consequences of Smoking: The Changing Cigarette.* Washington, D.C.: Government Printing Office.

U.S. DHHS. Surgeon General. 1982. *The Health Consequences of Smoking: Cancer.* Washington, D.C.: Government Printing Office.

U.S. DHHS. Surgeon General. 1986. *The Health Consequences of Involuntary Smoking.* Washington, D.C.: Government Printing Office.

U.S. DHHS. Surgeon General. 1988. *The Health Consequences of Smoking: Nicotine Addiction.* Washington, D.C.: Government Printing Office.

*U.S. DHHS. Surgeon General. 1989. *Reducing the Health Consequences of Smoking: 25 Years of Progress.* Washington, D.C.: Government Printing Office.

U.S. Department of Labor. Bureau of Labor Statistics. 1983. *Consumer Expenditure Survey: Diary Survey, 1980–1981.* Washington, D.C.: Government Printing Office.

U.S. Federal Trade Commission (U.S. FTC). 1981. *Staff Report on the Cigarette Advertising Investigation,* Matthew L. Meyers, chairman. Public version. Washington, D.C.: FTC.

U.S. FTC. 1984. *A Report to the Congress Pursuant to the Federal Cigarette Labelling and Advertising Act.* Washington, D.C.: Government Printing Office.

U.S. FTC. 1985. *A Report to the Congress Pursuant to the Federal Cigarette Labelling and Advertising Act.* Washington, D.C.: Government Printing Office.

U.S. General Accounting Office (U.S. GAO). 1980. *Indoor Air Pollution: A Growing Health Peril.* Report to the Congress. Washington, D.C.: GAO.

U.S. General Services Administration (U.S. GSA). 1986. Final Rule, Smoking Regulations. *Federal Register* 51:44258–59.

U.S. National Academy of Sciences (U.S. NAS). National Research Council. Committee on Airliner Cabin Air Quality. 1986a. *The Airliner Cabin Environment: Air Quality and Safety.* Washington, D.C.: National Academy Press.

U.S. NAS. National Research Council. Committee on Passive Smoking. 1986b. *Environmental Tobacco Smoke: Measuring Exposures and Assessing Health Effects.* Washington, D.C.: National Academy Press.

Victor, Kirk. 1987. Strange Alliances. *National Journal* 19:2076–81.

**Wald, Nicholas J.; Nanchahal, Kiran; Thompson, Simon G.; and Chuckle, Howard S. 1986. Does Breathing Other People's Tobacco Smoke Cause Cancer? *British Medical Journal* 293:1217–1222.

Walker, Jack L. 1977. Setting the Agenda in the U.S. Senate: A Theory of Problem Selection. *British Journal of Political Science* 7:423–46.

Warner, Kenneth E. 1981. Cigarette Smoking in the 1970s: The Impact of the Antismoking Campaign on Consumption. *Science* 211:729–31.

Warner, Kenneth E. 1985. Cigarette Advertising and Media Coverage of Smoking and Health. *New England Journal of Medicine* 312:384–88.

Warner, Kenneth E. 1987a. A Ban on the Promotion of Tobacco Products. *New England Journal of Medicine* 316:745–47.

Warner, Kenneth E. 1987b. Health and Economic Implications of a Tobacco-free Society. *Journal of the American Medical Association* 258:2080–86.

**Warner, K. E.; Ernster, V. L.; Holbrook, J. H.; Lewit, E. M., Pertschuk, M.; Steinfeld, J. L.; Tye, J. B.; and Whelan, E. M. 1986. Promotion of Tobacco Products: Issues and Policy Options. *Journal of Health Politics, Policy and Law* 11:367–92.

Watson, Gary. 1975. Free Agency. *Journal of Philosophy* 72:205–20.

Watson, Gary. 1977. Skepticism about Weakness of Will. *Philosophical Review* 86:316–39.

Weinberg, Jonathan. 1982. Note: Constitutional Protection of Commercial Speech. *Columbia Law Review* 82:720–50.

Weinkam, J. J.; Rosenbaum, W.; and Sterling, T. D. 1987. Smoking and Hospital Utilization. *Social Science and Medicine* 24:983–86.

*White, A. A. 1972. The Intentional Exploitation of Man's Known Weaknesses. *Houston Law Review* 9:889–927.

White, Larry C. 1988. *Merchants of Death: The American Tobacco Industry.* New York: Beach Tree Books, William Morrow.

**Wikler, Daniel. 1978. Persuasion and Coercion for Health: Ethical Issues in Government Efforts to Change Life-Styles. *Health and Society* (now *Milbank Quarterly*) 56:383–38. Reprinted in Sartorius, ed., 1983, pp. 35–59.

Wikler, Daniel. 1987. Personal Responsibility for Illness. In *Health Care Ethics,* ed. D. van de Veer and T. Regan, pp. 326–58. Philadelphia: Temple University Press.

Wilbert, Johannes. 1988. *Tobacco and Shamanism in South America.* New Haven, Conn.: Yale University Press.

Wildavsky, Aaron. 1977. Doing Better and Feeling Worse: The Political Pathology of Health Policy. *Daedalus* 106, no. 1:105–23.

Wildavsky, Aaron. 1980. Richer Is Safer. *Public Interest* 60:23–39.

Wilkinson, James. 1986. *Tobacco.* Harmondsworth: Penguin.

Will, George F. 1987. Foes of Smoking on Airliners Are Right. *International Herald Tribune,* September 10.

Winsten, Jay A., director. 1986. *Nicotine Dependency and Compulsive Tobacco Use.* A Research Status Report, Center for Health Communication, Harvard

School of Public Health. Reprinted in *Tobacco Product Liability Reporter* 1, no. 7.

Woodfield, Alan E. 1984. Costs and "Benefits" of Cigarette Smoking in Canada: A Comment. *Canadian Medical Association Journal* 130:118–20.

World Health Organisation (WHO). 1977. Alcohol-Related Disabilities. Offset Publication no. 32. Geneva: WHO.

WHO. 1978. *International Classification of Diseases*. 9th ed. Geneva: WHO.

WHO. 1986. *In Point of Fact*, no. 36. Geneva: WHO.

Yondorf, Barbara. 1979. Prostitution as a Legal Activity: The West German Experience. *Policy Analysis* 5:417–33

Index

Abortion, and fetal risk from passive smoking, 58–59
Addiction, nicotine. *See* Nicotine addiction
Addiction/habit distinction, 26, 95–100
Advertising, cigarette
 aggressive, 24–25
 aimed at children, 19–20, 54–55, 104, 106
 and brand switching, 106–7
 deceptive, 19–20, 104, 132
 ethics of, 103–7
 and the Fairness Doctrine, 53–55, 90–92, 104
 health warnings in, 16–19, 29–30, 42, 47n, 53–55, 118–19, 121–22
 possible limitations on, 7, 54–55, 103–7, 137. *See also* Bans
 in Third World countries, 118–19, 121–22
 "tombstone advertising," 105
Age of consent and smoking, 30. *See also* Children, Recruitment of new smokers, Teenage smokers
Aid to Families with Dependent Children (AFDC), 47
Air filters as remedy for passive smoking, 82. *See also* Technology
Airplanes, passive smoking in, 75, 82, 83
Alcohol. *See* Smoking/drinking attitudes linkage

"Alcohol dependence syndrome" and nicotine dependence compared, 128–30
Allergy risk from passive smoking, 63. *See also* Hypersensitivity and passive smoking
American Psychiatric Association (APA) on nicotine dependence, 26–30, 97
Anchoring fallacy and smoking risks, 22. *See also* Cognitive defects in thinking about smoking
Angina risk from passive smoking, 63
Anti-Cigarette League, 125
Antismoking commercials, 53–56. *See also* Fairness Doctrine
Antismoking policies, vi, vii, 3, 12, 41–56, 80–88. *See also* Policy options regarding smoking
Asthma and passive smoking, 63, 76, 77, 78–79. *See also* Hypersensitivity and passive smoking
Availability heuristic and smoking risks, 24. *See also* Cognitive defects

Bans
 on cigarette advertising, 7, 54–55, 103–4, 137
 on cigarette sales, 7, 54–55, 96n, 137

155